Birnbaum
Los Angeles

A BIRNBAUM TRAVEL GUIDE

Alexandra Mayes Birnbaum
EDITORIAL CONSULTANT

Lois Spritzer
Editorial Director

Laura L. Brengelman
Managing Editor

Mary Callahan
Senior Editor

David Appell
Patricia Canole
Gene Gold
Jill Kadetsky
Susan McClung
Associate Editors

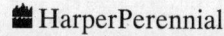

HarperPerennial
A Division of HarperCollinsPublishers

To Stephen, who merely made all this possible.

BIRNBAUM'S LOS ANGELES 95. Copyright © 1995 by HarperCollins Publishers. All rights reserved. Printed in the United States of America. No part of this book may be used or reproduced in any manner whatsoever without written permission except in the case of brief quotations embodied in critical articles and reviews. For information address HarperCollins*Publishers*, 10 East 53rd Street, New York, NY 10022.

FIRST EDITION

ISSN 0749-2561 (Birnbaum Travel Guides)
ISSN 1056-4462 (Los Angeles)
ISBN 0-06-278178-2 (pbk.)

95 96 97 ❖/RRD 5 4 3 2 1

Cover design © Drenttel Doyle Partners
Cover photograph © C. Moore/WestLight
Downtown skyline and freeway, Los Angeles

BIRNBAUM TRAVEL GUIDES

Bahamas, and Turks & Caicos
Berlin
Bermuda
Boston
Canada
Cancun, Cozumel & Isla Mujeres
Caribbean
Chicago
Country Inns and Back Roads
Disneyland
Eastern Europe
Europe
Europe for Business Travelers
France
Germany
Great Britain
Hawaii
Ireland
Italy
London
Los Angeles
Mexico
Miami & Ft. Lauderdale
Montreal & Quebec City
New Orleans
New York
Paris
Portugal
Rome
San Francisco
Santa Fe & Taos
South America
Spain
United States
USA for Business Travelers
Walt Disney World
Walt Disney World for Kids, By Kids
Washington, DC

Contributing Editors

Judith Krantz
Elise Nakhnikian
Anita Peltonen
Patti Covello Pietschmann
Merrill Shindler

Maps

Mark Carlson
Susan Carlson

Contents

Foreword...vii
How to Use This Guide...5

Getting Ready to Go

Practical information for planning your trip.

When to Go...9
Traveling by Plane...9
On Arrival...12
Package Tours...14
Insurance...16
Disabled Travelers...16
Single Travelers...19
Older Travelers...20
Money Matters...22
Time Zone...22
Business and Shopping Hours...22
Mail...23
Telephone...23
Medical Aid...24
Legal Aid...25
For Further Information...25

The City

A thorough, qualitative guide to Los Angeles, highlighting the city's attractions, services, hotels, and restaurants.

Introduction to Los Angeles...29

Los Angeles At-a-Glance
Seeing the City...32
Special Places...33

Sources and Resources
Tourist Information...43
Getting Around...44
Local Services...45
Special Events...46
Museums...47
Major Colleges and Universities...49
Shopping...50

Sports and Fitness...56
Theater...58
Music...59
Nightclubs and Nightlife...59

Best in Town
Checking In...60
Eating Out...70
Taking Tea...86

Diversions

A selective guide to a variety of unexpected pleasures, pinpointing the best places to pursue them.

Exceptional Pleasures and Treasures
Quintessential Los Angeles...91
A Few of Our Favorite Things...96
Performing Arts...97
Audience Participation: Getting into the Act...99
Oddities, Insanities, and Just Plain Fun...101
Grave Matters...103
Spas...105
Best Beaches...107
Great Sailing and Cruising...109
Best Golf Outside the City...110
A Shutterbug's Los Angeles...110

Directions

Eight of the best tours in and around Los Angeles.

Introduction...117

Tour 1: Downtown...119
Tour 2: Melrose Avenue...127
Tour 3: Fairfax/Farmers' Market...131
Tour 4: Beverly Hills...135
Tour 5: Hollywood...141
Tour 6: Westwood...145
Tour 7: Beach Towns: South Bay Beaches—Manhattan, Hermosa, Redondo...149
Tour 8: Catalina...153

Index...157

Foreword

For dyed-in-the-wool New Yorkers like me, being mean to Los Angeles is almost a requirement, and the urge to growl about the nation's second city has grown over the last decade or so. New Yorkers of a certain age watched ungraciously as California overtook New York as the most populous state in the union, and seethed as expatriate East Coasters returned from new residences on the West Coast with reports of a lifestyle that's both stimulating and slush-free, albeit occasionally sociologically and geologically explosive. You could cut the envy with a knife!

Although it probably would be genetically impossible (something to do with a virulent strain of skyscraper syndrome) to actually consider Los Angeles as a potential residence, I'm forced to confess that the last few years have witnessed an exponential increase in the number of excuses I've found to visit the City of Angels. To begin with, more and more friends have resettled beside the Pacific, so seeing them has required frequent hegiras to the warmth of Southern California. And once physically in the sway of the Pacific and the palm trees, it's hard to deny that the city has considerable appeal.

So this guide to Los Angeles is an attempt to demonstrate growing personal maturity and open-mindedness where Southern California is concerned. Just between us, it also provides a perfect excuse to spend a lot more time in LA.

That's why we've tried to create a guide to Los Angeles that's specifically organized, written, and edited for today's demanding traveler, one for whom qualitative information is infinitely more desirable than mere quantities of unappraised data. We realize that it's impossible for any single travel writer to visit thousands of restaurants (and nearly as many hotels) in any given year and provide accurate appraisals of each. And even if it were physically possible for one human being to survive such an itinerary, it would of necessity have to be done at a dead sprint, and the perceptions derived therefrom would probably be less valid than those of any other intelligent individual visiting the same establishments. It is, therefore, both impractical and undesirable (especially in a large, annually revised and updated guidebook *series* such as we offer) to have only one person provide all the data on the entire world. Instead, we have chosen what we like to describe as the "thee and me" approach to restaurant and hotel evaluation and, to a somewhat more limited degree, to the sites and sights we have included in the other sections of our text. What this really reflects is a personal sampling tempered by intelligent counsel from informed local sources.

This guidebook is directed to the "visitor," and such elements as restaurants have been specifically picked to provide the visitor with a representative, enlightening, and, above all, pleasant experience. Since so many extraneous considerations can affect the reception and service accorded a regular restaurant patron, our choices can in no way be construed as an exhaustive guide to resident dining. We think we've listed all the best places, in various price ranges, but they were chosen with a visitor's enjoyment in mind.

Other evidence of how we've tried to tailor our text to reflect modern travel habits is apparent in the section we call DIVERSIONS. Where once it was common for travelers to spend an urban visit seeing only the obvious sights, today's traveler is more likely to want to pursue a special interest or to venture off the beaten path. In response to this trend, we have collected a series of special experiences so that it is no longer necessary to wade through a pound or two of superfluous prose just to find exceptional pleasures and treasures.

Finally, I also should point out that every good travel guide is a living enterprise; that is, no part of this text is carved in stone. In our annual revisions, we refine, expand, and further hone all our material to serve your travel needs better. To this end, no contribution is of greater value to us than your personal reaction to what we have written, as well as information reflecting your own experiences while using the book. Please write to us at 10 E. 53rd St., New York, NY 10022.

We sincerely hope to hear from you.

Alexandra Mayes Birnbaum

ALEXANDRA MAYES BIRNBAUM, editorial consultant to the *Birnbaum Travel Guides*, worked with her late husband, Stephen Birnbaum, as co-editor of the series. She has been a world traveler since childhood and is known for her travel reports on radio on what's hot and what's not.

Los Angeles

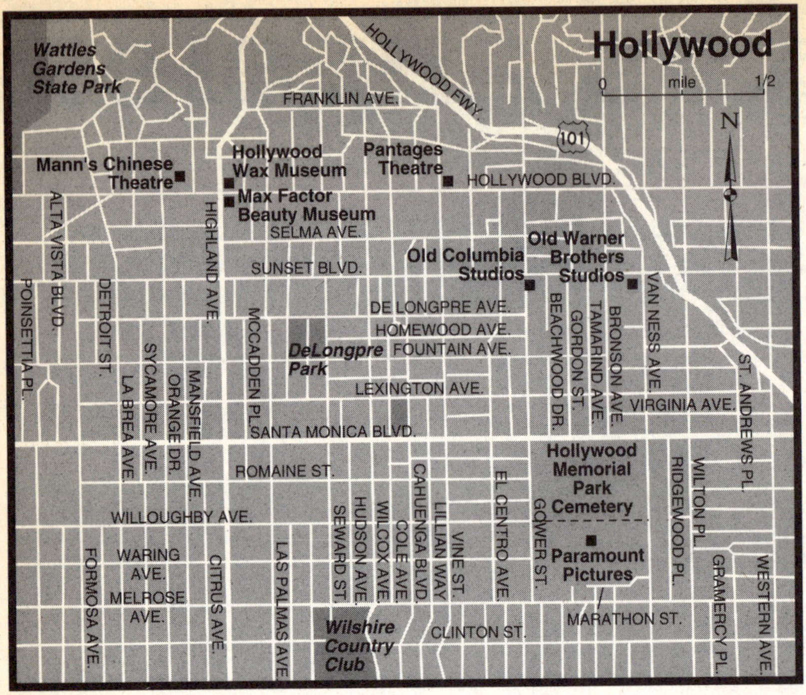
Hollywood
0
mile
1/2
N
101
Wattles Gardens State Park
FRANKLIN AVE.
HOLLYWOOD FWY.
Mann's Chinese Theatre
Hollywood Wax Museum
Pantages Theatre
HOLLYWOOD BLVD.
Max Factor Beauty Museum
SELMA AVE.
SUNSET BLVD.
Old Columbia Studios
Old Warner Brothers Studios
DE LONGPRE AVE.
HOMEWOOD AVE.
FOUNTAIN AVE.
DeLongpre Park
LEXINGTON AVE.
VIRGINIA AVE.
SANTA MONICA BLVD.
ROMAINE ST.
WILLOUGHBY AVE.
WARING AVE.
MELROSE AVE.
CLINTON ST.
MARATHON ST.
Hollywood Memorial Park Cemetery
Paramount Pictures
Wilshire Country Club
POINSETTIA PL.
ALTA VISTA BLVD.
DETROIT ST.
LA BREA AVE.
SYCAMORE AVE.
ORANGE DR.
MANSFIELD AVE.
HIGHLAND AVE.
MCCADDEN PL.
FORMOSA AVE.
CITRUS AVE.
LAS PALMAS AVE.
SEWARD ST.
HUDSON AVE.
WILCOX AVE.
COLE AVE.
CAHUENGA BLVD.
LILLIAN WAY
VINE ST.
EL CENTRO AVE.
GOWER ST.
BEACHWOOD DR.
GORDON ST.
TAMARIND AVE.
BRONSON AVE.
VAN NESS AVE.
RIDGEWOOD PL.
WILTON PL.
GRAMERCY PL.
ST. ANDREWS PL.
WESTERN AVE.

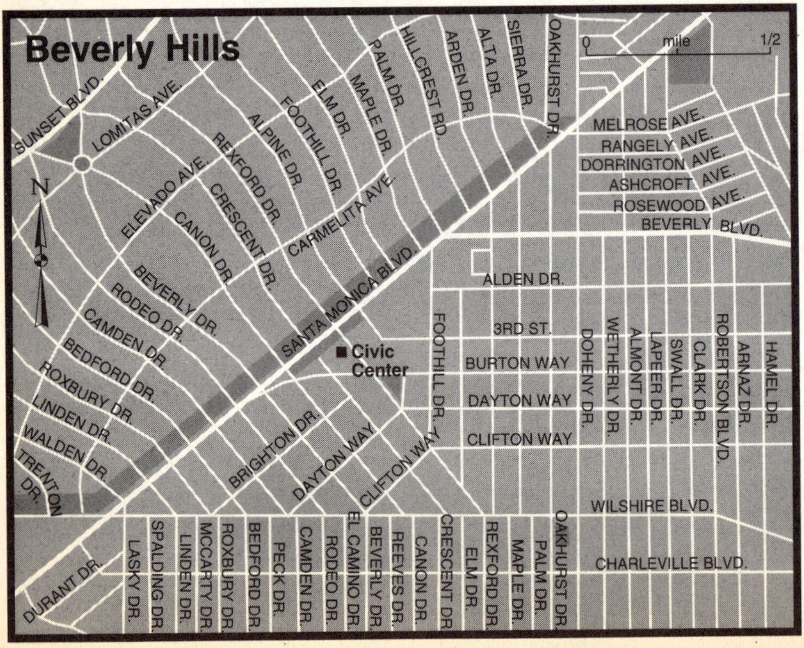
Beverly Hills
0
mile
1/2
N
SUNSET BLVD.
LOMITAS AVE.
ELEVADO AVE.
REXFORD DR.
ALPINE DR.
FOOTHILL DR.
ELM DR.
MAPLE DR.
PALM DR.
HILLCREST RD.
ARDEN DR.
ALTA DR.
SIERRA DR.
OAKHURST DR.
MELROSE AVE.
RANGELY AVE.
DORRINGTON AVE.
ASHCROFT AVE.
ROSEWOOD AVE.
BEVERLY BLVD.
CRESCENT DR.
CANON DR.
CARMELITA AVE.
BEVERLY DR.
RODEO DR.
CAMDEN DR.
BEDFORD DR.
ROXBURY DR.
LINDEN DR.
WALDEN DR.
TRENTON DR.
SANTA MONICA BLVD.
Civic Center
ALDEN DR.
3RD ST.
BURTON WAY
DAYTON WAY
CLIFTON WAY
FOOTHILL DR.
DOHENY DR.
WETHERLY DR.
ALMONT DR.
LAPEER DR.
SWALL DR.
CLARK DR.
ROBERTSON BLVD.
ARNAZ DR.
HAMEL DR.
BRIGHTON DR.
DAYTON WAY
CLIFTON WAY
WILSHIRE BLVD.
CHARLEVILLE BLVD.
DURANT DR.
LASKY DR.
SPALDING DR.
LINDEN DR.
MCCARTY DR.
ROXBURY DR.
BEDFORD DR.
PECK DR.
CAMDEN DR.
RODEO DR.
EL CAMINO DR.
BEVERLY DR.
REEVES DR.
CANON DR.
CRESCENT DR.
ELM DR.
REXFORD DR.
MAPLE DR.
PALM DR.
OAKHURST DR.

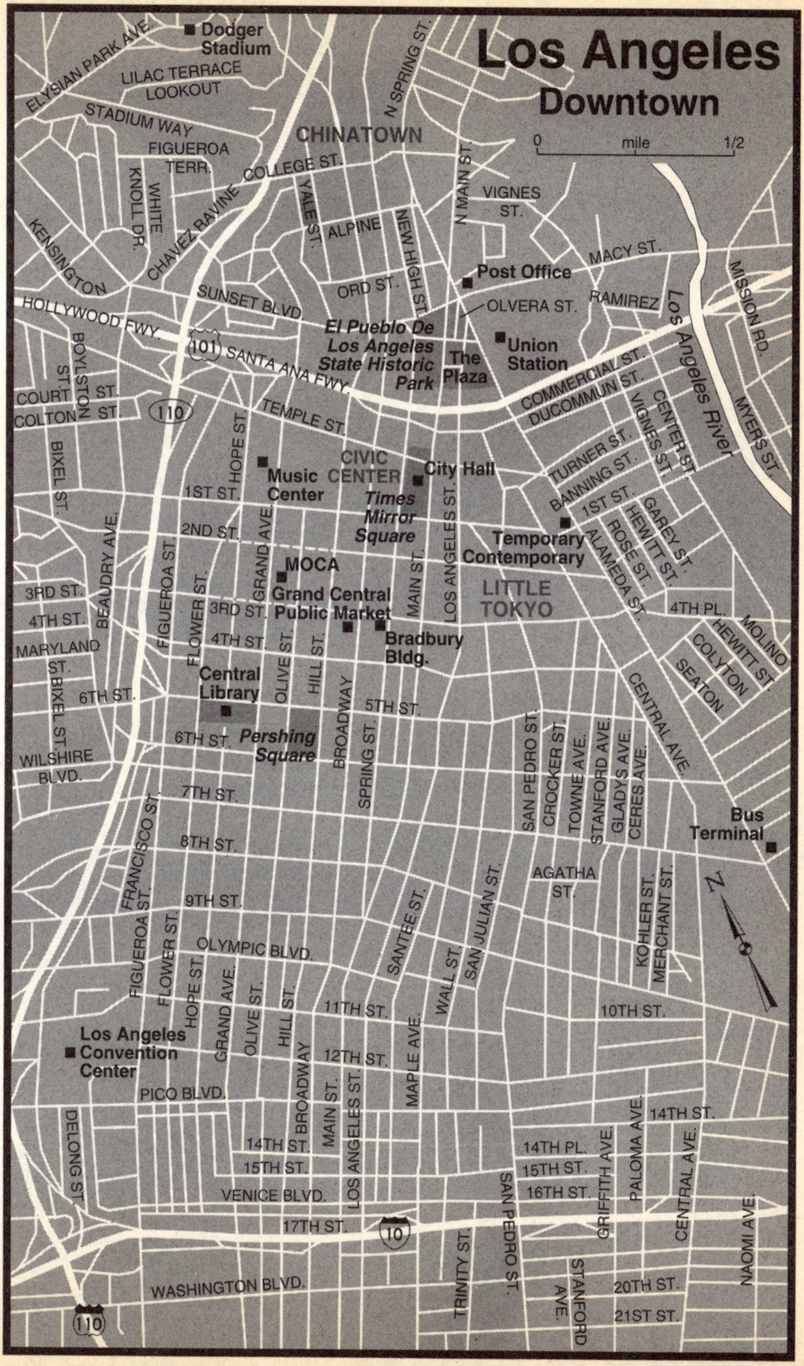

Los Angeles
Downtown
0 mile 1/2
Dodger Stadium
Elysian Park Ave.
Lilac Terrace Lookout
Stadium Way
Figueroa Terr.
Chinatown
N Spring St.
College St.
Knoll Dr.
White
Chavez Ravine
Yale St.
Alpine
New High St.
N Main St.
Vignes St.
Kensington
Macy St.
Post Office
Ord St.
Olvera St.
Ramirez
Mission Rd.
Sunset Blvd.
Hollywood Fwy.
101
Santa Ana Fwy.
El Pueblo De Los Angeles State Historic Park
The Plaza
Union Station
Los Angeles River
Boylston St.
Court St.
Colton St.
110
Temple St.
Commercial St.
Ducommun St.
Vignes St.
Center St.
Myers St.
Bixel St.
Hope St.
Music Center
Civic Center
City Hall
Turner St.
Banning St.
1st St.
Times Mirror Square
Los Angeles St.
Temporary Contemporary
Rose St.
Hewitt St.
Garey St.
Alameda St.
2nd St.
Beaudry Ave.
Figueroa St.
Flower St.
Grand Ave.
MOCA
Main St.
Little Tokyo
3rd St.
4th St.
Grand Central Public Market
4th Pl.
Maryland St.
Bradbury Bldg.
Hewitt St.
Molino
Colyton
Seaton
Olive St.
Hill St.
Central Library
6th St.
5th St.
Broadway
Central Ave.
Pershing Square
Spring St.
Wilshire Blvd.
San Pedro St.
Crocker St.
Towne Ave.
Stanford Ave.
Gladys Ave.
Ceres Ave.
7th St.
Bus Terminal
Francisco St.
8th St.
Agatha St.
9th St.
Santee St.
San Julian St.
Kohler St.
Merchant St.
N
Olympic Blvd.
Wall St.
11th St.
10th St.
Los Angeles Convention Center
12th St.
Maple Ave.
Pico Blvd.
14th St.
DeLong St.
14th St.
15th St.
14th Pl.
15th St.
16th St.
Griffith Ave.
Paloma Ave.
Central Ave.
Venice Blvd.
17th St.
10
Naomi Ave.
Trinity St.
San Pedro St.
Stanford Ave.
Washington Blvd.
20th St.
21st St.
110

How to Use This Guide

A great deal of care has gone into the special organization of this guidebook, and we believe it represents a real breakthrough in the presentation of travel material.

Our text is divided into four basic sections in order to present information in the best way on every possible aspect of a vacation to Los Angeles. Our aim is to highlight what's where and to provide basic information—how, when, where, how much, and what's best—to assist you in making the most intelligent choices possible.

Here is a brief summary of what you can expect to find in each section. We believe that you will find both your travel planning and en route enjoyment enhanced by having this book at your side.

GETTING READY TO GO

A mini-encyclopedia of practical travel facts with all the precise data necessary to create a successful trip to Los Angeles. Here you will find how to get where you're going, plus selected resources—including useful publications, and companies and organizations specializing in discount and special-interest travel—providing a wealth of information and assistance useful both before and during your trip.

THE CITY

Our individual report on Los Angeles offers a short-stay guide, including an essay introducing the city as a historic entity and a contemporary place to visit; an *At-a-Glance* section that's a site-by-site survey of the most important, interesting, and unique sights to see and things to do; *Sources and Resources*, a concise listing of pertinent tourist information, such as the address of the local tourist office, which sightseeing tours to take, where to find the best nightspot or hail a taxi, which are the shops which have the finest merchandise and/or the most irresistible bargains, and where the best museums and theaters are to be found; and *Best in Town*, which lists our collection of cost-and-quality choices of the best places to eat and sleep on a variety of budgets.

DIVERSIONS

This section is designed to help travelers find the best places in which to engage in a variety of exceptional experiences, without having to wade through endless pages of unrelated text. In every case, our particular suggestions are intended to guide you to that special place where the quality of experience is likely to be highest.

DIRECTIONS

Here are eight tours that cover Los Angeles and its outlying communities, its main thoroughfares and side streets, its most spectacular landmarks and sights, as well as a tour of nearby Catalina Island.

To use this book to full advantage, take a few minutes to read the table of contents and random entries in each section to get a firsthand feel for how it all fits together. You will find that the sections of this book are building blocks designed to help you put together the best possible trip. Use them selectively as a tool, a source of ideas, a reference work for accurate facts, and a guidebook to the best buys, the most exciting sights, the most pleasant accommodations, the tastiest foods—*the best travel experience* that you can possibly have.

Getting Ready to Go

Getting Ready to Go

When to Go

Los Angeles receives the most visitors from April through September. However, there really isn't a best time to visit. For the most part, the city enjoys spring-like temperatures and sunshine in abundant supply. There also are no real off-season periods when attractions are closed. Hotel rooms and car rental rates tend to be somewhat less expensive in winter; throughout the year, hotel rates also may be lower on weekends, when business travel is slow.

If you have a touch-tone phone, you can call *The Weather Channel Connection* (phone: 900-WEATHER) for current weather forecasts. This service, available from *The Weather Channel* (2600 Cumberland Pkwy., Atlanta, GA 30339; phone: 404-434-6800), costs 95¢ per minute; the charge will appear on your phone bill.

Traveling by Plane

SCHEDULED FLIGHTS

Airlines offering flights to *Los Angeles International Airport (LAX)* include *Alaska Airlines, America West, American, American Eagle, Carnival Air Lines, Continental, Delta, Delta Connection, Midwest Express, Northwest, NW Airlink, Southwest Airlines, Tower Air, TWA, TWA Express, United, United Express, USAir,* and *USAir Express.*

FARES The great variety of airfares can be reduced to the following basic categories: first class, business class, coach (also called economy or tourist class), excursion or discount, and standby, as well as various promotional fares. For information on applicable fares and restrictions, contact the airlines listed above or ask your travel agent. Most airfares are offered for a limited time. Once you've found the lowest fare for which you can qualify, purchase your ticket as soon as possible.

RESERVATIONS Reconfirmation is not generally required on domestic flights, although it is wise to call ahead to make sure that the airline has your reservation and any special requests in its computer.

SEATING Airline seats usually are assigned on a first-come, first-served basis at check-in, although you may be able to reserve a seat when purchasing your ticket. Seating charts sometimes are available from airlines and also are included in the *Airline Seating Guide* (Carlson Publishing Co., 11132 Los Alamitos Blvd., Los Alamitos, CA 90720; phone: 310-493-4877).

SMOKING US law prohibits smoking on flights scheduled for six hours or less within the US and its territories on both domestic and international carriers. A free wallet-size guide that describes the rights of nonsmokers under current regulations is available from *ASH* (*Action on Smoking and Health;* DOT Card, 2013 H St. NW, Washington, DC 20006; phone: 202-659-4310).

SPECIAL MEALS When making your reservation, you can request one of the airline's alternate menu choices for no additional charge. Though not always required, it is a good idea to reconfirm your request on the day before departure.

BAGGAGE On major airlines, passengers usually are allowed to carry on board one bag that will fit under a seat or in an overhead bin and to check two bags in the cargo hold. Specific regulations regarding dimensions and weight restrictions vary among airlines, but a checked bag usually cannot exceed 62 inches in combined dimensions (length, width, and depth), or weigh more than 70 pounds. There may be charges for additional, oversize, or overweight luggage, and for special equipment or sporting gear. Check that the tags the airline attaches are correctly coded for your destination.

CHARTER FLIGHTS

By booking a block of seats on a specially arranged flight, charter operators frequently can offer travelers bargain airfares. If you do fly on a charter, however, read the contract's fine print carefully. Federal regulations permit charter operators to cancel a flight or assess surcharges of as much as 10% of the airfare up to 10 days before departure. You usually must book in advance, and once booked, no changes are permitted, so buy trip cancellation insurance. Also, make your check out to the company's escrow account, which provides some protection for your investment in the event that the charter operator fails. For further information, consult the publication *Jax Fax* (397 Post Rd., Darien, CT 06820; phone: 203-655-8746; fax: 203-655-6257).

DISCOUNTS ON SCHEDULED FLIGHTS

COURIER TRAVEL In return for arranging to accompany some kind of freight, a traveler pays only a portion of the total airfare (and sometimes a small registration fee). One agency that matches up would-be couriers with courier companies is *Now Voyager* (74 Varick St., Suite 307, New York, NY 10013; phone: 212-431-1616; fax: 212-334-5243).

Courier Companies

Discount Travel International (169 W. 81st St., New York, NY 10024; phone/fax: 212-362-3636; and 801 Alton Rd., Suite 1, Miami Beach, FL 33139; phone: 305-538-1616; fax: 305-673-9376).

F.B. On Board Courier Club (10225 Ryan Ave., Suite 103, Dorval, Quebec H9P 1A2, Canada; phone: 514-633-0740; fax: 514-633-0735).

Halbart Express (147-05 176th St., Jamaica, NY 11434; phone: 718-656-8279; fax: 718-244-0559).

Midnite Express (925 W. Hyde Park Blvd., Inglewood, CA 90302; phone: 310-672-1100; fax: 310-671-0107).

Way to Go Travel (6679 Sunset Blvd., Hollywood, CA 90028; phone: 213-466-1126; fax: 213-466-8994).

Publications

Insiders Guide to Air Courier Bargains, by Kelly Monaghan (The Intrepid Traveler, PO Box 438, New York, NY 10034; phone: 212-569-1081 for information; 800-356-9315 for orders; fax: 212-942-6687).

Travel Unlimited (PO Box 1058, Allston, MA 02134-1058; no phone).

CONSOLIDATORS AND BUCKET SHOPS These companies buy blocks of tickets from airlines and sell them at a discount to travel agents or directly to consumers. Since many bucket shops operate on a thin margin, be sure to check a company's record with the *Better Business Bureau*—before parting with any money.

Council Charter (205 E. 42nd St., New York, NY 10017; phone: 800-800-8222 or 212-661-0311; fax: 212-972-0194).

International Adventures (60 E. 42nd St., Room 763, New York, NY 10165; phone: 212-599-0577; fax: 212-599-3288).

Travac Tours and Charters (989 Ave. of the Americas, New York, NY 10018; phone: 800-872-8800 or 212-563-3303; fax: 212-563-3631).

Unitravel (1177 N. Warson Rd., St. Louis, MO 63132; phone: 800-325-2222 or 314-569-0900; fax: 314-569-2503).

LAST-MINUTE TRAVEL CLUBS Members of such clubs receive information on imminent trips and other bargain travel opportunities. There usually is an annual fee, although a few clubs offer free membership. Despite the names of some of the clubs listed below, you don't have to wait until literally the last minute to make travel plans.

Discount Travel International (114 Forrest Ave., Suite 203, Narberth, PA 19072; phone: 215-668-7184; fax: 215-668-9182).

FLY ASAP (PO Box 9808, Scottsdale, AZ 85252-3808; phone: 800-FLY-ASAP or 602-956-1987; fax: 602-956-6414).

Last Minute Travel (1249 Boylston St., Boston, MA 02215; phone: 800-LAST-MIN or 617-267-9800; fax: 617-424-1943).

Moment's Notice (425 Madison Ave., New York, NY 10017; phone: 212-486-0500/1/2/3; fax: 212-486-0783).

Spur of the Moment Cruises (411 N. Harbor Blvd., Suite 302, San Pedro, CA 90731; phone: 800-4-CRUISES or 310-521-1070 in California; 800-343-1991 elsewhere in the US; 24-hour hotline: 310-521-1060; fax: 310-521-1061).

Traveler's Advantage (3033 S. Parker Rd., Suite 900, Aurora, CO 80014; phone: 800-548-1116 or 800-835-8747; fax: 303-368-3985).

Vacations to Go (1502 Augusta Dr., Suite 415, Houston, TX 77057; phone: 713-974-2121 in Texas; 800-338-4962 elsewhere in the US; fax: 713-974-0445).

Worldwide Discount Travel Club (1674 Meridian Ave., Miami Beach, FL 33139; phone: 305-534-2082; fax: 305-534-2070).

GENERIC AIR TRAVEL These organizations operate much like an ordinary airline standby service, except that they offer seats on not one but several scheduled and charter airlines. One pioneer of generic flights is *Airhitch* (2790 Broadway, Suite 100, New York, NY 10025; phone: 212-864-2000).

BARTERED TRAVEL SOURCES Barter—the exchange of commodities or services in lieu of cash payment—is a common practice among travel suppliers. Companies that have obtained travel services through barter may sell these services at substantial discounts to travel clubs, who pass along the savings to members. One organization offering bartered travel opportunities is *Travel World Leisure Club* (225 W. 34th St., Suite 909, New York, NY 10122; phone: 800-444-TWLC or 212-239-4855; fax: 212-564-5158).

CONSUMER PROTECTION

Passengers whose complaints have not been satisfactorily addressed by the airline can contact the *US Department of Transportation* (*DOT;* Consumer Affairs Division, 400 Seventh St. SW, Room 10405, Washington, DC 20590; phone: 202-366-2220). Also see *Fly Rights* (Publication #050-000-00513-5; *US Government Printing Office,* PO Box 371954, Pittsburgh, PA 15250-7954; phone: 202-783-3238; fax: 202-512-2250). If you have safety-related questions or concerns, write to the *Federal Aviation Administration* (*FAA;* 800 Independence Ave. SW, Washington, DC 20591) or call the *FAA Consumer Hotline* (phone: 800-322-7873).

On Arrival

FROM THE AIRPORT TO THE CITY

A taxi ride downtown from *Los Angeles International Airport (LAX)* can take from 30 minutes to over an hour, depending on traffic. Fares average between $25 and $30.

The *Metropolitan Transit Authority (MTA)* provides bus service between *LAX* and downtown Los Angeles at Broadway and Sixth Street; the trip takes about an hour and costs $1.10. Scheduled buses running to other parts of the city require one or more transfers; for information, call the *MTA* (phone: 310-273-0910 in Beverly Hills/west Los Angeles; 818-781-5890 in the San Fernando Valley).

A more efficient alternative is to use private transport companies, which can be called from courtesy phones at the airport and also are listed in the yellow pages. For instance, *Supershuttle* (phone: 56735 from airport courtesy phones; 213-775-6600 or 310-782-6600 from regular phones) offers van service between *LAX* and downtown hotels for $12 ($13 to Beverly Hills).

RENTING A CAR

You can rent a car through a travel agent or national rental firm before leaving home, or from a regional or local company once in Los Angeles. Reserve in advance.

Most car rental companies require a credit card, although some will accept a substantial cash deposit. The minimum age to rent a car is set by the company; some also may impose special conditions on drivers above a certain age. Electing to pay for collision damage waiver (CDW) protection will add to the cost of renting a car, but releases you from financial liability for the vehicle. Additional costs include drop-off charges or one-way service fees.

Car Rental Companies

Ajax Rent-A-Car (phone: 213-386-3363 or 310-278-0601).
Alamo (phone: 800-327-9633).
Avis (phone: 800-331-1212).
Bob Leech Auto Rental (phone: 800-635-1240 or 310-673-2727).
Budget (phone: 800-527-0700).
Dollar Rent A Car (phone: 800-800-4000).
Enterprise Rent-A-Car (phone: 800-325-8007).
Hertz (phone: 800-654-3131).
National (phone: 800-CAR-RENT).
Payless (phone: 800-PAYLESS).
Rocket Rent-A-Car (phone: 213-380-4866 or 310-674-1820).
Sears (phone: 800-527-0770).
Snappy (phone: 800-669-4802).
Thrifty (phone: 800-367-2277).
U-Save Auto Rental (phone: 800-272-USAV, 800-343-4833, or 310-649-5806).

NOTE

Rent-A-Wreck (phone: 800-421-7253 for locations of franchises nationwide; 800-423-2158 or 310-478-0676 for the Los Angeles office) rents cars that are well worn but (presumably) mechanically sound. *CEDI Exotic Car Rental* (phone: 800-537-0044 or 310-337-7827) and *LuxuryLine-Rent-A-Car* (phone: 800-826-7805 or 310-659-5555) rent luxury models. For larger vehicles, try *MPG Car Van Truck Rental* (phone: 213-746-2421).

Package Tours

A package is a collection of travel services that can be purchased in a single transaction. Its principal advantages are convenience and economy—the cost usually is lower than that of the same services purchased separately. Tour programs generally can be divided into two categories: escorted or locally hosted (with a set itinerary) and independent (usually more flexible).

When considering a package tour, read the brochure *carefully* to determine exactly what is included and any conditions that may apply, and check the company's record with the *Better Business Bureau*. The *United States Tour Operators Association* (*USTOA;* 211 E. 51st St., Suite 12B, New York, NY 10022; phone: 212-750-7371; fax: 212-421-1285) also can be helpful in determining a package tour operator's reliability. As with charter flights, to safeguard your funds, always make your check out to the company's escrow account.

Many tour operators offer packages focused on special interests such as the arts, local history, sports, and other recreations. *All Adventure Travel* (5589 Arapahoe St., Suite 208, Boulder, CO 80303; phone: 800-537-4025 or 303-440-7924; fax: 303-440-4160) represents such specialized packagers. Many also are listed in the *Specialty Travel Index* (305 San Anselmo Ave., Suite 313, San Anselmo, CA 94960; phone: 415-459-4900 in California; 800-442-4922 elsewhere in the US; fax: 415-459-4974). In addition, a number of local companies offer half- and full-day sightseeing tours in and around Los Angeles.

Package Tour Operators

Adventure Tours (10612 Beaver Dam Rd., Hunt Valley, MD 21030-2205; phone: 410-785-3500 in the Baltimore area; 800-638-9040 elsewhere in the US; fax: 410-584-2771).

Alaska Airlines Vacations (PO Box 68900, Seattle, WA 98168-0900; phone: 800-468-2248; fax: 206-433-3374).

American Airlines FlyAAway Vacations (offices throughout the US; phone: 800-321-2121).

Caravan Tours (401 N. Michigan Ave., Chicago, IL 60611; phone: 800-CARAVAN or 312-321-9800; fax: 312-321-9810).

Cartan Tours (2809 Butterfield Rd., Suite 350, Oak Brook, IL 60521; phone: 800-422-7826 or 708-571-1400; fax: 708-574-8074).

Certified Vacations (110 E. Broward Blvd., Ft. Lauderdale, FL 33302; phone: 800-233-7260 or 305-522-1440; fax: 305-357-4687).

Classic America (1 N. First St., San Jose, CA 95113; phone: 800-221-3949 or 408-287-4550; fax: 408-287-9272).

Collette Tours (162 Middle St., Pawtucket, RI 02860; phone: 800-752-2655 in New England; 800-832-4656 elsewhere in the US; fax: 401-727-4745).

Continental Grand Destinations (offices throughout the US; phone: 800-634-5555).

Dailey-Thorp (330 W. 58th St., New York, NY 10019-1817; phone: 212-307-1555; fax: 212-974-1420).

Dan Dipert Tours (PO Box 580, Arlington, TX 76004-0580; phone: 800-433-5335 or 817-543-3710; fax: 817-543-3729).

Delta's Dream Vacations (PO Box 1525, Ft. Lauderdale, FL 33302; phone: 800-872-7786).

Domenico Tours (751 Broadway, Bayonne, NJ 07002; phone: 800-554-8687, 201-823-8687, or 212-757-8687; fax: 201-823-1527).

Globetrotters SuperCities (139 Main St., Cambridge, MA 02142; phone: 800-333-1234 or 617-621-0099; fax: 617-577-8380).

Globus/Cosmos (5301 S. Federal Circle, Littleton, CO 80123; phone: 800-221-0090, 800-556-5454, or 303-797-2800; fax: 303-347-2080).

GOGO Tours (69 Spring St., Ramsey, NJ 07446-0507; phone: 201-934-3759).

Jefferson Tours (1206 Currie Ave., Minneapolis, MN 55403; phone: 800-767-7433 or 612-338-4174; fax: 612-332-5532).

Kerrville Tours (PO Box 79, Shreveport, LA 71161-0079; phone: 800-442-8705 or 318-227-2882; fax: 318-227-2486).

Le Ob's Tours (4635 Touro St., New Orleans, LA 70122-3933; phone: 504-288-3478; fax: 504-288-8517).

Maupintour (PO Box 807, Lawrence, KS 66044; phone: 800-255-4266 or 913-843-1211; fax: 913-843-8351).

New England Vacation Tours (PO Box 560, West Dover, VT 05356; phone: 800-742-7669 or 802-464-2076; fax: 802-464-2629).

Sunmakers (15375 SE 30th Pl., Suite 350, Bellevue, WA 98007; phone: 800-841-4321 or 206-643-8180; fax: 800-323-2231).

Tauck Tours (PO Box 5027, Westport, CT 06881; phone: 800-468-2825 or 203-226-6911; fax: 203-221-6828).

Tours and Travel Odyssey (230 E. McClellan Ave., Livingston, NJ 07039; phone: 800-527-2989 or 201-992-5459; fax: 201-994-1618).

TravelTours International (250 W. 49th St., Suite 600, New York, NY 10019; phone: 800-767-8777 or 212-262-0700; fax: 212-944-5854).

TWA Getaway Vacations (Getaway Vacation Center, 10 E. Stow Rd., Marlton, NJ 08053; phone: 800-GETAWAY; fax: 609-985-4125).

United Airlines Vacations (PO Box 24580, Milwaukee, WI 53224-0580; phone: 800-328-6877).

Companies Offering Day Tours

Burbury Wine Tours (2554 Lincoln Blvd., Suite 525, Marina del Rey, CA 90291; phone: 800-345-4265 or 310-208-0980; fax: 310-822-1360).

Casablanca Tours (*Hollywood Roosevelt Hotel,* 7000 Hollywood Blvd., Cabaña 4, Hollywood, CA 90028; phone: 800-49-TOUR-1 or 213-461-0156; fax: 213-465-8053).

Graveline Tours (PO Box 931694, Hollywood, CA 90093; phone: 213-469-3127 for recorded information; 213-469-4149 for customer assistance).
Gray Line Los Angeles (9830 Belanca St., Los Angeles, CA 90045; phone: 800-279-5800 or 310-337-3000; fax: 310-337-3003).
Heli USA Helicopters (3200 Airport Ave., Suite 6, Santa Monica, CA 90405; phone: 800-359-8727 or 310-553-4354; fax: 310-391-7134).
Hollywood Fantasy Tours (6731 Hollywood Blvd., Hollywood, CA 90028; phone: 800-782-7287 or 213-469-8184; fax: 213-466-9170).
Los Angeles Conservancy (727 W. Seventh St., Suite 955, Los Angeles, CA 90017; phone: 213-623-2489; fax: 213-623-3909).
Los Angeles Harbor Cruise (Village Boat House, Berth 78, Ports o' Call Village, San Pedro, CA 90731; phone: 310-831-0996; fax: 310-831-0599).
Magic Line Sightseeing Tours (5322 Wilshire Blvd., Suite 710, Los Angeles, CA 90036; phone: 800-956-2442 or 213-653-1090; fax: 213-937-4296).

Insurance

The first person with whom you should discuss travel insurance is your own insurance broker. You may discover that the insurance you already carry protects you adequately while traveling and that you need little additional coverage. If you charge travel services, the credit card company also may provide some insurance coverage (and other safeguards).

Types of Travel Insurance
Automobile insurance: Provides collision, theft, property damage, and personal liability protection while driving.
Baggage and personal effects insurance: Protects your bags and their contents in case of damage or theft at any point during your travels.
Default and/or bankruptcy insurance: Provides coverage in the event of default and/or bankruptcy on the part of the tour operator, airline, or other travel supplier.
Flight insurance: Covers accidental injury or death while flying.
Personal accident and sickness insurance: Covers cases of illness, injury, or death in an accident while traveling.
Trip cancellation and interruption insurance: Guarantees a refund if you must cancel a trip; may reimburse you for additional travel costs incurred in catching up with a tour or traveling home early.
Combination policies: Include any or all of the above.

Disabled Travelers

Make travel arrangements well in advance. Specify to all services involved the nature of your disability to determine if there are accommodations and facilities that meet your needs. For detailed information on accessibility, contact the *Junior League of Los Angeles* (*Farmers' Market,* Third and Fairfax, Los Angeles, CA 90036; phone: 213-937-5566; fax: 213-937-9844), which publishes *Around the Town with Ease.*

Organizations

ACCENT on Living (PO Box 700, Bloomington, IL 61702; phone: 800-787-8444 or 309-378-2961; fax: 309-378-4420).

Access: The Foundation for Accessibility by the Disabled (PO Box 356, Malverne, NY 11565; phone/fax: 516-887-5798).

American Foundation for the Blind (15 W. 16th St., New York, NY 10011; phone: 800-232-5463 or 212-620-2147; fax: 212-727-7418).

Information Center for Individuals with Disabilities (Ft. Point Pl., 27-43 Wormwood St., Boston, MA 02210; phone: 800-462-5015 in Massachusetts; 617-727-5540 elsewhere in the US; TDD: 617-345-9743; fax: 617-345-5318).

Mobility International (main office: 228 Borough High St., London SE1 1JX, England; phone: 44-171-403-5688; fax: 44-171-378-1292; US office: *MIUSA,* PO Box 10767, Eugene, OR 97440; phone/TDD: 503-343-1284; fax: 503-343-6812).

Moss Rehabilitation Hospital Travel Information Service (telephone referrals only; phone: 215-456-9600; TDD: 215-456-9602).

National Rehabilitation Information Center (8455 Colesville Rd., Suite 935, Silver Spring, MD 20910; phone: 301-588-9284; fax: 301-587-1967).

Paralyzed Veterans of America (*PVA;* PVA/ATTS Program, 801 18th St. NW, Washington, DC 20006; phone: 202-872-1300 in Washington, DC; 800-424-8200 elsewhere in the US; fax: 202-785-4452).

Royal Association for Disability and Rehabilitation (*RADAR;* 12 City Forum, 250 City Rd., London EC1V 8AF, England; phone: 44-171-250-3222; fax: 44-171-250-0212).

Society for the Advancement of Travel for the Handicapped (*SATH;* 347 Fifth Ave., Suite 610, New York, NY 10016; phone: 212-447-7284; fax: 212-725-8253).

Travel Industry and Disabled Exchange (*TIDE;* 5435 Donna Ave., Tarzana, CA 91356; phone: 818-368-5648).

Publications

Access Travel: A Guide to the Accessibility of Airport Terminals (Consumer Information Center, Dept. 578Z, Pueblo, CO 81009; phone: 719-948-3334).

Air Transportation of Handicapped Persons (Publication #AC-120-32; *US Department of Transportation,* Distribution Unit, Publications Section, M-443-2, 400 Seventh St. SW, Washington, DC 20590; phone: 202-366-0039).

The Diabetic Traveler (PO Box 8223 RW, Stamford, CT 06905; phone: 203-327-5832; fax: 203-975-1748).

Directory of Travel Agencies for the Disabled and Travel for the Disabled, both by Helen Hecker (Twin Peaks Press, PO Box 129, Vancouver, WA 98666; phone: 800-637-CALM or 206-694-2462; fax: 206-696-3210).

Guide to Traveling with Arthritis (Upjohn Company, PO Box 989, Dearborn, MI 48121; phone: 800-253-9860).

The Handicapped Driver's Mobility Guide (American Automobile Association, 1000 AAA Dr., Heathrow, FL 32746-5080; phone: 407-444-7000; fax: 407-444-7380).

Handicapped Travel Newsletter (PO Box 269, Athens, TX 75751; phone/fax: 903-677-1260).

Handi-Travel: A Resource Book for Disabled and Elderly Travellers, by Cinnie Noble (Canadian Rehabilitation Council for the Disabled, 45 Sheppard Ave. E., Suite 801, Toronto, Ontario M2N 5W9, Canada; phone/TDD: 416-250-7490; fax: 416-229-1371).

Incapacitated Passengers Air Travel Guide (International Air Transport Association, Publications Sales Department, 2000 Peel St., Montreal, Quebec H3A 2R4, Canada; phone: 514-844-6311; fax: 514-844-5286).

Ticket to Safe Travel (American Diabetes Association, 1660 Duke St., Alexandria, VA 22314; phone: 800-232-3472 or 703-549-1500; fax: 703-836-7439).

Travel for the Patient with Chronic Obstructive Pulmonary Disease (Dr. Harold Silver, 1601 18th St. NW, Washington, DC 20009; phone: 202-667-0134; fax: 202-667-0148).

Travel Tips for Hearing-Impaired People (American Academy of Otolaryngology, 1 Prince St., Alexandria, VA 22314; phone: 703-836-4444; fax: 703-683-5100).

Travel Tips for People with Arthritis (Arthritis Foundation, 1314 Spring St. NW, Atlanta, GA 30309; phone: 800-283-7800 or 404-872-7100; fax: 404-872-0457).

Traveling Like Everybody Else: A Practical Guide for Disabled Travelers, by Jacqueline Freedman and Susan Gersten (Modan Publishing, PO Box 1202, Bellmore, NY 11710; phone: 516-679-1380; fax: 516-679-1448).

The Wheelchair Traveler, by Douglass R. Annand (123 Ball Hill Rd., Milford, NH 03055; phone: 603-673-4539).

Package Tour Operators

Accessible Journeys (35 W. Sellers Ave., Ridley Park, PA 19078; phone: 800-846-4537 or 215-521-0339; fax: 215-521-6959).

Accessible Tours/Directions Unlimited (Attn.: Lois Bonnani, 720 N. Bedford Rd., Bedford Hills, NY 10507; phone: 800-533-5343 or 914-241-1700; fax: 914-241-0243).

Beehive Business and Leisure Travel (1130 W. Center St., N. Salt Lake, UT 84054; phone: 800-777-5727 or 801-292-4445; fax: 801-298-9460).

Classic Travel Service (8 W. 40th St., New York, NY 10018; phone: 212-869-2560 in New York State; 800-247-0909 elsewhere in the US; fax: 212-944-4493).

Evergreen Travel Service (4114 198th St. SW, Suite 13, Lynnwood, WA 98036-6742; phone: 800-435-2288 or 206-776-1184; fax: 206-775-0728).

Flying Wheels Travel (143 W. Bridge St., PO Box 382, Owatonna, MN 55060; phone: 800-535-6790 or 507-451-5005; fax: 507-451-1685).

Good Neighbor Travel Service (124 S. Main St., Viroqua, WI 54665; phone: 800-338-3245 or 608-637-2128; fax: 608-637-3030).

The Guided Tour (7900 Old York Rd., Suite 114B, Elkins Park, PA 19117-2339; phone: 800-783-5841 or 215-782-1370; fax: 215-635-2637).

Hinsdale Travel (201 E. Ogden Ave., Hinsdale, IL 60521; phone: 708-325-1335 or 708-469-7349; fax: 708-325-1342).

MedEscort International (*ABE International Airport,* PO Box 8766, Allentown, PA 18105-8766; phone: 800-255-7182 or 215-791-3111; fax: 215-791-9189).

Prestige World Travel (5710-X High Point Rd., Greensboro, NC 27407; phone: 800-476-7737 or 910-292-6690; fax: 910-632-9404).

Sprout (893 Amsterdam Ave., New York, NY 10025; phone: 212-222-9575; fax: 212-222-9768).

Weston Travel Agency (134 N. Cass Ave., Westmont, IL 60559; phone: 708-968-2513 in Illinois; 800-633-3725 elsewhere in the US; fax: 708-968-2539).

SPECIAL SERVICES

Wheelchair Getaways (main office: PO Box 605, Versailles, KY 40383; phone: 800-642-2042; phone/fax: 606-873-4973; Los Angeles area office: 24252 Tahoe Court, Laguna Niguel, CA 92656; phone: 800-659-1972 or 714-831-1972; fax: 714-362-2414) rents vans designed to accommodate wheelchairs.

Single Travelers

The travel industry is not very fair to people who vacation by themselves—they often end up paying more than those traveling in pairs. There are services catering to single travelers, however, that match travel companions, offer travel arrangements with shared accommodations, and provide information and discounts. Useful publications include *Going Solo* (Doerfer Communications, PO Box 123, Apalachicola, FL 32329; phone/fax: 904-653-8848) and *Traveling on Your Own*, by Eleanor Berman

(Random House, Order Dept., 400 Hahn Rd., Westminster, MD 21157; phone: 800-733-3000; fax: 800-659-2436).

Organizations and Companies
- *Contiki Holidays* (300 Plaza Alicante, Suite 900, Garden Grove, CA 92640; phone: 800-466-0610 or 714-740-0808; fax: 714-740-0818).
- *Gallivanting* (515 E. 79th St., Suite 20F, New York, NY 10021; phone: 800-933-9699 or 212-988-0617; fax: 212-988-0144).
- *Globus/Cosmos* (5301 S. Federal Circle, Littleton, CO 80123; phone: 800-221-0090, 800-556-5454, or 303-797-2800; fax: 303-347-2080).
- *Jane's International and Sophisticated Women Travelers* (2603 Bath Ave., Brooklyn, NY 11214; phone: 718-266-2045; fax: 718-266-4062).
- *Marion Smith Singles* (611 Prescott Pl., N. Woodmere, NY 11581; phone: 516-791-4852, 516-791-4865, or 212-944-2112; fax: 516-791-4879).
- *Partners-in-Travel* (11660 Chenault St., Suite 119, Los Angeles, CA 90049; phone: 310-476-4869).
- *Singles in Motion* (545 W. 236th St., Riverdale, NY 10463; phone/fax: 718-884-4464).
- *Singleworld* (401 Theodore Fremd Ave., Rye, NY 10580; phone: 800-223-6490 or 914-967-3334; fax: 914-967-7395).
- *Solo Flights* (63 High Noon Rd., Weston, CT 06883; phone: 800-266-1566 or 203-226-9993).
- *Suddenly Singles Tours* (161 Dreiser Loop, Bronx, NY 10475; phone: 718-379-8800 in New York City; 800-859-8396 elsewhere in the US; fax: 718-379-8858).
- *Travel Companion Exchange* (PO Box 833, Amityville, NY 11701; phone: 516-454-0880; fax: 516-454-0170).
- *Travel Companions* (Atrium Financial Center, 1515 N. Federal Hwy., Suite 300, Boca Raton, FL 33432; phone: 800-383-7211 or 407-393-6448; fax: 407-451-8560).
- *Travel in Two's* (239 N. Broadway, Suite 3, N. Tarrytown, NY 10591; phone: 914-631-8301 in New York State; 800-692-5252 elsewhere in the US).
- *Umbrella Singles* (PO Box 157, Woodbourne, NY 12788; phone: 800-537-2797 or 914-434-6871; fax: 914-434-3532).

Older Travelers

Special discounts and more free time are just two factors that have given older travelers a chance to see the world at affordable prices. Many travel suppliers offer senior discounts—sometimes only to members of certain senior citizens organizations (which provide benefits of their own). When considering a particular package, make sure the facilities—and the pace of the tour—match your needs and physical condition.

Publications

The Mature Traveler (PO Box 50820, Reno, NV 89513-0820; phone: 702-786-7419).

The Senior Citizen's Guide to Budget Travel in the US and Canada, by Paige Palmer (Pilot Books, 103 Cooper St., Babylon, NY 11702; phone: 516-422-2225; fax: 516-422-2227).

Take a Camel to Lunch and Other Adventures for Mature Travelers, by Nancy O'Connell (Bristol Publishing Enterprises, PO Box 1737, San Leandro, CA 94577; phone: 510-895-4461 in California; 800-346-4889 elsewhere in the US; fax: 510-895-4459).

Unbelievably Good Deals & Great Adventures That You Absolutely Can't Get Unless You're Over 50, by Joan Rattner Heilman (Contemporary Books, 1200 Stetson Ave., Chicago, IL 60601; phone: 312-782-9181; fax: 312-540-4687).

Organizations

American Association of Retired Persons (*AARP;* 601 E St. NW, Washington, DC 20049; phone: 202-434-2277).

Golden Companions (PO Box 754, Pullman, WA 99163-0754; phone: 208-858-2183).

Mature Outlook (Customer Service Center, 6001 N. Clark St., Chicago, IL 60660; phone: 800-336-6330).

National Council of Senior Citizens (1331 F St. NW, Washington, DC 20004; phone: 202-347-8800; fax: 202-624-9595).

Package Tour Operators

Elderhostel (75 Federal St., Boston, MA 02110-1941; phone: 617-426-7788; fax: 617-426-8351).

Evergreen Travel Service (4114 198th St. SW, Suite 13, Lynnwood, WA 98036-6742; phone: 800-435-2288 or 206-776-1184; fax: 206-775-0728).

Gadabout Tours (700 E. Tahquitz Canyon Way, Palm Springs, CA 92262; phone: 800-952-5068 or 619-325-5556; fax: 619-325-5127).

Grand Circle Travel (347 Congress St., Boston, MA 02210; phone: 800-221-2610 or 617-350-7500; fax: 617-423-0445).

Grandtravel (6900 Wisconsin Ave., Suite 706, Chevy Chase, MD 20815; phone: 800-247-7651 or 301-986-0790; fax: 301-913-0166).

Interhostel (*University of New Hampshire,* Division of Continuing Education, 6 Garrison Ave., Durham, NH 03824; phone: 800-733-9753 or 603-862-1147; fax: 603-862-1113).

Mature Tours (c/o *Solo Flights,* 63 High Noon Rd., Weston, CT 06883; phone: 800-266-1566 or 203-226-9993).

OmniTours (104 Wilmot Rd., Deerfield, IL 60015; phone: 800-962-0060 or 708-374-0088; fax: 708-374-9515).

Saga International Holidays (222 Berkeley St., Boston, MA 02116; phone: 800-343-0273 or 617-262-2262; fax: 617-375-5950).

Money Matters

CREDIT CARDS AND TRAVELER'S CHECKS

Most major credit cards enjoy wide domestic and international acceptance; however, not every hotel, restaurant, or shop in Los Angeles accepts all (or in some cases any) credit cards. It's also wise to carry traveler's checks while on the road, since they are widely accepted and replaceable if stolen or lost. You can buy traveler's checks at banks and some are available by mail or phone. Keep a separate list of all traveler's checks (noting those that you have cashed) and the names and numbers of your credit cards. Both traveler's check and credit card companies have numbers to call for information or in the event of loss or theft.

CASH MACHINES

Automated teller machines (ATMs) are increasingly common worldwide, and most banks participate in ATM networks such as *CIRRUS* (phone: 800-4-CIRRUS) and *PLUS* (phone: 800-THE-PLUS). Cardholders can withdraw cash from any machine in the same network using either a "bank" card or, in some cases, a credit card. Additional information on ATMs and networks can be obtained from your bank or credit card company.

SENDING MONEY

Should the need arise, you can have money sent to you in Los Angeles via the services provided by *American Express MoneyGram* (phone: 800-926-9400 for information; 800-866-8800 for money transfers) or *Western Union Financial Services* (phone: 800-325-6000 or 800-325-4176).

Time Zone

Los Angeles is in the pacific standard time zone. Daylight saving time is observed from the first Sunday in April until the last Sunday in October.

Business and Shopping Hours

Los Angeles maintains business hours that are fairly standard throughout the US: 9 AM to 5 PM, Mondays through Fridays. Although banking hours generally are weekdays from 9 AM to 3 PM, some banks stay open until 5 or 6 PM on Fridays, and some also offer Saturday morning hours. Retail stores usually are open Mondays through Saturdays from 10 AM to 6 PM; many also are open on Sundays from noon to 5 PM. Most malls and department stores in the Los Angeles area stay open until 9 PM on weekdays and Saturdays, and until 6:30 or 7 PM on Sundays.

Mail

Los Angeles's main post office (7101 S. Central Ave.; Los Angeles, CA 90001; phone: 213-586-1723) is open weekdays from 7 AM to 7 PM and Saturdays from 7 AM to 3 PM. Near *LAX,* the *World Way* post office (5800 Century Blvd.; Los Angeles, CA 90009; phone: 310-337-8885) is open 24 hours daily. The Beverly Hills branch (235 N. Maple Dr., Los Angeles, CA 90210; phone: 310-247-3400) is open weekdays from 8:30 AM to 5 PM. For other branches, call the main post office or check the yellow pages.

Stamps also are available at most hotel desks, some supermarkets and other stores, and from public vending machines. For rapid, overnight delivery to other cities, use *Express Mail* (available at post offices), *Federal Express* (phone: 800-238-5355), or *DHL Worldwide Express* (phone: 800-225-5345).

You can have mail sent to you care of your hotel (marked "Guest Mail, Hold for Arrival") or to the main post office (sent "c/o General Delivery" to the address above). *American Express* offices in Los Angeles also will hold mail for customers ("c/o Client Letter Service"); information is provided in their pamphlet *Travelers' Companion.*

Telephone

The area code for central Los Angeles and Hollywood is 213; Beverly Hills is split between the 213 and 310 area codes. The 310 area code also includes West Hollywood, as well as Malibu, Santa Monica, Venice, and other coastal areas. The San Fernando Valley and the upper half of the San Gabriel Valley are in the 818 area code. The Ventura/Santa Barbara area is in the 805 area code. The area code for Orange County is 714.

To make a long-distance call, dial 1 + the area code + the local number. The nationwide number for information is 555-1212; you also can dial 411 for local information. If you need a number in another area code, dial 1 + the area code + 555-1212. (If you don't know an area code, dial 555-1212 or 411 for directory assistance.)

Although you can use a telephone company calling card number on any phone, pay phones that take major credit cards (*American Express, MasterCard, Visa,* and so on) are increasingly common. Also available are combined telephone calling/bank credit cards, such as the *AT&T Universal Card* (PO Box 44167, Jacksonville, FL 32231-4167; phone: 800-423-4343). Similarly, *Sprint* (8140 Ward Pkwy., Kansas City, MO 64114; phone: 800-THE-MOST or 800-800-USAA) offers the *VisaPhone* program, through which you can add phone card privileges to your existing *Visa* card. Companies offering long-distance phone cards without additional credit card privileges include *AT&T* (phone: 800-CALL-ATT), *Executive Telecard*

International (4260 E. Evans Ave., Suite 6, Denver, CO 80222; phone: 800-950-3800), *MCI* (323 Third St. SE, Cedar Rapids, IA 52401; phone: 800-444-4444; and 12790 Merit Dr., Dallas, TX 75251; phone: 800-444-3333), *Metromedia Communications* (1 International Center, 100 NE Loop 410, San Antonio, TX 78216; phone: 800-275-0200), and *Sprint* (address above).

Hotels routinely add surcharges to the cost of phone calls made from their rooms. Long-distance telephone services that may help you avoid this added expense are provided by a number of companies, including *AT&T* (International Information Service, 635 Grant St., Pittsburgh, PA 15219; phone: 800-874-4000), *MCI* (address above), *Metromedia Communications* (address above), and *Sprint* (address above). Note that even when you use such long-distance services, some hotels still may charge a fee for line usage.

Useful resources for travelers include the *AT&T 800 Travel Directory* (phone: 800-426-8686 for orders), the *Toll-Free Travel & Vacation Information Directory* (Pilot Books, 103 Cooper St., Babylon, NY 11702; phone: 516-422-2225; fax: 516-422-2227), and *The Phone Booklet* (Scott American Corporation, PO Box 88, W. Redding, CT 06896; no phone).

Medical Aid

In an emergency: Dial 911 for assistance, 0 for an operator, or go directly to the emergency room of the nearest hospital.

Hospitals
California Medical Center (1401 S. Hope St.; phone: 213-748-2411).
Cedars Sinai Medical Center (8700 Beverly Blvd.; phone: 310-855-5000).
University of Southern California Medical Center (1200 N. State St.; phone: 213-226-2622).

24-Hour Pharmacies
Kaiser Pharmacy (*Kaiser Hospital;* 6041 Cadillac Ave. and La Cienega Blvd.; phone: 213-857-2155).
Kaiser Pharmacy (1526 Edgemont Ave. and Sunset Blvd.; phone: 213-667-8301).
Savon (6360 W. Third St.; phone: 213-937-3030).

Additional Resources
International SOS Assistance (PO Box 11568, Philadelphia, PA 19116; phone: 800-523-8930 or 215-244-1500; fax: 215-244-2227).
Medic Alert Foundation (2323 Colorado Ave., Turlock, CA 95382; phone: 800-ID-ALERT or 209-668-3333; fax: 209-669-2495).
Travel Care International (*Eagle River Airport,* PO Box 846, Eagle River, WI 54521; phone: 800-5-AIR-MED or 715-479-8881; fax: 715-479-8178).

Legal Aid

If you don't have, or cannot reach, your own attorney, most cities offer legal referral services maintained by county bar associations. These services ensure that anyone in need of legal representation gets it and can match you with a local attorney. For legal assistance in Los Angeles, contact the *Los Angeles County Bar Association Lawyer Referral and Information Service* (PO Box 55020, Los Angeles, CA 90055-2020; phone: 213-243-1525 for lawyer referral service; 213-243-1500 for "SmartLaw" 24-hour automated legal information hotline). If you must appear in court, you are entitled to court-appointed representation if you can't obtain a lawyer or can't afford one.

For Further Information

Tourist information is available from the *Los Angeles Convention & Visitors Bureau* (685 Figueroa St., Los Angeles, CA 90017; phone: 213-624-7300; 213-689-8822 for recorded information; fax: 213-624-1992). Information on Los Angeles also can be obtained from the *California Trade and Commerce Agency, Division of Tourism* (801 K St., Suite 1600, Sacramento, CA 95814; phone: 800-GO-CALIF or 916-322-2881; fax: 916-322-3402; mailing address: PO Box 1499, Sacramento, CA 95814). For additional sources of tourist information for Los Angeles, see *Sources and Resources* in THE CITY.

The City

Los Angeles

In Los Angeles, the movie capital of the world, despite all adversity, almost everything has a happy ending—although last year had its share of skeptics. On January 17, 1994, Angelenos—the people of the city of Los Angeles—were rudely awakened by a devastating earthquake that measured 6.8 on the Richter scale and killed dozens of apartment dwellers and destroyed homes, buildings, freeways, and bridges as it snaked from its epicenter in Northridge, in the San Fernando Valley, southwest to the Santa Monica beaches. The most powerful in the city's history, this destructive tremor and consequent aftershocks caused billions of dollars in damage, not to mention emotional toll on city residents still reeling from the fires, mudslides, and riots of recent years.

As the year progressed, however, souls slowly mended while freeways and other structures were repaired at breakneck speed. Of the handful of hotels, restaurants, and businesses that suffered damage, the vast majority were repaired and back in business within months. However, a few closed their doors forever. (At press time we checked on the status of those that had been affected and reported what we found, but you are advised to call ahead for updated information.) Transportation returned to normal surprisingly quickly, too, with roads like the collapsed San Diego Freeway reopened in April 1994, and most others speedily repaired. One large attraction ravaged by the quake, the Los Angeles Memorial Coliseum *(home of the* Raiders *and the* University of Southern California *football teams), was undergoing repairs that would cost nearly $40 million and was scheduled to reopen at press time (again, call for updates).*

Back in business once again, Los Angeles has fulfilled the dream of living happily ever after—and then some. Read on.

Whatever you have heard—or think you know—about Los Angeles is probably wrong. Or misleading. Or hyperbole. This is a city that leads the league in misconceptions. To set the record straight on a few points:

- Despite the palm trees, Los Angeles is not tropical.
- Los Angeles is not a clutch of countless suburbs in search of a city, but rather it's a vast metropolis encompassing the City of Los Angeles plus a sprawl of municipalities and unincorporated areas.
- One cannot swim comfortably in the Pacific during the winter, when cold Alaskan currents often drop the water temperature into the 50s.
- Debilitating smog is rare, most often occurs in summer, and usually is worst in valley areas.
- It is possible to visit Los Angeles happily without spending every minute inside a car.

- The arts—music, theater, dance—can be readily enjoyed, are flourishing, and have made Los Angeles a leading cultural city.
- The city has more people than swimming pools.
- Gang violence and other street crime continue to plague the inner city, just as in most other major metropolises.
- Sunglasses are not issued to residents at birth.

Los Angeles, like it or not, is a city of dreams, myths, and misunderstandings. It is our nation's Olympus, where certain of our gods live and cavort and where both good and bad are inflated to larger-than-life proportions. Yes, certainly, there is glitter and foolishness and often much about which to chuckle. Yes, admittedly, there are the curses of snarled traffic and eye-tearing smog.

But much of the rest can be sublime.

To begin with, the 8.6 million people who call the LA metropolitan area home care little about the City of Angels' skewed—and skewered—reputation. They are there, for the most part, not for the glitz and hijinks but for the quality of life.

There is no doubt that Los Angeles is one of the world's most beautifully situated and climate-blessed cities (except for the earthquakes and the smog). The mile-high San Gabriel Mountains skirt Los Angeles to the north and the Santa Monica Mountains bisect it, thus allowing Angelenos to enjoy magnificent vistas and offering the unusual opportunity for secluded hillside living in the midst of a vast metropolis. These lofty ranges also mean that this is one of the few places on the globe where it is possible in the same day both to ski and to surf (though you'll want to wear a wetsuit while surfing in winter).

On the other hand, many visitors are stunned to learn that Los Angeles isn't always favored with blue skies and perpetual sunshine. Late summer and early fall usually are the hottest times of year, when the dusty, dry Santa Ana winds blow out of the nearby eastern desert to elevate temperatures into the 90s—and sometimes 100s—and escalate temperaments into the danger zone. This is the time, wrote LA crime novelist Raymond Chandler, that wives finger the sharp edges of knives and study the contour of their husbands' necks. Oddly enough, spring and early summer can bring the dullest weather of the year—chill fog and overcast skies. Winter is the rainy season and can be glorious or awful—and normally is both, in spurts. Rainfalls can be quick and violent, giving way to clear warm days and cool nights. Although the city has experienced occasional severe floods in recent years, there is little danger of it being transformed into swampland.

Despite these vicissitudes, it is virtually inevitable that *New Year's Day* will dawn bright and sunny, with temperatures in the 80s, and that the achingly beautiful panoramas seen by the tens of millions watching the *Rose Bowl* game on television only will reinforce the LA legend.

Los Angeles traces its origins to a dusty little settlement founded in 1781 by order of a Spanish colonial governor. The settlers gave it the monumental name of El Pueblo de Nuestra Señora la Reina de los Angeles (The Town of Our Lady the Queen of the Angels). In 1850, after California was ceded to the United States (following the Mexican-American War), it had a population of only 1,610, and by the year 1900, it was the home of only a few more than 100,000 residents.

Still largely composed of citrus groves and bean fields at the turn of the century, Los Angeles retained much of the character of its Spanish and Mexican roots until the massive American migration to the West Coast began in the 1920s. California was the country's last frontier, a chance to start a new life and make one's fortune, and the city, along with the state, boomed. In the 1930s, the area attracted those rendered homeless and near hopeless by the Great Depression; in the 1940s, servicemen on their way home from World War II stopped here to put the past behind them. The 1950s and 1960s saw LA develop into a center for new businesses—the technological and aerospace industries of the future.

The film industry had begun to develop here in the 1920s, with the arrival of the early movie moguls who were drawn from New York by the sun, which permitted outdoor filming year-round. Later, the city attracted the television and music businesses as well. To much of the rest of the nation, however, Los Angeles was still "the Coast," a place dismissed laughingly and almost automatically as provincial and self-absorbed.

Meanwhile, Los Angeles began an effort to shed its second class mantle. The archaic ordinance that limited downtown buildings to the height of *City Hall* (presumably for earthquake protection) was scrapped, and a skyline began to rise. Major league sports arrived in 1946 with the *NFL Rams* from Cleveland, followed by professional teams in the top ranks of baseball, basketball, and hockey. Finally, in 1964, the city proudly opened the ambitious, multi-theater complex called the *Music Center*.

Over the years, Los Angeles also has become a favorite vacation destination and now welcomes more than 60 million visitors annually from all over the world, making *Los Angeles International Airport* the fourth-busiest in the country. Travelers are lured to LA not only by its salubrious weather and the chance of glimpsing a movie or TV personality but also by its theaters, symphony orchestras, opera and light opera companies, dance troupes, museums, and scores of top professional and college sporting events. Specific areas of Los Angeles have become attractions in themselves: Hollywood and its *Mann's Chinese Theatre,* with its footprints and handprints of the stars embedded in cement; Beverly Hills and its expensive shops and Rolls-Royce lifestyle; Westwood, with its footloose university-town ambience; and the casual but wealthy beach communities stretching from Malibu to the Palos Verdes Peninsula. The more traditional tourist sites and activities—*Disneyland, Universal Studios, Movieland, Knott's Berry Farm, Marineland,* and so on—continue to draw many visitors to Los Angeles and its surrounding areas as well.

Today, LA is a sophisticated city boasting the kinds of hotels, restaurants, shopping, nightlife, museums, and cultural events that befit the second-largest city in the nation. It also has a state-of-the-art regional commuter rail service (*Metrolink*) that connects downtown with a host of cities from north to south between Ventura and Oceanside and west to east to San Bernadino. There's also a fledgling subway system—the first leg of the *Metro Red Line* (a 4.4-mile segment between *Union Station* and *MacArthur Park*) opened in 1993. The underground train will eventually cover 22.7 miles of the city. The $5.3-billion project was designed to ease the city's traffic congestion; and tax-paying Angelenos surely hope it does.

To further ease the area's transportation problems, the new *Glenn Anderson Freeway* (Rte. 105) opened last year linking *LAX* (the airport), the *Great Western Forum* (the sports arena), and *Hollywood Park* (the racetrack) via one major thoroughfare. The route runs between El Segundo and Norwalk and includes bus and car pool lanes and a light rail route, down the center, to be used when the *Metro Green Line* opens (it is scheduled to be ready for public use by the end of this year). The *Green Line,* part of the city's expanded rail system, will link 13 communities, from Norwalk to Redondo Beach, with 14 stations and 10 parking lots along the route. By the end of this year, shuttle buses are expected to be available to take airport passengers directly to trains headed for downtown LA, with transfers to the *Blue Line* at Imperial and Wilmington, or to trains headed south to Long Beach (also on the *Blue Line*). For more information, see *Getting Around,* below.

Los Angeles also has the largest convention center on the West Coast, thanks to a 1993 expansion that added 2.5 million square feet to the downtown *Los Angeles Convention Center.* Improvements included 685,000 square feet of exhibit hall space, two 400-seat restaurants, food courts, a picturesque plaza landscaped with palm trees, and two 150-foot-high glass lobby pavilions.

The City of Angels still has its critics. Its vast size (the city itself is almost half as big as the entire state of Rhode Island) may make it seem uncomfortably spread out and sometimes difficult to negotiate. But most people find LA a pleasant and easy city in which to live and to visit. Beneath the official municipal veneer, away from the sunshine, and removed from the artificial glitter of show biz, Los Angeles has an essentially solid, all-American soul. Add the fascination of the ethnic mix—European, African, and Mexican stock, plus Chinese, Japanese, Korean, Vietnamese, Russian, and Thai—as well as its environmental meld of sea, mountain, and desert, and Los Angeles indisputably retains its status as one of the great cities of the world.

Los Angeles At-a-Glance

SEEING THE CITY

There are at least two great places to go for a fantastic view of Los Angeles. The most famous is Mulholland Drive, a twisting road that winds through the Hollywood Hills. Another is the top of Mount Olympus, in Laurel Canyon, north of Sunset Boulevard.

SPECIAL PLACES

OLD HOLLYWOOD: MEMORIES AND EMPTY BUILDINGS

A walk along Hollywood Boulevard from Vine Street to Highland Avenue and beyond will delight anyone who loves the great movies that made Hollywood famous. The area is no longer the physical center of film production, however, and its glamour is, sadly, long gone. X-rated movies now seem to outnumber the kinds of films that made Hollywood world renowned. Hollywood Boulevard usually bustles with tourists and a smattering of locals night and day. There is a lot to enjoy here, much of it at little or no cost. For additional details, see *Tour 5: Hollywood* in DIRECTIONS.

MANN'S CHINESE THEATRE Known to movie fans around the world as *Grauman's Chinese Theatre,* this is probably the most visited site in Hollywood. If you wander down Hollywood Boulevard looking for the *Grauman's* sign, however, you'll never find it. Several years ago, Ted Mann took over the theater, added it to his movie chain, and replaced Syd Grauman's name with his. The *Chinese Theatre* forecourt is world-famous for its celebrity footprints and handprints immortalized in cement. If you join the crowd of visitors outside the box office, you'll probably find imprints of your favorite stars from the 1920s to the present. If you buy a ticket to get in, you'll be treated to one of the world's most impressive and elaborate movie palaces. The ornate carvings, high, decorative ceiling, traditionally plush seats, heavy curtains that whoosh closed when the film ends, and the enormous screen itself are all part of a Hollywood that no longer exists. The less opulent *Chinese Twin* next door also shows films. 6925 Hollywood Blvd. (phone: 213-464-8111).

HOLLYWOOD WAX MUSEUM If the *Chinese Theatre* makes you nostalgic for the faces belonging to celluloid souls, stop in at the *Hollywood Wax Museum.* Here images of many of the immortals of the film industry are captured both in and out of character—in wax. Marilyn Monroe, Jean Harlow, Paul Newman, Raquel Welch, Michael Jackson, Madonna, Sylvester Stallone as Rambo, and many more fill the star-studded display cases. There's also the *Academy Award Film Library,* a horror chamber, and a re-creation of the Last Supper. Open Sundays through Thursdays until midnight, Fridays and Saturdays to 2 AM. No admission charge for children under six. 6767 Hollywood Blvd. (phone: 213-462-8860).

HOLLYWOOD STUDIO MUSEUM If nostalgia is what you seek, you can find it at the largest single historic movie artifact in existence. Called the *De Mille Barn,* it was the production site of the first feature-length film made in Hollywood—Cecil B. De Mille's *The Squaw Man.* Designated a California Cultural Landmark in 1956, it was moved by *Paramount Studios* to the *Hollywood Bowl* parking lot and turned into the *Hollywood Studio Museum* in 1979. Inside are a replica of De Mille's office and stills from silent motion pictures. The outside of the building is interesting too: When it was on the back lot of *Paramount Studios,* it often was used in Westerns and, for many years, was seen as the railroad station in the "Bonanza" TV series. In addition, there's a gift shop, filled with old autographs, books, and pictures. The museum is open weekends only in winter; also open Friday afternoons in summer. No admission charge for children under six. 2100 N. Highland Ave., across from the *Hollywood Bowl* (phone: 213-874-2276).

PARAMOUNT PICTURES At one time, *RKO Studios* adjoined the *Paramount* lot. After *RKO* folded in 1956, its studio became the home of television's Desilu Productions, which in turn sold its property to next-door *Paramount.* Close to the Bronson Avenue intersection with Melrose is the famous *Paramount Gate,* the highly decorative studio entrance that many people will remember from the film *Sunset Boulevard.* The Gower Street side of today's *Paramount* was the old front entrance to *RKO.* It once featured Art Deco doors and a marquee with distinctive Deco neon letters spelling out *RKO.* Today, it's simply an unimpressive back door to *Paramount,* painted in that dull, flat beige many studios use to protect their exterior walls. *Paramount* extends from Melrose Avenue on the south to Gower Street on the west, Van Ness Avenue on the east, and Willoughby Avenue on the north (phone: 213-956-5000).

GOWER STREET This was once the center for so many small film studios that it became known in the biz as "Gower Gulch." It was also nicknamed "Poverty Row," since so many of its independent producers were perpetually strapped for production money. Poverty Row's most famous studio was *Columbia Pictures,* which ultimately grew healthy enough to acquire most of the smaller parcels of studio real estate in the neighborhood. *Columbia*'s old studios still stand at Gower Street and Sunset Boulevard, although *Columbia* moved out several years ago. (It found a new home in Burbank.)

WARNER BROTHERS During the late 1920s, when Warner's was introducing "talkies" to America, its pictures were filmed here. This also was the home of *Warner*'s radio station at the time, KFWB. Today the old studio is the headquarters for KTLA-TV and KMPC radio. The stately Southern mansion that served as *Warner*'s administration building still stands on Sunset Boulevard. Sunset Blvd. and Van Ness Ave.

MAX FACTOR BEAUTY MUSEUM The only museum in the world devoted to makeup is housed in the famous Max Factor Building, just off Hollywood Boulevard, where (since the 1930s) the stars came to have their faces painted, their hair styled, and to be fitted for wigs or toupees. There are exhibits of beauty techniques used in the early days of Hollywood, and some outlandish makeup tools invented by Max Factor. One of the most unusual displays is a collection of special head blocks of famous stars, used to create wigs and toupees without the actors and actresses having to spend hours being fitted and styled. There is also "The Scroll of Fame," one of the most extensive collections of movie star autographs around. Closed Sundays. No admission charge. Free parking. 1666 N. Highland Ave. (phone: 213-463-6668).

"HOLLYWOOD": ALIVE AND WELL

"Hollywood," meaning the film business, is no longer geographically in the district bearing that name. If your nostalgic walking tour of Old Hollywood has made you curious about modern production methods, we suggest a tour of one of the following Los Angeles studios.

UNIVERSAL STUDIOS HOLLYWOOD Only during a trip to *Universal Studios Hollywood* can one encounter a 30-foot, 6.5-ton King Kong, beam up to the starship *Enterprise,* and experience 15 minutes in the life of a "Miami Vice" cop. The combination movie studio tour and theme park has been attracting more than five million people a year. There is a guided tram tour past all the attractions on the grounds, which include some of the 34 sound stages and other production facilities; the house used in Alfred Hitchcock's *Psycho;* re-created sets from such movies as *All Quiet on the Western Front, Jaws,* and *The Sting;* a burning house; a collapsing bridge; a multimedia special-effects show; the parting of the Red Sea; the *Doomed Glacier Expedition,* where you get to plunge down an alpine avalanche; and an earthquake simulation called *The Big One.* If this isn't enough, there are other tricks and treats: *An American Tale,* a musical production; *The Riot Act,* a western stunt show; *Backdraft,* a vivid re-creation of the burning warehouse from the movie; and *Back to the Future,* which reveals how the special effects were created for that movie series. You also can travel through time on *Back to the Future: The Ride.* Fans of the late Lucille Ball will enjoy *Tribute to Lucy,* a dazzling display of memorabilia and highlights of the comedienne's TV and movie career. Meanwhile, Flintstone fans will flip over the new *Flintstone Show,* a fanciful extravaganza with comedic dictabirds, lava-spewing volcanoes, and characters like "Walter Concrete" and "Masadonna." Open daily. No admission charge for children under three. Hollywood Frwy. to Lankershim exit, Universal City (phone: 818-508-9600).

WARNER BROTHERS STUDIOS To take a look at a real production studio rather than the Universal extravaganza, try these studios in Burbank—home of Warner Brothers, as well as many independent production companies. Nothing on the tour is staged, so visitors watch whatever is happening on that particular day. Not only do you get to see some actual shooting whenever possible, you also witness behind-the-scenes action—scenery construction, sound recording, and prop selection. Since tours are limited to 12 people (children under 10 are not permitted), reservations are required a week in advance. Tours are at 10 AM and 2 PM; closed Sundays. Admission charge. 4000 Warner Blvd. (phone: 818-954-1744).

UNIVERSAL CITYWALK If the studio tours aren't enough to keep you entertained, stroll over to this $100-million shopping and entertainment extravaganza—a four-block stretch of retail shops, restaurants, theaters, and offices created by the folks at MCA Development Company, owners of Universal Studios. It's worth the trip if only for an affordable pizza at the *Wolfgang Puck Café* (phone: 818-985-9653), where the Italian pies cost a fraction of their higher priced cousins at *Spago,* or for the show at the *Wizardz Magic Theater* (phone: 818-506-0066), where the world's top magicians strut their illusionary stuff. You can even walk down a replica of Olvera Street and grab a bite of authentic Mexican fare at *Camacho's Cantina* (phone: 818-622-3333). Then enjoy a cup of coffee with a good book at *Upstart Crow,* a coffee bar/bookstore (phone: 818-763-1811). And if you're too nervous for a real roller coaster ride, you can get your thrills vicariously at *Cinemania: The Motion Simulation Theater* (phone: 818-752-3399), which lets you experience the sensation through visual effects. The complex also houses the *Museum of Neon Art* (see *Museums,* below), *Gladstone's 4 Fish* restaurant (phone: 818-622-3474), and a 14-classroom *UCLA Extension Center. CityWalk* is located in the center of Universal City and is accessible from the Universal off-ramps of the Hollywood (101) Frwy. via Lankershim, Cahuenga, or Barham Blvd. entrances; Universal Center Dr.

BEVERLY HILLS After a hard day on the lot, movie stars still living in Beverly Hills return to their mansions for a good night's sleep. Even during the sunshiny daylight hours, Beverly Hills's residential section is remarkably tranquil, with only a handful of people on the streets. Without a doubt the most affluent and elegant neighborhood in Southern California, Beverly Hills is a must-see. If you want to window-shop or purchase high-fashion clothing, stroll along Rodeo Drive between Santa Monica and Wilshire Boulevards. To guarantee that you won't make an impulsive (and expensive) purchase, go during the evening or on Sundays, when many stores are closed. *Gray Line* is one of several companies offering van and limousine tours of the area (phone: 213-856-5900). From June through *Labor Day,* an old-fashioned trolley, which departs from in front of the *Chanel* boutique on Rodeo Drive, tours Beverly Hills daily (phone: 310-271-8174). For additional details, see *Tour 4: Beverly Hills* in DIRECTIONS.

DOWNTOWN LOS ANGELES

To see a Los Angeles that most people don't know about, take a walking tour downtown. (Also see *Tour 1: Downtown* in DIRECTIONS.)

EL PUEBLO DE LOS ANGELES If you're wondering what LA looked like before shopping centers were created, go to *El Pueblo de Los Angeles,* where the city was born in 1781. Today, the 44-acre Mexican-style site is a state historic park. At the center of the park is the Old Plaza, a wide historic square that is the scene of tours and monthly fiestas. The *Old Plaza Church,* which dates from 1822, has a curious financial history: It was partially paid for by the sale of seven barrels of brandy. The city's first firehouse is here—it is now the *Plaza Firehouse* museum (phone: 213-628-1274). The museum is closed Mondays. No admission charge. Colorful local anecdotes are retold during a narrated 45-minute walking tour of the Plaza, offered hourly Tuesday through Saturday mornings. For information, contact *El Pueblo de Los Angeles State Historic Park* on the Plaza (845 N. Alameda St.; phone: 213-628-1274).

OLVERA STREET The music from the Plaza fiestas spills over to this block-long pedestrian alley filled with colorful Mexican shops, restaurants, and stalls selling spicy food. The oldest house in Los Angeles is here—the 1818 adobe *Avila House* (E10 Olvera St.; phone: 213-628-1274). It is closed Mondays. No admission charge. The first brick house also is here, but now it's home to *La Golondrina* restaurant (W17 Olvera St.; phone: 213-628-4349). There is a *Visitors' Center* in the 1887 *Sepulveda House* (622 N. Main St.; phone: 213-628-1274). The center, which is closed Sundays, offers a free 18-minute film on the history of Los Angeles.

LOS ANGELES CIVIC CENTER AND MALL An unusually quiet, well-landscaped city mall, it features tropical plants, gently splashing fountains, and sculptures half hidden among the lush greenery. It's the first and only mall of shops and restaurants to be built on LA *City Hall* property. The covered bridge between *East City Hall* and *City Hall* features changing art exhibits. The mall is open daily. *City Hall* is between Main and Spring Sts. (phone: 213-485-2121).

THIRD AND BROADWAY Several places in this area are worth noting. First is the skylit, five-story indoor court of the *Bradbury Building,* now a registered historic landmark (closed weekends). You can ride an old hydraulic elevator to the top balcony and walk down a magnificent staircase guaranteed to evoke visions of bygone splendors. Across the corner from the *Bradbury Building* is the *Million Dollar Theater*—Syd Grauman's first—with a fascinating interior; it's currently a Spanish-language picture palace. Just south of the theater is the entrance to the *Grand Central Public Market,* a conglomeration of stalls selling food from all over the world amid the sounds and smells of a Mexican *mercado.*

LITTLE TOKYO This is the social, economic, cultural, and religious center of the largest Japanese-American community in the US. There are four specialty shopping centers here, as well as the *Japanese Cultural Center* and many fine restaurants. First and San Pedro Sts. (phone: 213-620-8861).

MUSIC CENTER The best time to visit the *Music Center* is during a concert or performance, but it's worth seeing anytime. This large cultural complex encompasses three performance halls (with another in the works). The *Ahmanson Theater* is the base of a branch of the *Center Theater Group;* it stages classical dramas, comedies, and international premieres with big-name stars. The *Mark Taper Forum,* a small, award-winning theater, houses the branch of the *Center Theater Group* that specializes in new works and experimental material. The glittering *Dorothy Chandler Pavilion,* a 3,200-seat auditorium best known as the site of the Academy Awards ceremonies, is the home of the *Los Angeles Philharmonic* and the *Los Angeles Master Chorale.* It's also the setting for most of the season of the *Los Angeles Opera Company.* The orchestra season runs from October through May; musical theater is presented generally in summer, when the orchestra moves to the *Hollywood Bowl.* If you take the free guided tour of the theaters, you will get a sneak preview of the *Walt Disney Concert Hall*—a mega-million-dollar, 2,380-seat, Frank Gehry–designed facility; scheduled to open in 1997, it will house the *Los Angeles Philharmonic.* Made possible by a $50-million grant from Lillian B. Disney in memory of her husband, the hall will contain four theaters, an outdoor park, and gardens. First St. and Grand Ave. (phone: 213-972-7483 for tour information; 213-972-7211 for general information).

NATURAL HISTORY MUSEUM With exhibits illustrating the cultural and technological changes of the 20th century, this museum has a wing devoted to American history, a dazzling hall of gems and minerals, the *Ralph W. Schreiber Hall of Birds,* a large taxidermy collection of North American and African mammals imaginatively posed in picturesque display cases, and ever-changing, traveling exhibitions. The *Ralph M. Parsons Discovery Center* is entertaining and educational. Learning is easy with hands-on exhibits that are as much fun for adults as they are for children. Closed Mondays. No admission charge on the first Tuesday of each month. 900 Exposition Blvd. (phone: 213-744-3466).

CHINATOWN LA's Chinatown has the usual assortment of restaurants, vegetable stores, and weird little shops selling ivory chess sets and acupuncture charts. The 900 block of N. Broadway.

MUSEUM OF CONTEMPORARY ART This is one museum in two buildings: the *MOCA* building at California Plaza, designed by Arata Isozaki (and a work of modern art in itself), and the *Temporary Contemporary,* a renovated warehouse about 10 blocks away, on Bunker Hill downtown. Both house artworks from the 1940s to the present. In addition, the Media and Performing Arts Program at *MOCA*'s *Ahmanson Auditorium* looks at performance—contemporary dance, theater, film, and video—as an art form. There's also a gift shop, as well as a pleasant café. Closed Mondays. Admission charge (except Thursdays from 5 to 8 PM). One ticket covers admission to both buildings on the same day. (*Note:* The *Temporary Contemporary* was closed for construction at press time but scheduled to reopen this year; call for details.) *MOCA:* 250 S. Grand Ave. at California Plaza (phone: 213-621-2766; 213-626-6222 for recorded information); *Temporary Contemporary:* 152 N. Central Ave.

MIDTOWN

FARMERS' MARKET Here you'll find just about everything within the reach of gastronomic imagination—both fresh produce and prepared dishes. There are more than 160 stalls of American, Mexican, Italian, and Chinese food and any number of exquisite bakeries and fruit and candy shops. If you don't like to eat standing up, there are tables set among the aisles of this indoor covered market. It's a great place to be hungry. Open daily. 6333 W. Third St. at Fairfax Ave. (phone: 213-933-9211). For additional details, see *Tour 3: Fairfax/Farmers' Market* in DIRECTIONS.

LA BREA TAR PITS These pools of sticky, bubbling asphalt, dating back some 40,000 years, are one of the world's most famous fossil sites. Once part of a Mexican land grant called Rancho La Brea, the pits are now part of *Hancock Park,* thanks to oil magnate Captain G. Allan Hancock, who deeded the property to the county in 1916. A natural phenomenon, tar pits develop when asphalt seeps to the earth's surface and forms pools, primarily during warm weather. For thousands of years, unsuspecting animals and at least one human—the 9,000-year-old La Brea Woman—became trapped in the pits, and their skeletons eventually fossilized. Scientists have recovered literally millions of animal and plant fossils from the La Brea site. For two months each summer, visitors can watch a pit excavation. Also in the park near the pits is the colorful *George C. Page Museum of La Brea Discoveries,* which has in excess of one million fossils from the Ice Age, as well as entire skeletons of prehistoric animals that were trapped in the tar pits. There are specimens of plants, reptiles, insects, birds, and mammals. One of the museum's more unusual exhibits is the open paleontological laboratory, where one may observe the cleaning and identification of fossils found in the pits. Also of interest are two films, the *La Brea Story,* which runs every half hour at the *La Brea Story Theater,* and *A Whoppingly Small Dinosaur,* which is shown continuously in the *Dinosaur Theater.* Also near the pits is the *Los Angeles Museum of Art* (see below). Closed Mondays. Admission charge (combination *Museum of Art* and *Page Museum* tickets are available). 5801 Wilshire Blvd. (phone: 213-936-2230).

LOS ANGELES MUSEUM OF ART With five buildings surrounding a spacious central court at the *La Brea Tar Pits* (see above), this is one of the top museums in the country and the largest in the West. The permanent collection features paintings, sculpture, graphic arts, photography, costumes, textiles, and decorative arts from a wide range of cultures and periods from prehistoric times to the present. The museum's holdings include American and European painting, sculpture, and decorative arts; 20th-century arts; pre-Columbian Mexican art; a unique assemblage of glass from Roman times to the 19th century; the renowned Gilbert collection of mosaics and monumental silver; and Indian and Islamic art. Major traveling loan exhibitions also are presented, along with lectures, films, concerts, and other educational events in the 600-seat *Leo S. Bing Theater.* The *Pavilion for Japanese Art* houses the internationally renowned *Shin'enkan Collection* of Japanese paintings, as well as Japanese ceramics, sculpture, lacquerware, screens, scrolls, and prints. Closed Mondays. Admission charge. 5905 Wilshire Blvd. (phone: 213-857-6000).

FARTHER AFIELD

GRIFFITH PARK AND THE LOS ANGELES ZOO The largest municipal park in the country, *Griffith* has three golf courses, a wilderness area and bird sanctuary, tennis courts, three miniature railroads, a carousel, pony rides, and picnic areas within its 4,043 acres. On top of all that, this is where you'll find the famous *Los Angeles Zoo,* home to more than 1,500 mammals, birds, and reptiles. Be sure to check out the *Tiger Fall,* an 18-foot waterfall in the wild cats' enclosure. The zoo is closed *Christmas Day.* No admission charge for children under two (5333 Zoo Dr.; phone: 213-666-4650). If you like railroads, you'll love *Travel Town,* a unique outdoor museum of old railroad engines, cars, railroad equipment, and fire trucks, also located in the park. The *Griffith Observatory* (2800 E. Observatory Rd.; phone: 213-664-1191) near Mt. Hollywood houses a 500-seat planetarium/theater, a twin-refracting telescope, and the *Hall of Science.* Most park facilities are open daily. Admission charge for planetarium shows. The park is in the Las Feliz district; call for details of how to reach it by car (phone: 213-665-5188).

SIX FLAGS MAGIC MOUNTAIN A 260-acre family theme park, featuring 100-plus rides, shows, and other attractions, this is the home of Bugs Bunny and his Looney Tunes friends in *Bugs Bunny World.* In addition to the mighty *Colossus* (a huge, wooden roller coaster) and the spine-tingling *Revolution* (a 360-degree vertical loop coaster), there's also the challenge of *Roaring Rapids* (a whitewater rafting experience), the *Z Force* mock starship ride, and a magic show run by the wily rabbit himself. *Ninja,* the West Coast's only suspended roller coaster, promises a delightfully terrifying trip. Other attractions include *Batman the Ride,* a 50-mile-per-hour, two-minute romp through Gotham City, complete with hair-raising spins, loops, and turns; the six-coaster *Psyclone,* a replica of Coney Island's *Cyclone;* and *Flashback,* a thrilling roller coaster that shoots through six 180° dives, fast switchbacks, and a startling 540° spiral. The *Viper* is one of the world's largest—and LA's scariest—multiple-looped roller coasters. The dolphin show and a children's village and petting zoo also are worthwhile. Open daily from *Memorial Day* through *Labor Day,* weekends only the rest of the year. No admission charge for children under three. Twenty-five minutes north of Hollywood on the Golden State Frwy., Magic Mountain exit in Valencia (phone: 818-367-2271 or 805-255-4100; 805-255-4111 or 818-367-5965 for recorded information).

PORTS O' CALL VILLAGE Some 60 specialty shops here feature merchandise from around the world. You can take a boat or helicopter tour of Los Angeles Harbor and dine in your choice of 25 restaurants and snack shops. Open daily. Berths 76–79 at the foot of the Harbor Frwy., San Pedro (phone: 310-831-0287).

REDONDO BEACH MARINA A delightful waterfront recreation showplace, the marina offers boat cruises and sport fishing. Open daily. 181 N. Harbor Dr., Redondo Beach. Take the Harbor Frwy. to the Torrance Blvd. exit and proceed west to the ocean (phone: 310-374-3481). For more information see *Tour 7: Beach Towns* in DIRECTIONS.

FOREST LAWN MEMORIAL PARK A major tourist attraction, this huge cemetery is the final resting place of Humphrey Bogart, Walt Disney, W. C. Fields, Clark Gable, and Bette Davis, among others; it advertises on huge billboards overlooking the freeways. The cemetery also contains a major collection of art treasures and marble sculptures including the largest religious painting in the world, Jan Styka's 195-by-45-foot *The Crucifixion*. And don't be surprised if you also find a real live bride and groom—some people like to get married here. Donations appreciated. 1712 S. Glendale Ave., Glendale (phone: 818-241-4151). For more information, see *Grave Matters* in DIVERSIONS.

QUEEN MARY SEAPORT You can explore the 81,000-ton ship, now permanently docked in Long Beach, from stem to stern, either on your own or with one of the daily guided tours; you even can spend the night—some 365 converted staterooms now make up the *Queen Mary* hotel. When she was launched in 1936, the *Queen* was the ultimate transatlantic travel experience of its time. In 1971, after retiring from a long career on the high seas, she was "relaunched" in this picturesque harbor by the Disney Company. After Disney pulled out in late 1992, the behemoth boat closed down for several months before being bought and reopened by a local entrepreneur. Open daily. Admission charge. Long Beach Frwy. to *Queen Mary* exit (phone: 310-435-3511).

CATALINA ISLAND Here you can spend the day wandering around the flower-filled hills, swimming, sightseeing, playing golf, or riding horses. There are places to stay overnight, but be sure to reserve in advance during the summer; for additional details, see *Tour 8: Catalina* in DIRECTIONS. Boats operated by *Catalina Cruises* (phone: 213-253-9800) leave daily from *Catalina Landing* (320 Golden Shore Blvd., downtown Long Beach); the super-fast *Catalina Express* boats (phone: 310-519-1212 or 310-519-7957) depart from the *Queen Mary* terminal in Long Beach and from the *Catalina Terminal Building* (foot of Harbor Frwy., Berths 95 and 96, San Pedro); travel time: an hour from Long Beach, an hour and a half from San Pedro.

J. PAUL GETTY MUSEUM The home of Vincent van Gogh's masterpiece, *Irises,* this museum also houses an extensive collection of Greek and Roman antiquities; pre-20th-century Western European paintings, drawings, sculpture, illuminated manuscripts, and decorative arts; and 19th- and 20th-century American and European photographs. The museum building is patterned after a 1st-century Roman country villa that was buried at Herculaneum in AD 79 by the eruption of Mt. Vesuvius. Closed Mondays. No admission charge. Parking is by reservation only. 17985 Pacific Coast Hwy. (phone: 310-458-2003).

ORANGE COUNTY

DISNEYLAND For many people, this is the most compelling magnet in all of Southern California—and the inspired creation that forever changed the image of theme and amusement parks. More than 50 attractions delight visitors of all ages including the ever-popular *Pirates of the Caribbean;* the intergalactic thriller *Star Tours; Main Street,* a re-creation of a typical 1890s American street; and *Fantasmic!,* a dazzling display of streaking lasers and wild pyrotechnics between *Frontierland* and *Tom Sawyer's Island,* featuring Mickey Mouse as master of ceremonies. *Birnbaum's Disneyland* (Hyperion; $10.95) can provide complete details about this still-expanding wonderland. Located 40 minutes from downtown LA, *Disneyland* is open daily. Admission charge. 1313 Harbor Blvd., Anaheim (phone: 714-999-4565). Also see *Quintessential Los Angeles* in DIVERSIONS.

MOVIELAND WAX MUSEUM About a 10-minute drive from *Disneyland,* this museum has more than 250 movie and television stars depicted in wax, molded into stances from their most famous roles. Newer arrivals include Bette Davis, Marlon Brando, and Clint Eastwood. The original props and sets from many films are here too. At the *Chamber of Horrors,* 15 sets with wax figures re-create the special effects that made movies such as *Psycho* and *The Exorcist* famous. Open daily. Admission charge. 7711 Beach Blvd., Buena Park (phone: 714-522-1154).

MEDIEVAL TIMES An arena set in a castle-like structure is the site of evenings of 11th-century entertainment featuring colorfully attired knights on horseback competing in medieval games, jousting, and sword fighting. The show comes with dinner (whole roasted chicken, spareribs, and various other finger foods, since people in those days didn't use forks). Open daily. Admission charge. Across the street from the *Movieland Wax Museum,* 7662 Beach Blvd., Buena Park (phone: 714-521-4740; 800-899-6600).

KNOTT'S BERRY FARM The theme of this amusement park is the Old West. An old-fashioned stagecoach and an authentic steam coach take visitors around the grounds, which are divided into five sections (*Fiesta Village,* a *Roaring Twenties* area, a *Ghost Town,* an early-California-Spanish area, and *Camp Snoopy,* a children's park featuring the world's largest Snoopy, a 38-foot tall replica of the cartoon canine). Among the attractions are rides with such names as the *Whirlpool, Mountain Log Ride, Sky Jump, XK-1, Tumbler, Slammer,* and *Slingshot;* a mine train; *Montezooma's Revenge,* the multiple-looped *Boomerang* roller coaster; and the exciting *Kingdom of the Dinosaurs.* The *Pacific Pavilion* features delightful aquatic attractions, and you can play games in the largest arcade west of the Mississippi. Top country-and-western artists perform here frequently; there are also cancan dancers, marionettes, and a great ice show during the *Christmas* season. There's plenty of good eating right on the grounds: Stop in at *Mrs. Knott's Chicken Dinner Restaurant,* which is older than the park, or any of the stands selling Sicilian pizza, extra-juicy hot dogs, and barbecued ribs. Open daily. Admission charge. Located 10 minutes from *Disneyland* at 8039 Beach Blvd., Buena Park (phone: 714-827-1776; 714-220-5200 for recorded information).

> **EXTRA SPECIAL**
>
> For one of the most spectacular drives in California, follow the Pacific Coast Highway (Rte. 1) north about 95 miles from LA to Santa Barbara, a picturesque California mission town facing the Pacific, where bougainvillea bursting with purple and magenta blossoms adorn Mediterranean-style buildings of white adobe. A "red tile" walking tour zigzags through the historic district and runs along downtown State Street—a truly Spanish experience down to the last tile-enclosed trash bin and mailbox. The Spanish-Moorish courthouse is worth a visit for its opulent interior and the incomparable panorama from the tower. The city center owes its harmonious look to the strict architectural guidelines for reconstruction that were imposed after the devastating earthquake of 1925. Overnighters can opt for a hacienda-style hostelry, such as the *Four Seasons Biltmore* (1260 Channel Dr.; phone: 805-969-2261); Charlie Chaplin's favorite hotel, the *Montecito Inn* (1295 Coast Village Rd.; phone: 805-969-7854); an exclusive hideaway such as the *San Ysidro Ranch* (see *Checking In*), with its excellent French *Stonehouse* restaurant; the Victorian *Upham* hotel (1404 De la Vina; phone: 805-962-0058), which features *Louie's,* a highly regarded restaurant serving California fare; or one of many period bed and breakfast establishments. The *Cold Spring Tavern* (5995 Stagecoach Rd.; phone: 805-967-0066), about 10 miles northwest of Santa Barbara on Route 154, goes back to the old stagecoach days. Chili is popular at lunch. At dinner, the menu tends more toward chicken, steaks, and game.

Sources and Resources

TOURIST INFORMATION

For free information, brochures, and maps, contact the *Los Angeles Visitors' and Convention Bureau* (633 W. Fifth St., Suite 6000, Los Angeles, CA 90071; phone: 213-624-7300). Closed Sundays. For all the latest information on events and happenings, call the *Visitors' and Convention Bureau Events Hotline* (phone: 213-689-8822); the service is available 24 hours a day in English, Spanish, French, Japanese, and German. Another information line, run by the *City of Los Angeles Cultural Affairs Department,* provides a recorded events listings covering the fine arts, museum exhibitions, and upcoming festivals (phone: 213-688-ARTS).

Contact the California state hotline (800-TO-CALIF) for maps, calendars of events, health updates, and travel advisories. Also, *West Hollywood*

Marketing Corporation provides free brochures, maps, and information (phone: 310-274-7294).

LOCAL COVERAGE The *Los Angeles Times* and the *Daily News,* published in the San Fernando Valley, are daily morning newspapers. *Los Angeles* is a monthly magazine, and *LA Weekly* and *LA Reader* are free weekly newspapers with local listings of events about town.

For the best (albeit most expensive) maps of the Los Angeles area, as well as travel books, try *Thomas Bros. Maps & Books* (603 W. Seventh St.; phone: 213-627-4018); their *Los Angeles County Street Guide and Directory* (Thomas Bros.; $15.95) is particularly useful. For a lively guide to sights around town, see *Los Angeles Access* (HarperCollins; $18). To really get a handle on this massive metropolis, pick up a copy of *50 Maps of LA* (H. M. Gousha, $9.95). This whimsical yet informative tome—a compilation of hot spots from artists, movie stars, and critics in map form—includes such gems as where Nancy Reagan gets her facials and a diagram of celebrity seating at *Lakers* games.

TELEVISION STATIONS KCBS Channel 2–CBS; KNBC Channel 4–NBC; KABC Channel 7–ABC; KTTV Channel 11–Fox; and KCET Channel 28–PBS.

RADIO STATIONS AM: KLAC 570 (country); KABC 790 (talk); KFWB 980 (all news); and KNX 1070 (all news). FM: KCRW 89.9 (public); KUSC 91.5 (public); KCBS 93.1 (oldies); KXEZ 100.3 (adult contemporary); KRTH 101.1 (oldies); KBIG 104.3 (adult contemporary); and KNAC 105.5 (Top 40).

TELEPHONE The area code for central Los Angeles is 213. For Santa Monica, Inglewood, Beverly Hills, West Los Angeles, and Long Beach, the area code is 310. The 818 area code covers the San Fernando Valley and the upper half of the San Gabriel Valley. The 805 area code covers the Ventura–Santa Barbara area; the 714 area code, Orange County. All telephone numbers in this chapter include area codes.

SALES TAX The sales tax is 8.25%; there also is a 12.5% hotel tax.

GETTING AROUND

It's always more convenient to have a car for exploring Los Angeles; however, there are buses, taxis, tour operators, and the *Metrolink* rail service.

BUS For city bus route and schedule information, call the *Metropolitan Transportation Authority* (*MTA;* phone: 310-273-0910 in the Beverly Hills/West LA area; 213-626-4455 in Hollywood/central LA; and 818-781-5890 in the San Fernando Valley). The bus fare is $1.10. *DASH* minibuses (phone: 213-485-7201 for information), run by the *MTA,* travel through downtown's most scenic areas—from the *Civic Center* district to California Plaza, Broadway, or Pershing Square—24 hours a day, Mondays through Saturdays. The minibus fare is a mere 25¢.

CAR RENTAL For information on renting a car, see GETTING READY TO GO.

SUBWAY The city's underground rail system is still in the works, but part of the *Red Line* has been in operation since 1993. It runs between *Union Station* (Alameda St. at Sunset Blvd.) and *MacArthur Park* from 5 AM to 7 PM daily with stops at the *Civic Center* (First and Hill Sts.), Pershing Square (Fifth and Hill Sts.), Seventh Street, and *Westlake-MacArthur Park*. Tokens and tickets are available from vending machines at each station and cost $1.10 each.

TAXI Cabs *don't* cruise the streets in LA. Check at your hotel desk; different firms serve different areas. A few companies to try: *Bell Cab* (phone: 213-221-1112); *LA Taxi* (phone: 213-627-7000); and *United Independent Taxi* (phone: 213-653-5050).

TRAIN If all goes according to schedule, LA's first major rail system—linking *Los Angeles International Airport (LAX)* with downtown LA, Long Beach, and major attractions along the way—should be in full swing by the end of this year. Passengers arriving at *LAX* will be able to hop a free shuttle bus to *Union Station*. To reach downtown, they will then take the new *Green Line* to *Imperial/Wilmington* station, and transfer to the *Blue Line*. The *Green Line* will connect 13 communities between Norwalk and Redondo Beach. At press time the fare was slated to be $1.10, with tokens available in vending machines at the station. For information, contact the *MTA* (see *Bus*, above).

TOURS *Star Line/Gray Line* (541 Hollywood Blvd., Hollywood; phone: 213-856-5900) is one of many companies offering tours of downtown LA (including the *Music Center*, Chinatown, Little Tokyo, Olvera St., and more) and of the Hollywood–Beverly Hills area, as well as *Disneyland*, *Knott's Berry Farm*, and *Universal Studios Hollywood*. There are tours that offer more than the usual sights, including tasteful trips through Southern California wine country given by *Burbury Wine Tours* (2554 Lincoln Blvd., Marina del Rey; phone: 310-208-0980; 800-345-4265) and the ghoulish *Grave Line Tours* (PO Box 931694, Hollywood, CA 90093; phone: 213-876-4286), which visits scenes of scandals, crimes, and misdemeanors in a renovated hearse. For further information on companies offering tours in and around Los Angeles, see GETTING READY TO GO.

LOCAL SERVICES

AUDIOVISUAL EQUIPMENT *Ametron Rents* (phone: 213-466-4321).

BABY-SITTING *Weston's Babysitters Guild* (phone: 213-658-8792) and *Community Job Shop* (phone: 818-345-2950).

BUSINESS SERVICES *Century Secretarial Service* (2040 Ave. of the Stars, Suite 400, Century City; phone: 310-277-3329); *HQ Headquarters Company* (2121 Ave. of the Stars; phone: 310-277-6660 and 310-551-6666), which offers word processing, conference rooms, and telex and fax machines; and *Word Shop* (phone: 213-381-3801) for word processing. Many hotels also offer business services (see *Checking In*).

DRY CLEANERS/TAILORS *The Cleaning Baron* (510 Washington Blvd.; phone: 310-823-8003), which offers free pickup and delivery, and *Top Hat Cleaners* (8122 Santa Monica Blvd., W. Hollywood; phone: 213-654-5595).

LIMOUSINE *Brentwood Limousine* (phone: 310-395-0932; 800-296-5466); *Carey Limousine* (phone: 310-275-4153 or 310-272-0081); and *Classic Fleet Limousine Service* (phone: 213-753-4384).

MECHANIC *Bliss & Bothwell Auto Service* (2110 Kotner Ave.; phone: 310-444-9958).

MEDICAL EMERGENCY For information on area hospitals and pharmacies, see GETTING READY TO GO.

MESSENGER SERVICES *Jet Delivery Inc.* (phone: 213-749-0123). Many hotels also can make arrangements.

PHOTOCOPIES *Barbara's Place* (7925 Santa Monica Blvd., W. Hollywood; phone: 213-654-5902) is open 24 hours Mondays through Thursdays, until 10 PM Fridays, and from 10 AM to 4 PM Saturdays; *Copy Print* (404 S. Figueroa Ave., in the *Bonaventure* hotel; phone: 213-620-6279) offers 24-hour service, pickup, and delivery.

POST OFFICES For information on local branch offices, see GETTING READY TO GO.

PROFESSIONAL PHOTOGRAPHERS *Atkinson Business Photography* (phone: 213-624-5950) and *Wayne Seidel* (phone: 213-467-0552).

TELECONFERENCE FACILITIES Most of the city's luxury hotels have teleconferencing facilities (see *Checking In*).

TRANSLATORS *Berlitz* (3345 Wilshire Blvd.; phone: 213-380-1144).

WESTERN UNION/TELEX *Western Union* (phone: 800-325-6000) has offices throughout the city. For information on money transfers, see GETTING READY TO GO.

SPECIAL EVENTS

Los Angeles is bustling with activity all year long. No matter what time of year you arrive, some not-to-be-missed festival or event will probably be taking place. For complete listings, check the local publications listed above or call the *Los Angeles Visitors' and Convention Bureau* (see *Tourist Information*, above).

The year kicks off with the *Tournament of Roses Parade* in Pasadena and the *Rose Bowl*, the traditional *New Year's Day* gridiron spectacle held at the *Pasadena Rose Bowl*. Then there's more sports action during the *Los Angeles Open Golf Tournament*, which takes place in February at the *Riviera Country Club* in Pacific Palisades; the *Los Angeles Marathon*, which is held in the city in March; and the *Long Beach Grand Prix Formula One Auto Racing* in April. *Cinco de Mayo,* one of Mexico's most popular holidays, commemorating Mexican victory over the French in 1862, is celebrated May 5 at the *El Pueblo de Los Angeles Historic Park.* In mid-May strawberry lovers celebrate their favorite fruit at the two-day *Strawberry Festival. Disneyland's Easter Parade, UCLA's Mardi Gras,* and the *Manhattan Beach Art Festival* also take place in May. The *Playboy Jazz Festival* is at the *Hollywood Bowl* in June. *Fourth of July* fireworks are on display at *Anaheim Stadium* and the *Pasadena Rose Bowl,* as well as at the *Hollywood Bowl* and *Burton Chase Park* in Marina del Rey. The *All-Star Shrine Football Game* is usually held in the *Pasadena Rose Bowl* in July. The *Lotus Festival* celebrates Asian Pacific cultures every July in *Echo Park.* Held in late July or August at Manhattan, Hermosa, Torrance, and Redondo Beaches, the *International Surf Festival* has no surfing competitions, but does offer a series of races and contests. The *Nisei Japanese Festival,* a week-long display of cultural pride featuring food, music, and dancing, is held in early to mid-August in Little Tokyo. Hundreds of works of art are displayed at the *Festival of the Arts and Pageant of the Masters* festival, held in August in scenic Laguna Beach; the pageant features re-creations of great works of art using live models. *SeaFest* is an August festival held at Long Beach. During the months of August and September at *Rancho Cienega Park,* the *African Marketplace & Cultural Fair* showcases arts and crafts from 23 different African cultures along with "tastes of Africa," a culinary sampling from local restaurants. The *Los Angeles County Fair,* the world's largest annual county fair, runs a full 18 days from mid-September to early October and has something for everyone. Established in 1935, the *Los Angeles Bach Festival,* featuring the works of Bach and other legendary composers, is presented annually in October at the *First Congregational Church.* Late in October at *Hancock Park,* the *International Festival of Masks* features the traditional dances of the Sudan, the Middle East, Hawaii, Guatemala, and Greece performed in authentic native costumes. The *Hollywood Christmas Parade* and Pasadena's irreverent *DooDah Parade* take place in November; and the *Christmas Boat Parade* sets sail in Marina del Rey in December.

MUSEUMS

In addition to those described in *Special Places,* the following are other fine museums in LA:

ARMAND HAMMER MUSEUM OF ART Rembrandts, van Goghs, Cézannes, and Goyas are among the masterpieces that the late industrialist collected during his lifetime. Closed Mondays. Admission charge. 10899 Wilshire Blvd. (phone: 310-443-7000).

GENE AUTRY WESTERN HERITAGE MUSEUM Featuring art and artifacts from the Wild West, this nonprofit collection, sponsored and run by the legendary Western singer–film star's Autry Foundation, spans the years from the late 17th century to the present. Fun for the whole family; many of the hands-on displays were created by the Walt Disney Imagineering design firm. Closed Mondays. Admission charge. 4700 Western Heritage Way, Hollywood (phone: 213-667-2000).

JAPANESE AMERICAN NATIONAL MUSEUM Dedicated to preserving the history of Japanese-Americans, this museum is housed in poignant and appropriate quarters. The building, erected in 1925 as a Buddhist temple, was used as a warehouse for the possessions of Japanese-Americans when they were herded into internment camps during World War II. The exhibits, which change quarterly, include photographs, moving images, letters, tools, clothing, works of art, and personal possessions that have been passed from generation to generation. Closed Mondays. Admission charge. 369 E. First St. (phone: 213-625-0414).

LOS ANGELES CHILDREN'S MUSEUM There are 18 hands-on exhibits and special workshops for children of all ages. Open daily. No admission charge for children under two. 310 N. Main St. (phone: 213-687-8800).

MUSEUM OF FLYING A collection of vintage flying machines is on display along with a simulator ride and a theater showing various films on topics related to air travel, such as old airplanes and the history of flight technology. Closed Mondays. Admission charge. 2772 Donald Douglas Loop N., Santa Monica (phone: 310-392-8822).

MUSEUM OF NEON ART Calling this "art" is debatable, but still you're bound to get a charge out of this whimsical collection of neon and electric signs, including sculpture and classic theater marquees. Closed Sundays and Mondays. Admission charge. 1000 Universal Center Dr., No. 154 *CityWalk* (phone: 213-617-0274).

MUSEUM OF SCIENCE AND INDUSTRY Hands-on science, mathematics, aerospace, energy, and health exhibits encourage children to take an active role in their own education. One of the newer additions to the museum's permanent exhibitions is *Our Urban Environment,* an innovative ecological exploration. Also be sure to check out the *Space Garden,* with a DC-8 and a real Apollo space capsule on display—a treat for children and adults alike. Open daily. Admission charge for the *IMAX* theater only (phone: 213-744-2014). 700 S. State, *Exposition Park* (phone: 213-744-7400).

NORTON SIMON MUSEUM OF ART The rich industrialist's multimillion-dollar collection includes five centuries of European art from the Renaissance to the 20th century. You'll find Rembrandts, such as *The Bearded Man in the Wide Brimmed Hat, Self Portait,* and *Titus;* a sizable collection of Picasso's paintings, sketches, and sculptures, highlighted by his famous *Woman with Book;* and a Degas gallery, featuring *Waiting,* one of Degas's many masterpieces. The museum's collection of Impressionist art (with works by van Gogh, Monet, and Renoir) and its selections of early Renaissance and Baroque art also are impressive. In addition, there's Asian sculpture spanning a period of 2,000 years. The only thing the museum lacks is a place to eat. Closed Mondays through Wednesdays. Admission charge. 411 W. Colorado Blvd., Pasadena (phone: 818-449-6840).

RICHARD NIXON LIBRARY & BIRTHPLACE Opened in 1990, it includes a 52,000-square-foot, Spanish-style library with exhibits chronicling the former president's life and career, as well as an art gallery with changing shows. Also on the property are the modest frame house in which Nixon was born in 1913 and his grave. Open daily. Admission charge. 18001 Yorba Linda Blvd., Yorba Linda (phone: 714-993-3393).

ROY ROGERS AND DALE EVANS MUSEUM An exact replica of a frontier fort features highlights of the lives of this famed Wild West celluloid couple, who trotted their way through dozens of motion pictures. There's a tribute to Roy's faithful steed Trigger and Dale's Buttermilk—the horses themselves are preserved and mounted on pedestals. Open daily. Admission charge. 15650 Seneca Rd., Victorville (phone: 619-243-4547).

SIMON WIESENTHAL CENTER BEIT HASHOAH MUSEUM OF TOLERANCE A $50-million, 165,000-square-foot museum and educational center, it was founded in 1993 to "challenge visitors to confront bigotry and racism and understand the Holocaust in both historical and contemporary contexts." Besides a permanent exhibition level, the center features a multimedia learning facility with 30 workstations from which visitors can access extensive historical data; an extensive archival collection; and the dramatic *Tower of Witness*, which showcases more than 2,000 photographs of victims of Auschwitz-Birkenau. The eight-level complex also features a theater, an auditorium, a memorial plaza, and a temporary exhibit area. Closed Saturdays. Admission charge. 9786 W. Pico Blvd. (phone: 310-553-8403 or 310-553-9036).

SOUTHWEST MUSEUM Devoted to the anthropology of the American Southwest, this museum contains some of the finest examples of Native American art and artifacts in the US. Periodically there are special displays dealing with Indian culture and lore. Closed Mondays. Admission charge. 234 Museum Dr., near *Dodger Stadium* (phone: 213-221-2163).

MAJOR COLLEGES AND UNIVERSITIES

There are many major university campuses spread throughout the LA area, in addition to dozens of colleges and junior colleges. The *University of California, Los Angeles (UCLA)* is among the top-ranked universities in the nation and is known to college football and basketball fans for its *Bruins* teams (main campus at 405 Hilgard Ave.; phone: 310-825-4321). The *University of Southern California (USC)* also is a major institution and, with teams like the *Trojans*, is *UCLA*'s arch rival in football (Exposition Blvd. and Figueroa St.; phone: 213-740-2311). *California Institute of Technology* counts more than 20 Nobel laureates among its alumni and past and present faculty (main campus at 1201 E. California Blvd., Pasadena; phone: 818-356-6326).

SHOPPING

For many, shopping is as much as part of the LA experience as celebrity sightings (if you're lucky, you can combine the two). The city's browsing and buying opportunities are nothing short of outstanding.

RODEO DRIVE AND ENVIRONS

No single street on this planet so typifies consumer excess as Rodeo Drive in Beverly Hills. Few mortals will be able to afford the prices, but window-shopping along this avenue for the affluent is as much fun as studying the boutiques along Paris's Rue du Faubourg-St.-Honoré, London's Bond Street, or New York's Fifth Avenue. In fact, many of the shop names are the same. Only a few are homegrown, such as *Fred Hayman* (see below). Don't miss *Two Rodeo,* a charming enclave of pricey shops and boutiques set on Italianate cobblestone lanes that surround a piazza, travertine fountains, and an elaborate staircase similar to the *Spanish Steps* in Rome. The retail newcomers who have settled here represent the crème-de-la-crème in high fashion and jewelry. Here is a list of the top emporia along and near Rodeo.

Bally of Switzerland High-style shoes for men (340 N. Rodeo Dr.; phone: 310-271-0666) and for women (409 N. Rodeo Dr.; phone: 310-275-0962).

Barneys New York A five-level, 108,000-square-foot cathedral of cutting-edge fashion. Also on the premises is the *Chelsea Passage Gift Department,* offering marvelous collectibles from all over the world. 9570 Wilshire Blvd. (phone: 310-888-2200).

Bijan Where the rich and famous shop for men's clothing; by appointment only. 420 N. Rodeo Dr. (phone: 310-273-6544). *Bijan USA,* where no appointment is required, is at 431 N. Rodeo Dr. (phone: 310-285-1800).

Bulgari A long-established purveyor of fine jewelry, also known for exquisitely designed bangles and baubles. 201 N. Rodeo Dr. (phone: 310-858-9216).

Carroll & Co. Ivy League clothing for men. 466 N. Rodeo Dr. (phone: 310-273-9060).

Cartier Internationally renowned jewelers since 1847, with two locations on Rodeo. 370 N. Rodeo Dr. (phone: 310-275-4272) and 220 N. Rodeo Dr. (phone: 310-275-4855).

Chanel Boutique Clothes, scents, and accessories from the famous fashion house, which in 1993 moved to a new, greatly expanded facility. 400 N. Rodeo Dr. (phone: 310-278-5500).

Charles Jourdan Clothes, shoes, and accessories from the French firm. 201 N. Rodeo Dr., in the *Two Rodeo* complex (phone: 310-273-3507).

Christian Dior In the spiffy *Two Rodeo* complex, this is a replica of the Paris flagship store, with Louis XVI furnishings. It features women's ready-to-wear, cosmetics, men's and women's accessories, jewelry, and watches. 230 N. Rodeo Dr. (phone: 310-859-4700).

David Orgell Crystal, china, antique and modern silver, and jewelry. 320 N. Rodeo Dr. (phone: 310-273-6660).

Dyansen Galleries Fine art. 339 N. Rodeo Dr. (phone: 310-275-0165).

Elliott Katt's Books on the Performing Arts Crammed with a tremendous selection of rare books pertaining to the performing arts, this amazingly informative shop is frequented by professionals in the movie and theater industries, who thumb through the vast casting and agency directories. Owner Katt stocks biographies of actors and directors, books on film, scores from famous Broadway musicals, as well as how-to books on everything from writing for television to getting a job in the music industry. 8568 Melrose Ave. (phone: 310-652-5178).

Ferragamo A large selection of the famous Ferragamo shoes and leather goods, women's ready-to-wear, and men's furnishings—ties, dress shirts, polo shirts, silk robes. Jason Robards and Ricardo Montalban shop here. 357 N. Rodeo Dr. (phone: 310-273-9990).

Frances Klein Antique and estate jewelry. 310 N. Rodeo Dr. (phone: 310-273-0155).

Fred Hayman A Beverly Hills shopping landmark, this supposed model for the title store of Judith Krantz's steamy novel *Scruples* sold its name and wildly successful fragrance to Avon. It's now home of the "273" and "Touch" fragrances, FHBH signature leather goods and evening bags, and collections from hot, young designers such as Eva Chun, Zang Toi, Christian Francis Roth, and C. D. Greene. There's a stand-up bar with complimentary drinks for shoppers. 273 N. Rodeo Dr. (phone: 310-271-3000).

Fred Joaillier Expensive jewelry, leather goods, and gifts. 401 N. Rodeo Dr. (phone: 310-278-3733).

Giorgio Armani Boutique The designer's coveted clothes for men and women. 436 N. Rodeo Dr. (phone: 310-271-5555).

Gucci Italian leather goods, jewelry, clothing, and accessories. 347 N. Rodeo Dr. (phone: 310-278-3451).

Harry Winston Exquisite, expensive jewelry. 371 N. Rodeo Dr. (phone: 310-271-8554).

Hermès Classic signature scarves, famous perfumes (including Caléche, Parfum d'Hermès, Amazone, and Equipage), and sumptuous leather goods from France. 343 N. Rodeo Dr. (phone: 310-278-6440).

Krizia The Italian designer's boutique. 410 N. Rodeo Dr. (phone: 310-276-5411).

Louis Vuitton Famous French handbags, accessories, and luggage. 307 N. Rodeo Dr. (phone: 310-859-0457).

Neiman Marcus The specialty store from Dallas for those who have almost everything (but want to buy more). 9700 Wilshire Blvd. (phone: 310-550-5900).

Polo/Ralph Lauren Every Lauren item you ever wanted and then some. Goldie Hawn, Tom Selleck, and Sally Field are among the regulars. 444 N. Rodeo Dr. (phone: 310-281-7200).

The Rodeo Collection A posh half-block mall; *Gianni Versace, Sonia Rykiel, Merletto, Fogal,* and *Furla* are among the designer boutiques. 421 N. Rodeo Dr. (phone: 310-858-7580).

Samuel French This West Coast outlet for the oldest play publishers in the world (since 1833) has an extensive collection of drama books, biographies of film directors and stars, and a tremendous selection of plays. 7623 Sunset Blvd. (phone: 310-876-0570).

Scriptorium This gallery sells the autographs of a wide variety of famous people—mostly historical figures such as Jimmy Carter, Abraham Lincoln, Lillian Gish, and Andy Warhol, although there are a few signatures of contemporary celebrities as well. Closed Mondays. 427 N. Canon Dr. (phone: 310-275-6060).

Sharper Image The very latest in high-tech toys. 9550 Santa Monica Blvd. (phone: 310-271-0515).

Superior Stamp & Coin Gold coins and rare stamps. 9478 W. Olympic Blvd. (phone: 310-203-9855).

Tiffany & Co. Fine jewelry in the famous blue boxes. 210 N. Rodeo Dr. (phone: 310-273-8880).

Williams-Sonoma Dining-table and kitchen outfitters. 317 N. Beverly Dr. (phone: 310-274-9127).

Yves Saint Laurent Boutique One of only two in the US (the other is in New York City), this Beverly Hills branch of the chic Paris boutique is a must-see (and looking is all most can afford). It is a sensational showcase for the French designer's fashions, jewelry, shoes, furs, fragrances, and cosmetics, framed by a theatrical limestone arch outside. A majestic staircase leads from the plush ground floor to a luminous mezzanine. Closed Sundays. 428 N. Rodeo Dr. (phone: 310-859-2389).

SPECIALTY STORES

For shopping with a more native character, browse in several burgeoning areas, such as the following:

MELROSE AVENUE Traveling eastward on Melrose, the stores run the gamut from upscale to funky to weird, with Gallery Row situated roughly between Doheny Drive and Fairfax Avenue. *LA Impressions* (8318 Melrose Ave.;

phone: 310-659-3336), open by appointment only, specializes in Mexican art. At *Gemini Gel* (8365 Melrose Ave.; phone 213-651-0513), a superb creator and exhibitor of limited-edition prints, customers watch the printing process through upstairs gallery windows. For an offbeat souvenir, try *Wild Blue* (7220 Melrose Ave.; phone: 213-939-8434) where the ceramics and crockery seem to have a sense of humor.

Finals (7374 ½ Melrose Ave.; phone: 213-653-8292) is filled with unique leather jackets, denim shirts, and such. For those who never left the 1960s behind, *Retail Slut* (7264 Melrose Ave.; phone: 213-934-1339) is a must for its collection of campy shoes, clothing, and tacky accessories. Antiques and gift shops, fashion boutiques, restaurants, and small theaters prosper all the way to La Brea Boulevard. Also see *Quintessential Los Angeles* in DIVERSIONS.

WEST THIRD STREET Due to the rising rents on Melrose Avenue, many merchants have relocated to West Third Street and other blocks nearby. The *Craft and Folk Art Museum Gift Shop* (5800 Wilshire Blvd.; phone: 213-937-5544) features outstanding handcrafts by American artisans. *Freehand* (8413 W. Third St.; phone: 213-655-2607) boasts three rooms of beautiful ceramics; handloomed, raw-silk clothing; and imaginative jewelry. Next door, *New Stone Age* (8407 W. Third St.; phone: 213-658-5969) features one-of-a-kind, artist-designed goods that have to be seen to be believed. Among the items for sale are baskets woven out of telephone wire, reconditioned radios painted Day-Glo colors, ceramics, vases, and jewelry made out of God-knows-what.

Sonrisa (7609 Beverly Blvd., phone: 213-935-8438), a Taos transplant, is the place to go for unique crafts from New Mexico and Mexico. Located in the decorator showroom district, *Tesoro* (319 S. Robertson Blvd.; phone: 310-273-9890) showcases functional and wearable art. Pick out a sculpted bowl for a wedding gift, have dinnerware made to match your decor, or buy jewelry that looks like sugar candy.

MONTANA AVENUE A cornucopia of small shops has sprung up between Seventh and 17th Streets along this Santa Monica thoroughfare, making it a window-shopper's delight. Among the pricey and super-specialized boutiques are *Lisa Norman* (1134 Montana Ave.; phone: 310-451-2026; also at 8595 Sunset Blvd.; phone: 310-854-4422), selling silk lingerie; *Where's My Conga!* (1615 Montana Ave.; phone: 310-451-1879) for funky, retro clothing ; and *Private Stock* (1617A Montana Ave.; phone: 310-451-9431), which features unusual men's apparel. After making your selections, quench your thirst with a brew at *Father's Office* (1018 Montana Ave.; phone: 310-393-BEER), a fun, English-style (albeit *nonsmoking*) pub.

MALLS AND SHOPPING CENTERS

Lest anyone forgo the rather overwhelming experience of shopping in a mall, LA offers some of the finest, as well as some of the most eclectic, merchandise marts in the country. Among the largest shopping complexes are *Beverly Center* (8500 Beverly Blvd.; phone: 310-854-0070); *Century City Shopping Center* (10250 Santa Monica Blvd.; phone: 310-277-3898); *Del Amo Shopping Center* (Hawthorne Blvd. and Carson St.; phone: 310-542-8525); *Glendale Galleria* (100 W. Broadway; administrative offices: 2148 Glendale Galleria; phone: 818-240-9481); *South Coast Plaza* (3333 Bristol St.; phone: 714-435-2000); *One Colorado* (24 E. Union St., Pasadena; phone: 818-564-1066); *Sherman Oaks Galleria* (15301 Ventura Blvd.; phone: 818-884-7090); *Westside Pavilion* (10800 W. Pico Blvd.; phone: 310-474-5940); and *Woodland Hills Promenade* (6100 Topanga Canyon; phone: 818-884-7090).

DISCOUNT STORES

Though it's better known for its sky-high prices, LA does not lack for places offering bargains (or very expensive items at somewhat lower prices). Here are the area's top discount spots:

The Address A resale boutique offering designer duds by Adolfo, Chanel, Armani, and Valentino from some star-studded closets. 1116 Wilshire Blvd., Santa Monica (phone: 310-394-1406).

Alandale's Armani for the masses. These men's suits, of the finest Italian fabrics, come from the same factory that makes Giorgio Armani's upscale line, only without the label—and about half the price. 10500 W. Pico Blvd. (phone: 310-838-8100).

Almost (and) Perfect English China This is in the Valley and well worth a trip. Top-quality English china at discount prices. 14519 Ventura Blvd., Sherman Oaks (phone: 818-905-6650).

Black & White This is a great place for women's clothing—primarily the Karen Kane label—at rock-bottom prices. Most of the merchandise costs twice as much in other stores. 1240-1 S. Broadway (phone: 213-746-5841).

Chic Conspiracy Another snazzy resale shop selling designer clothes, shoes, and accessories at great prices. 10955 W. Pico Blvd., West Los Angeles (phone: 310-475-5542).

Citadel Factory Outlet Center Housed in an incredibly beautiful replica of an Assyrian castle, it features 44 outlet stores that sell goods from fashion to home furnishings at 30% to 75% off. Big-name stores include *Adolfo II, Ann Taylor, Eddie Bauer, The Gap, Linen Club,* and *Perry Ellis Shoes. The Citadel* has it all, and it's only minutes from downtown LA. 5675 E. Telegraph Rd., City of Commerce (phone: 213-888-1220).

Cooper Building Located in the heart of the Garment District, this is an entire building of clothing manufacturers' outlet shops. Check out the building directory if you know what you're looking for; if not, just start at the top and work your way down. Designer clothes for women can be had for 50%

off, and popular, casual clothes for men can be scooped up at savings of from 33% to 50%. 860 S. Los Angeles St. (phone: 213-622-1139).

Designer Labels for Less A shopper's wonderland of women's and men's designer fashions for 40% to 80% below department store prices. 1924 S. Main St., Downtown LA (phone: 213-745-4101).

Factory Merchants Outlet Plaza (Barstow) More than 50 major discount outlets, including *Anne Klein, Evan-Picone, Lenox China, Levi's, London Fog* and *Ralph Lauren,* can be found here. There's something for everyone at rock-bottom prices, 20% to 70% off retail. Located in Barstow, a desert town a little over two hours from Los Angeles, this complex is often referred to simply as "Barstow." To get here, take the No. 15 Freeway north and exit at Lenwood Road, just south of Barstow, and follow the signs to the *Plaza*—it's visible from the freeway. If you're a committed shopper, the trip is well worth it. 2837 Lenwood Rd., Barstow (phone: 619-253-7342 or 619-253-7354). *Note:* Buckita Leff's *Outlet Shopping Tours* (1559 Pacific Coast Hwy., Suite 249, Hermosa Beach; phone: 310-372-9930; fax: 310-376-0966) offers an all-day excursion to Barstow; minimum group size is 30, but individual shoppers can join if there's room.

For Kids Only Some of the finest names in children's togs, at 30% to 60% off. An incredible collection of European imports—shoes, too! 746 N. Fairfax Ave., Los Angeles (phone: 213-650-4885).

Freeport International This is a wholesale perfume distributor with the genuine article: top-name scents at top savings. No watered-down formulas here. 1058 S. Main St., Downtown LA (phone: 213-745-3000).

Jean's Star Apparel Savvy women shoppers flock here for designer clothing sold at a fraction of the original prices. Chanel, Adolfo, and Armani are just a few of the names represented. 15136 Ventura Blvd., Sherman Oaks (phone: 818-789-3710).

The Place and Company A first-rate resale boutique for designer casual and evening wear. 8820 S. Sepulveda Blvd., Los Angeles (phone: 310-645-1539).

Silk Factory This is the place for affordable silks, linen, and quality cotton garments in women's larger sizes. 3100 Wilshire Blvd., Los Angeles (phone: 213-487-0087).

VINTAGE SHOPPING

It doesn't get any hipper or more happening than *American Rag,* an Art Deco complex of five affiliated shops set along one city block on the east side of La Brea Avenue. The place showcases a mixed bag of high-ticket haute couture, outrageous accessories, and budget-friendly fashions, but even if you're not in a shopping mood, stroll through to see Margot Werts's riveting window displays with their lifelike mannequins. The shops sport a French countryside motif with high, vaulted ceilings and funky flooring.

American Rag (150 S. La Brea Ave.; phone: 213-935-3154), the main store, proffers new and vintage fashions from designer jeans to outlandish leather jackets priced as high as $8,000; happily, most of the clothes are more affordable. *Maison et Café* (148 S. La Brea Ave.; phone: 213-935-3157), next door and accessible through an inside passageway, is a perky sidewalk café and curio shop rolled into one. Enjoy a cappuccino and baguette or browse among unique bric-a-brac and artifacts. For collectors, there are antique Pernod bottles and rare books, marvelous mosaic tile tables, and hand-picked European dinnerware. A short walk away is *Shoes* (144 S. La Brea Ave.; phone: 213-931-6903), a Moroccan-style bootery featuring everything from French and Italian sandals to sneakers. *Colours* (124 S. La Brea Ave.; phone: 213-931-6903), a super-hip bargain outlet, is popular with rock and rap stars; nothing here costs more than $30. Next door is *Youth* (136 S. La Brea Ave.; phone: 213-965-1404), a stylish kid's shop with unusual togs, accessories, and playthings.

SPORTS AND FITNESS

There is no question that Southern California is a paradise for sports lovers.

BASEBALL The Los Angeles *Dodgers* play at *Dodger Stadium* (1000 Elysian Park Ave.; phone: 213-224-1500); *Anaheim Stadium* (2000 State College Blvd., Anaheim; phone: 714-937-7200) is the home of the California *Angels*.

BASKETBALL The *NBA Lakers'* home court is at the *Great Western Forum* (3900 Manchester Blvd., Inglewood; phone: 310-419-3100 or 310-419-3182 for tickets). The *Clippers* play at the *LA Memorial Coliseum and Sports Arena* (3939 S. Figueroa; phone: 213-748-6131).

BICYCLING Biking is great around the Westwood *UCLA* campus, *Griffith Park* (see *Special Places*), and on the oceanside, where there is a 19-mile bike path between the cities of Torrance and Pacific Palisades.

FISHING Power and sailboats can be rented from *Rent-A-Sail* (13719 Fiji Way, Marina del Rey; phone: 310-822-1868). Fishermen catch halibut, bonito, and bass off the LA shores. Sport fishing boats leave daily from San Pedro, site of the LA port, about 20 minutes from downtown Los Angeles, and from the Redondo Beach Marina in Redondo Beach.

FITNESS CENTERS *Bally's Sports Connection* (8612 Santa Monica Blvd., West Hollywood; 310-652-7440) caters to starlets, models, and movie industry types. This branch of a Southern California chain is equipped with Nautilus machines, weight rooms, steamrooms, saunas, a pool, and a Jacuzzi, and offers a full schedule of exercise classes. The shortest membership term is two weeks. *Sports Club LA* (1835 Sepulveda Blvd.; phone: 310-473-1447), a $22-million fitness center complete with state-of-the-art amenities, is where the city's "power" players work out; some regulars are Madonna, Debra Winger, and Brooke Shields. It is open to non-members for a fee. *Nautilus and Aerobics Plus,* on the ground floor of the International Tower

Building (888 Figueroa St.; phone: 213-488-0095), offers aerobics classes and has a Jacuzzi and sauna. It also has branches all over the metropolitan area which are open to non-members for a fee. Many hotels have their own health clubs too (see *Checking In*).

FOOTBALL Champions of the Big 10 and Pacific 10 college conferences meet in the *Pasadena Rose Bowl* (1001 Rose Bowl Dr.; phone: 818-577-3100) every *New Year's Day*. *UCLA* plays its home games at the *Pasadena Rose Bowl*, and *USC* takes the field at the *Coliseum* (3939 S. Figueroa; phone: 213-747-7111 or 213-748-6131). The *NFL Rams* play at *Anaheim Stadium* (see *Baseball*, above; phone: 213-625-1123 or 714-937-6767). The *NFL Raiders* kick off at the *Coliseum* (see above).

GOLF The *Industry Hills Golf Club* (1 Industry Hills Pkwy., City of Industry; phone: 818-810-HILL) boasts two 18-hole golf courses, designed by William Bell, with 160 sand bunkers, eight lakes, and miles of astoundingly long fairways. The club also has an ultramodern, lighted driving range and four practice putting greens. For information on golf courses beyond Los Angeles (but worth the trip), see *Best Golf Outside the City* in DIVERSIONS. Some of the world's top golfers compete in the *Los Angeles Open,* which takes place in February at the *Riviera Country Club* (Pacific Palisades; phone: 310-454-6591).

HOCKEY The *Kings* make their home at the *Great Western Forum* (3900 Manchester Blvd., Inglewood; phone: 310-673-1300 or 310-480-3282 for tickets). And the *Mighty Ducks* push their pucks at *The Pond of Anaheim* (2695 Katella Ave.; phone: 714-704-2400 for tickets).

HORSE RACING If you like to spend your nights at the track, make tracks for *Los Alamitos.* There's harness, quarterhorse, and thoroughbred racing year-round. Take Freeway 605 south to the Katella Avenue exit in Orange County (phone: 310-431-1361 or 714-995-1234). If you prefer daytime action, try *Hollywood Park* between mid-April and late July and from early November to *Christmas Eve* (near *Los Angeles International Airport* between Manchester and Century Blvds.; phone: 310-419-1500). From late December to mid-April and in October and November, there's also thoroughbred racing at *Santa Anita Park,* home of the *Breeder's Cup* (Huntington Dr. and Baldwin Ave., Arcadia; phone: 818-574-7223).

JOGGING Downtown, run around *Echo Park Lake* (a little less than a mile) during the day only; get there by going up Sunset and taking a right onto Glendale. In *Griffith Park,* run in the woodsy Ferndale area near the Vermont Avenue entrance; get to the park via the Golden State Freeway and watch for the sign to turn off (also see *Special Places*). In Westwood, *UCLA* has a hilly 4-mile perimeter course and a quarter-mile track. Four blocks from Century City, *Cheviot Hills Park* (at 2551 Motor Ave.) has a runners' course. And in Beverly Hills, jog in *Roxbury Park* (entrance at 471 S. Roxbury Dr.

and Olympic) or along the 1½ mile stretch of Santa Monica Boulevard between Doheny and Wilshire. Jogging also is popular along the oceanside bike path between Marina del Rey and the Palos Verdes Peninsula, in Santa Monica's *Palisades Park* on Ocean Avenue, and along San Vicente Boulevard from Brentwood to Ocean Avenue.

POLO *Will Rogers State Park* (14253 Sunset Blvd., Pacific Palisades; phone: 310-454-8212) has free morning and afternoon matches on weekends year-round, weather permitting. The *Santa Barbara Polo Club* (3375 Foothill Rd., Carpinteria; phone: 805-684-6683) has Sunday afternoon matches from April through October.

SWIMMING AND SURFING For swimming, the best beaches are El Porto Beach in Manhattan Beach, Will Rogers State Beach in Pacific Palisades, and Zuma Beach, north of Malibu. For surfing, Malibu Surfrider Beach, Hermosa Beach, El Porto Beach, and Zuma Beach are tops. Also see *Best Beaches* in DIVERSIONS.

TENNIS *Griffith Park,* featuring one of the top 25 municipal tennis facilities in the US according to *Tennis* magazine, boasts 12 outdoor courts, all with lights for night play (Riverside and Los Feliz; phone: 213-664-1191). Reservations can be made for a small fee. At the *Racquet Centre* (10933 Ventura Blvd., Studio City; phone: 818-760-2302), there are 20 lighted courts, a tennis shop, and a locker room and showers. The *Tennis Place* (5880 W. Third St.; phone: 213-931-1715), with a prime LA location, has 16 lighted, hard-surface courts; lessons and practice sessions with a ball machine are also available. Top-seeded players on the pro circuit generally show up for the *Volvo/Los Angeles Pro Tournament* held in July at *UCLA* (phone: 310-208-0730).

VOLLEYBALL If volleyball is your game, you won't have any trouble having a hands-on or a spectator's experience here. There are nets up on most beaches in Los Angeles County, and both amateur and professional tournaments take place year-round. At Manhattan and Hermosa Beaches, 26 professional competitions are held during March and September. For a schedule of the competitions, contact the *Association of Volleyball Professionals* (phone: 310-337-4842). Indoor volleyball is also popular and played regularly by local leagues at most of the area's 150 public parks. For more information, contact the *Southern California Volleyball Association* (phone: 310-320-9440) or the *Valley Municipal Sports Office* (phone: 818-989-8070).

THEATER

There is no shortage of stages in LA, despite the overshadowing presence of the film industry. The *Center Theater Group* performs at the *Music Center*'s *Ahmanson Theater,* which offers mainstream Broadway plays and musicals, and at the *Mark Taper Forum,* where the performances are more cutting edge (see *Special Places*). Also downtown is the *Los Angeles Theatre Center*

(514 S. Spring St.; phone: 213-627-6500), where you can enjoy a variety of entertainment—from live theater and dance to performance art and readings. The revived *State Theatre of California* is at the *Pasadena Playhouse* (39 S. El Molina Ave.; phone: 818-356-7529), which generally offers new and experimental theater. Other Los Angeles theaters include the *Doolittle Theatre* (1615 N. Vine St., Hollywood; phone: 213-462-6666 or 213-972-0700); the *Shubert Theatre* (in the *ABC Entertainment Center*, 2020 Ave. of the Stars, Century City; phone: 310-201-1500; 800-233-3123 for information and credit card reservations); the *Odyssey Theatre Ensemble,* which performs in three small theaters (all at 2055 S. Sepulveda; phone: 310-477-2055); and the *Pantages Theatre* (6233 Hollywood Blvd.; phone: 310-468-1700). The *Westwood Playhouse* (10886 Le Conte Ave.; phone: 310-208-5454) often headlines a celebrity or two in its Broadway and off-Broadway productions. Tickets for all major events can be ordered over the telephone through *Ticketmaster* (phone: 213-480-3232). For more information, see *Performing Arts* in DIVERSIONS.

MUSIC

All kinds of music can be heard in LA's concert halls and clubs. The *Los Angeles Philharmonic* plays at the *Dorothy Chandler Pavilion* at the *Music Center* (see *Special Places*). The *Hollywood Bowl* (2301 N. Highland Ave., Hollywood; phone: 213-850-2000) is a 17,000-seat hillside amphitheater that features famous guest entertainers and is the summer home of the *Philharmonic.* Leading popular performers in a wide range of musical styles play year-round at the *Universal Amphitheatre* (Hollywood Frwy. at Lankershim Blvd.; phone: 818-980-9421). The *Greek Theatre* (2700 N. Vermont Ave.; phone: 213-665-1927) is a 6,200-seat indoor theater with concerts by top names. The *Roxy* (9009 Sunset Blvd.; phone: 310-276-2222) is also good for concerts. For country music, check out the *Palomino Club* (6907 Lankershim Blvd., N. Hollywood; phone: 818-764-4010). Rock and jazz buffs should try the *Palace* (1735 N. Vine, near Hollywood and Vine; phone: 213-462-3000), where the rock theater–dance club downstairs often has live shows, as well as dancing. Upstairs, the *Palace Court* has live jazz on weekends; another Art Deco rock and jazz (and sometimes bluegrass) place is the *Wiltern Theatre* (3790 Wilshire Blvd.; phone: 213-380-5005). Other choices include the *Cinegrille,* an Art Deco cabaret with blues, jazz, and Broadway show performances at the *Radisson Hollywood Roosevelt* hotel (see *Checking In*); and *Kingston 12* (814 Bwy., Santa Monica; phone: 310-451-4423) for reggae. Also see *Performing Arts* in DIVERSIONS.

NIGHTCLUBS AND NIGHTLIFE

Anything goes in LA, especially after dark. Swinging nightspots open and close quickly, since the restless search for what's "in" keeps people on the move. *Doug Weston's Troubadour Club* (9081 Santa Monica Blvd., West Hollywood; phone: 310-276-6168) has introduced a number of top rock music acts. Another place that seems to be able to hold its own with live rock shows nightly is *Whisky A Go-Go* (8901 Sunset Blvd.; phone: 310-652-4202). *Roxbury* (8225 Sunset, W. Hollywood; phone: 213-656-1750) is popular with celebrities and the wannabe crowd. There are three levels for entertainment, a good restaurant, and an exclusive VIP room. Other hot nightspots include *Club Lingerie* (6507 Sunset Blvd., Hollywood; phone: 213-466-8557), a hip, happening rock club; *Hollywood Athletic Club* (6525 Sunset Blvd.; phone: 213-962-6600), with pool tables plus the latest rock groups; and *Café Largo* (432 Fairfax, Hollywood; phone: 213-852-1073), a modern cabaret with a mix of rock 'n' roll, folk, country, and oldies. In downtown LA, step out at the hip *Mayan* (1038 Hill St.; phone: 213-746-4287) or *Glam Sam* (333 S. Boylston; phone: 213-747-4849), owned by the singer formerly known as Prince, where a well-heeled crowd gathers on weekend nights to dine and dance until 4 AM. If you want to mingle with LA's trendiest, try to make the scene at the *Olive* (119 S. Fairfax Ave.; phone: 213-939-2001); admission here depends on who you are, who you know, and how you're dressed. Since it's not often easy to get in the door at these hot spots, *LA NightHawks* (phone: 310-392-1500) has club-hopping tours conducted in stretch limousines that travel to your choice of 250 popular nighttime nooks. Prices vary depending on destinations and include cover charges and a bottle of French champagne.

For blues buffs there's *Mint* (6010 W. Pico Blvd.; phone: 213-937-9630), a neighborhood bar, and the *House of Blues* (across the street from *The Comedy Club* in W. Hollywood at 8439 W. Sunset Blvd.; phone: 310-652-0247), the 1,000-seat music club/restaurant opened last year by Dan Aykroyd and *Aerosmith*.

With Movietown's pool of talent, comedy clubs here are a better bet than elsewhere. Among the options: *Improvisation* (8162 Melrose Ave.; phone: 213-651-2583, and at 321 Santa Monica Blvd., Santa Monica; phone: 310-394-8664), the grandparent of them all; and the *Comedy Store* (8433 Sunset Blvd.; phone: 213-656-6225), another survivor. If you want to get into the act, head over to *All That Glitz* (1911 Sunset Blvd.; phone: 310-278-7712), where musical comedy comes with a twist—cast members "roast" certain folks in the audience. Comedy is king at the *Groundling Theater* (7307 Melrose Ave., W. Hollywood; phone: 213-934-9700), LA's answer to Chicago's *Second City* and the launching pad for *Saturday Night Live* funny man Phil Hartman.

Best in Town

CHECKING IN

Los Angeles is the city where mere mortals stand the best chance of checking in alongside a movie star, although, obviously, the privilege will cost you dearly. (Note: The *Beverly Hills* hotel, one of the most popular with members of the film industry, has temporarily closed while it undergoes a complete renovation; it's not expected to reopen before the spring of this year at the earliest. The situation is the same for the sumptuous *L'Ermitage*, which is undergoing a change of ownership as well and is expected to reopen this year. For updated information on either, contact the *Los Angeles Visitors' and Convention Bureau;* the phone number is listed above, in *Tourist Information.*) If you're looking for someplace simply to shower and sleep, you'll be happier at one of the smaller hotels or motels sprinkled throughout the area. Generally speaking, accommodations are less expensive in the San Fernando and San Gabriel Valleys than in Hollywood or downtown. Most of Los Angeles's major hotels have complete facilities for the business traveler. Those hotels listed below as having "business services" usually offer such conveniences as meeting rooms, photocopiers, computers, translation services, and express checkout, among others. Call the hotel for additional information. Expect to pay $245 or more (sometimes *much* more) per night for a double room at hotels we've described as very expensive; between $140 and $240 at those places listed as expensive; between $80 and $140 at places in the moderate category; and less than $80 at places listed as inexpensive. (Be sure to ask about special commercial rates and weekend package deals.) For statewide information on bed and breakfast accommodations, contact *Eye Openers Bed & Breakfast* (PO Box 694, Altadena, CA 91001; phone: 213-684-4428 or 818-797-2055) or *California Houseguests International* (605 Lindley Ave., Suite 6, Tarzana, CA 91356; phone: 818-344-7878). Unless otherwise indicated, all hotels have air conditioning, private baths, TV sets, and telephones. Twenty-four-hour room service is the norm, unless otherwise noted. All telephone numbers below include area codes.

For an unforgettable experience in Los Angeles, we begin with our favorites, followed by our recommendations of cost and quality choices of accommodations, listed by price category.

GRAND HOTELS AND SPECIAL HAVENS

Bel-Air In the fashionable Bel-Air district of Los Angeles, this member of the prestigious Relais & Châteaux group has been a favorite hideaway of Gary Cooper, Howard Hughes, Grace Kelly, Sophia Loren, Marilyn Monroe, and other celebs since it opened during the 1920s. The hotel's perfectly appointed 92 rooms (39 of which are suites) are in one- and two-story mission-style buildings and bungalows scattered amid 11.5 exquisitely landscaped acres; privacy prevails. Executive chef Gary Clausen caters to the sophisticated tastes of patrons of *The Bel-Air Dining Room* with "back to basics" culinary artistry: Meat is lightly marinated rather than doused in rich sauces, and herbs are grown on the premises. Business services are available, and there's also a very gracious and helpful concierge desk. 701 Stone Canyon Rd. (phone: 310-472-1211; 800-648-4097 outside California; fax: 310-476-5890).

Four Seasons Located in a residential area referred to as "Beverly Hills adjacent," this elegant place is reminiscent of a grand European manor house. But instead of making guests feel self-conscious, the attentive service puts one at ease. The 285 rooms are large and luxuriously appointed. The decor is pleasantly subdued, with an emphasis on comfort, yet there are all the services you would expect in a world class hotel, and then some: Instead of providing the usual little in-room sewing kits, the hotel offers an on-premises seamstress 24 hours a day. On the fourth-floor rooftop terrace is a heated pool/spa area surrounded by palm trees and lounge chairs, with a small exercise area nearby. The *Gardens* restaurant, bright, cheery, and casually elegant, is a delight for lunch, dinner, or a lavish Sunday buffet brunch; it's also known for its oversize club sandwiches. All rooms have computer modems. Other conveniences include a concierge and business services. 300 S. Doheny Dr. (phone: 310-273-2222; 800-332-3442; fax: 310-859-3824).

Peninsula Beverly Hills A world class hotel, this stylish property has 200 rooms, suites, and villas, but its intimate scale, residential location (complete with lavish gardens and winding gravel pathways), antique furnishings, and fine artworks give it the feel of a private palazzo. An additional 16 rooms and suites are located in five villas, some of which offer private terraces and fireplaces. The wonderful rooftop deck has its own lush garden—it even boasts a manicured lawn and Moroccan-style cabañas. A health spa features a weight room, a lap pool, a whirlpool, a steam/sauna sun deck, and masseuses. *The Living Room,* a lobby lounge, serves traditional afternoon tea, and the *Belvedere* restaurant, with its handsome bar, is one of the most popular (and priciest) dining spots in town. Business services are available. A room attendant is on call 24 hours on each floor. 9882 Santa Monica Blvd., Beverly Hills (phone: 310-273-4888; 800-462-7899; fax: 310-788-2319.)

Regent Beverly Wilshire Built in 1928, this Beaux Arts jewel—a favorite spot of celebrities and visiting royalty—sits at the foot of Rodeo Drive. In the tower wing, all the rooms are done in different color schemes, furniture styles, and themes. The Wilshire Wing (our favorite) has 147 units, as well as three restaurants (the *Dining Room* is the best) and bars. There are 294 rooms in all, and the marble bathrooms are particularly plush. With the addition of a health spa, heated pool, hot tubs, and sauna, who could ask for more? Other services include a concierge desk and business services. 9500 Wilshire Blvd., Beverly Hills (phone: 310-275-5200; 800-545-4000; fax: 310-274-3709).

St. James's Club The first American link in this international hotel chain—with branches in London, Paris, and Antigua—its West Coast outpost is located smack-dab in the middle of the Sunset Strip, in the lovingly restored 1931 Art Deco *Sunset Tower* building. To rub shoulders with celebrities (Joan Collins, Quincy Jones, and David Bowie to name just a few regular guests), check into one of the 18 rooms or 44 suites, or have dinner at the *St. James* restaurant (formerly the *Members Room*). 8358 Sunset Blvd., W. Hollywood (phone: 213-654-7100; 800-225-2637; fax: 213-654-9287).

San Ysidro Ranch Originally owned by Franciscan missionaries, this 540-acre ranch, which opened in 1893 near Santa Barbara, enjoyed a long season as the choice vacation spot of the rich and the famous: Laurence Olivier and Vivien Leigh were married here; John F. Kennedy honeymooned here with Jackie; John Galsworthy, Aldous Huxley, Sinclair Lewis, Winston Churchill, Somerset Maugham, Bing Crosby, Jack Benny, and many others stayed here; and Ronald Colman owned the place from the mid-1930s until his death in 1958. But during the 1960s, the legend began to fade, and the inn was well down the road to total ruin when a former president of New York's great *Plaza* hotel put up the money to clean up, fix up, and paint. Today the 45 cottages, two tennis courts, stables, restaurant, and swimming pool all are as spiffy as they were when Galsworthy revised his *Forsyte Saga* here, with some added extras: 10 of the guest cottages now have their own Jacuzzis. Mix with fellow guests in the *Plow & Angel* bar, or the *Stonehouse* restaurant, where chef Gerard Tompson creates fine regional American fare. Special meals grace the tables on holidays. The ranch is one of only 21 American members of the prestigious Relais & Châteaux hotel group. 900 San Ysidro La., Montecito (phone: 805-969-5046; 800-368-6788).

VERY EXPENSIVE

Bel Age This hotel with a European ambience offers 188 suites, gracefully decorated with hand-carved rosewood and pecan wood furniture. *La Brasserie* is the hotel's casual café; *Diaghilev,* its more formal dining room, serves Franco-Russe cuisine. Also on the premises is a heated rooftop pool. A concierge and business services are available. 1020 N. San Vicente Blvd., W. Hollywood (phone: 310-854-1111; 800-424-4443; fax: 310-854-0926).

Century Plaza Extensively renovated last year, the 750-room hotel and the 322-room tower (which boasts spectacular views from spacious rooms and private balconies, and had a major face-lift last year) are run separately but share many facilities. The 24,000-square-foot ballroom has undergone an $8.5 million renovation; it reopened last year to host more Hollywood spectaculars. This hotel is a favorite spot for conventiongoers. There are plenty of shops in which to browse and several fine restaurants on the premises, including the casual seafood bar and grill, *Waters Edge,* and the California-continental *La Chaumière* (see *Eating Out*). Located in Century City, near the *ABC Entertainment Center,* it offers complimentary town car service for trips within a 5-mile radius. Other amenities include a concierge desk and business services. 2025 Ave. of the Stars, Century City (phone: 310-277-2000; 800-228-3000; fax: 310-551-3355).

Checkers Kempinski This 188-room property in the center of Los Angeles's financial district is geared to the needs of the business traveler. To ease the stress of the work day, there's a guest library, as well as a rooftop spa with a sauna, a steamroom, and exercise equipment. And for mixing business with pleasure, *Checkers* restaurant, open for "power" breakfasts and lunches, as well as dinners, serves sophisticated American fare. Complimentary limousine service is available to downtown business locations, and guests may choose from six complimentary newspapers each day. Full business services are available, and there's also a concierge desk. 535 S. Grand Ave. (phone: 213-624-0000; 800-426-3135; fax: 213-626-9906).

Doubletree Across the road from Marina del Rey—the world's largest manmade small-craft harbor—this 338-room seaside resort, with ocean and mountain views, is a short ride (by free shuttle) from the airport. Sailing, jogging, swimming, and bicycling are among the relaxing amenities. Two restaurants are on the property. There is a concierge, and business services are available. 4100 Admiralty Way, Marina del Rey (phone: 310-301-3000; 800-528-0444; fax: 310-213-301-6890).

J. W. Marriott On spacious grounds in Century City, this is Marriott's West Coast luxury flagship, designed in fashionable château style. The lobby is opulent yet intimate, with art objects and a resident live cockatoo. The hotel features 375 rooms, of which more than half are suites, and indoor and outdoor pools. Among the extra-special touches here is a loofah and natural sponge by each tub. There's a concierge desk and business services. 2151 Ave. of the Stars (phone: 310-277-2777; 800-228-9290; fax: 310-785-9240).

Marina del Rey Casual and California-style, this property is practically a peninsula as it is surrounded by boats on three sides. The 160 rooms and suites all have patios and balconies. Request a "Main Channel" room for the best views. There are two restaurants, a pool, and complimentary airport shuttle service. Other conveniences include a concierge and business services. 13534 Bali Way, Marina del Rey (phone: 310-301-1000; 800-8-MARINA within California; 800-882-4000 elsewhere in the US; fax: 310-301-8167).

Marina International Don't be misled by the less-than-grand exterior, for the meandering tile walkways eventually lead to spacious accommodations in wooden, shingled buildings. There are 135 rooms, but request one of the 25 bungalows decorated in soothing pastels. Although there is no restaurant on the premises, there are plenty within walking distance, and a continental breakfast and light fare are available in the downstairs coffee shop. There's a pool and a Jacuzzi, and complimentary transportation to the airport is offered. Business services are available. 4200 Admiralty Way, Marina del Rey (phone: 310-822-1010; 800-421-8145 or 800-8-MARINA within California; 800-882-4000 elsewhere in the US; fax: 310-301-6687).

Ritz-Carlton Marina del Rey This Los Angeles outpost borders the world's largest pleasure-craft harbor. There are sailboats for rent and a shore promenade, as well as tennis courts, a pool and fitness center, and 306 rooms with traditional decor. The club-like *Grill* serves dinner; all meals are provided in *The Café,* which has both indoor and outdoor seating with marina views. Afternoon tea and after-dinner cordials are served in the handsome library and lounge. Transportation to and from *LAX* is complimentary. Other amenities include a concierge and business services. 4375 Admiralty Way, Marina del Rey (phone: 310-823-1700; 800-241-3333; fax: 310-823-2403).

Sheraton Grande Pampering on a grand scale—this is the only hotel in town with personal butler service on every floor and other services beyond the call of duty. The 469 spacious rooms are tastefully decorated. There's a pool (but no health club), and each guest receives a complimentary membership to the *YMCA,* right across the street via a pedestrian bridge. Other amenities include a ballroom, concierge services, and business services. 333 S. Figueroa St. (phone: 213-617-1133; 800-325-3535; fax: 213-613-0291).

Shutters on the Beach Perched smack on the sand, this adorable, plantation-style hostelry gracefully mixes old Southern-style comfort with modern conveniences. The 198 rooms are decorated with dark walnut furniture, country prints, and tufted lounge chairs; terry robes and Jacuzzi tubs are among the creature comforts, as are a health club, a pool, an outdoor Jacuzzi, two restaurants, and a waterfront saloon. The concierge can arrange for most business needs. 1 Pico Blvd., Santa Monica (phone: 310-458-0030; 800-336-3000; fax: 310-458-4589).

Westwood Marquis This is a favorite among business who appreciate quality. The attractive high-rise holds 258 suites, and the bustling college town of Westwood is all around. The *Garden Terrace Room* is popular for Sunday brunch, and the elegant *Dynasty Room* (see *Eating Out*) serves California-French food. The *UCLA* running track is less than a half-mile away. There's also a lovely pool surrounded by cabañas and a concierge desk. 930 Hilgard Ave., Westwood (phone: 310-208-8765; 800-421-2317; fax: 310-824-0355).

EXPENSIVE

Beverly Hilton It's not quite as convenient to downtown Beverly Hills as the *Regent Beverly Wilshire* (see above), but if you plan to spend a lot of time in the hotel, you'll be happy in this self-contained 579-room establishment. *Trader Vic's* is a consistently good restaurant, and *L'Escoffier,* under the exclusive direction of executive chef Michel Blanchet, now offers superb food along with entertainment and dancing (see *Eating Out*). Other amenities include a concierge desk and business services. 9876 Wilshire Blvd., Beverly Hills (phone: 310-274-7777; 800-922-5432; fax: 310-285-1313).

Biltmore The grande dame of downtown hotels offers dramatic interiors that combine the classical architecture typical of European palaces with contemporary luxury (even more plush after an early 1990s renovation). There are 700 well-appointed rooms, an indoor pool, and a Jacuzzi. Other pluses include the fine French restaurant *Bernard's* and the *Grand Avenue* bar, with great jazz nightly. There's also a concierge and business services. 506 S. Grand Ave. (phone: 213-624-1011; 800-245-8673; fax: 213-612-1545).

Doubletree LA Airport If it's Tuesday, this must be LA—a mile from the airport, this 750-room hotel (formerly the *Westin LA Airport*) announces the day of the week on its elevators' carpets. With travelers often adjusting to time changes from faraway places like the Orient, this thoughtful touch could save the day. There is an outdoor swimming pool and a health club, the *Trattoria Grande,* and the *Charisma Café.* Half of the 42 suites have private outdoor Jacuzzis. Additional amenities include a concierge desk and business services. 5400 W. Century Blvd., Los Angeles (phone: 310-216-5858; 800-222-TREE; fax: 310-645-8053).

Hyatt Regency This 485-room super-modern place is another convention favorite. There are two restaurants, the *Brasserie* and the *Pavan* (serving northern Italian fare), and a fitness center. Other amenities include a concierge and business services. 711 S. Hope St. (phone: 213-683-1234; 800-233-1234; fax: 213-629-3230).

Inter-Continental Los Angeles Downtown's newest hotel, this massive 469-room establishment is geared to business travelers. Business services are available, and two restaurants, a pool, and a health club are also on the premises. 251 S. Olive St. (phone: 213-617-3300; 800-327-0200; fax: 213-617-3399).

Loews Santa Monica Loews' first venture on the West Coast, this 349-room property provides 20th-century comfort in a 19th-century setting, recalling an era when the area flourished as a resort community. A five-story atrium affords spectacular Pacific views; there's also an extensive fitness center with a personal trainer, an indoor/outdoor pool, and a Jacuzzi. The beach is a few steps away. The decor features antique ironwork, cool Pacific colors, and marine themes in paintings and sculptures by local artists. There are two restaurants, the contemporary Italian *Riva* and the more casual

Coast Café, and a lobby bar that also serves afternoon tea. A concierge and business services are also available. 1700 Ocean Ave., Santa Monica (phone: 310-458-6700; fax: 310-458-6721).

Le Mondrian This contemporary 188-room establishment on Sunset Strip pays homage to Piet Mondrian with its checkerboard exterior and its original paintings by the Dutch artist. The suites provide stunning city views, and the decor is upbeat and sophisticated—rock stars, models, and other Hollywood types are among the clientele. There's a pool, a fitness center, a beauty salon, and a restaurant featuring northern Italian cooking. The jazz lounge provides entertainment nightly. Business services are available. There is also a concierge desk. *Note:* At press time it was uncertain whether the hotel still would be operating under the same name and management this year. 8440 Sunset Blvd., W. Hollywood (phone: 213-650-8999; 800-255-5168; fax: 213-650-5215).

Le Montrose This property is considered one of the best bargains (a relative term in LA) in the city. The 107 rooms are all suites; some have balconies and kitchenettes. It's a favorite extended-stay place for people in the music and movie industries. The hotel restaurant has no name, but it does have its own chef who prepares continental cuisine. There is a rooftop pool, a Jacuzzi, and tennis courts. Business services are available. 900 Hammond St., W. Hollywood (phone: 310-855-1115; 800-424-4443 fax: 310-657-9192).

Nikko at Beverly Hills East meets West in this high-tech, Japanese-style hostelry. Busy executives will appreciate the full-service business center, as well as the 304 guestrooms, each of which is equipped with a fax, computer hookup, voice mail, oversize desk, and a multi-line computer phone that also controls the lights, stereo, and TV set. Other features include a private bar, terry robes, and a Japanese soaking tub in each striking, black marble bathroom. The hotel also has a small swimming pool; a well-equipped fitness center; and the *Panagaea* restaurant, specializing in Pacific Rim dishes. *Arnie Morton's of Chicago* is located next door (see *Eating Out*). 465 S. La Cienega Blvd. (phone: 310-247-0400; 800-NIKKO-US; fax: 310-247-0315).

Radisson Bel Air Summit Ideally located, this spot offers a light, breezy atmosphere. All 162 rooms have balconies, and there is a swimming pool, a tennis court, a cocktail lounge, and a dining room. Free parking is available, as are business services. 11461 Sunset Blvd. (phone: 310-476-6571; 800-333-3333; fax: 310-471-6310).

Ritz-Carlton, Huntington Pasadena's Spanish-style landmark, razed after it was declared earthquake-unsafe, has risen like the proverbial phoenix, albeit Ritz-Carlton–style. Set on 23 acres, the 1920s building has been reconstructed, complete with its imposing Alamo Arch at the entrance, Japanese horseshoe gardens, six cottages, and leaded crystal chandeliers. Other features include the hotel chain's signature dark woods, art and antiques in 385 guestrooms, an Olympic-size pool, a Jacuzzi and fitness center, three tennis courts, three restaurants, and three lounges. Other amenities include a concierge and business services. 1401 S. Oak Knoll Ave., Pasadena (phone: 818-568-3900; 800-241-3333; fax: 818-568-3159).

Sheraton at LAX This conference center at the airport features 810 rooms and *Landry's,* a fine restaurant with an excellent sushi bar. A concierge and full business services are available. 6101 W. Century Blvd. (phone: 310-642-1111; fax: 310-410-1276).

Sofitel Ma Maison The broad carved staircase, country French furniture, and gaily patterned wall-and-window treatments create a fittingly homey atmosphere in this 311-room, château-style property whose name includes the French words for "My House." The *Ma Maison* restaurant, airy and plant-filled, features expertly prepared French-California fare. For less formal dining, there's the bistro, *La Cajole,* an approximate re-creation of an old Parisian artists' hangout. Additional amenities include business services and a 24-hour concierge desk. 8555 Beverly Blvd. (phone: 310-278-5444; 800-521-7772; fax: 310-657-2816).

Sunset Marquis If you're looking for a romantic hideaway, this Mediterranean-style paradise is just the ticket. Lush tropical gardens dotted with *koi* ponds and inhabited by exotic birds shelter guests from the outside world; the privacy is just what the many celebrities who stay here are looking for. The 118 luxury suites and villas are furnished with canopy beds, fireplaces, saunas, and Jacuzzis; each has its own butler to cater to guests' needs. Amenities include two restaurants, two pools, a swinging bar called *Whiskey,* a full health club with personal trainers available, a concierge, and full business services. There is also a state-of-the-art recording studio, where musicians and wanna-bes can cut albums, score films, or just play around with music mixing (for a fee). 1200 N. Alta Loma Rd., W. Hollywood (phone: 310-657-1333; 800-858-9758; fax: 310-652-5300).

Westin Bonaventure Hotel and Suites This 1,474-room giant is a major downtown convention hotel that boasts an all-suite tower with 94 guest units designed especially for the business traveler (extras for tower guests include free local phone calls and a complimentary breakfast). Its cylindrical, mirrored towers are an LA skyline landmark, and it is especially convenient for downtown activities. This city within a city has 20 restaurants and lounges. The rooms, however, do not live up to the promise of the lobby and public spaces. Other amenities include a concierge desk and business services. 404 S. Figueroa St. (phone: 213-624-1000; fax: 213-612-4800).

MODERATE

Barnabey's Possibly the best value in Southern California, with the charm of an English country inn and a convenient location less than 3 miles from the airport and within walking distance of Manhattan Beach. All 123 rooms are furnished with antiques, and breakfast is included in the rate. Dine in *Barnabey's* restaurant and relax at *Rosie's Pub*. There's also complimentary 24-hour shuttle service to and from the airport, beach, and shopping. Room service is available until 10 PM. Business services also are available. Sepulveda Blvd. at Rosecrans Ave., Manhattan Beach (phone: 310-545-8466; 800-552-5285; fax: 310-545-8621).

Beverly Prescott Hotelier Bill Kimpton took over the former *Beverly Hillcrest* and transformed the place into another one of his snazzy boutique hotels. Perched on a hilltop—with private balconies overlooking Beverly Hills, Century City, Hollywood, and the Pacific Ocean—this 140-room hostelry has a palm-tree–lined, canopied entrance, a jewelry-box reception desk inlaid with onyx and mother of pearl, and gardens in its indoor/outdoor lobby. Each room has its own balcony; executive suites come with fax machines, computers, and printers. Other highlights include a health club, an outdoor pool with cabañas and food service, the newspaper delivered to your door, room service, and a great restaurant, *Rox*, run by Hans Rockenwagher. There's also a concierge and business services. 1224 S. Beverwil Dr., W. Los Angeles (phone: 310-277-2800; 800-421-3212; fax: 310-203-9537).

Century Wilshire In Westwood, the movie theater capital of LA and home of *UCLA*, this 99-room spot offers kitchen units, complimentary coffee, and continental breakfast (no room service or restaurant, though). There's a concierge desk, and business services are available. 10776 Wilshire (phone: 310-474-4506; 800-421-7223 outside California; fax: 310-474-2535).

Mikado Best Western The twisting canyon roads separating Hollywood from the San Fernando Valley are among the most scenic parts of LA. Set between Coldwater and Laurel Canyons, where cottages and modern glass and wood homes hang dramatically from cliffs, propped up only by stilts, this 58-room hostelry has a pool, a Jacuzzi, a restaurant, and a cocktail lounge. There's no room service, but guests receive complimentary American breakfast. Business services are available. 12600 Riverside Dr. (phone: 818-763-9141; 800-433-2239 in California; 800-826-2759 elsewhere in the US; fax: 818-752-1045).

New Otani Within walking distance of the *Music Center*, it has 448 rooms featuring Japanese luxury and service in a lovely garden-like setting—a soothing respite from the madness of downtown LA. The suites have an authentic tatami room and futon bedding, as well as deep bathtubs. *A Thousand Cranes* is its serene Japanese restaurant (see *Eating Out*). For more casual dining, the cheery *Azalea Restaurant & Bar* serves breakfast, lunch, and dinner. There's also a shopping arcade and a Japanese health club that offers shiatsu massage and acupuncture therapy. Other amenities include a concierge and business services. 120 S. Los Angeles St. (phone: 213-629-

1200; 800-252-0197 within California; 800-421-8795 elsewhere in the US; fax: 213-622-0980).

Radisson Hollywood Roosevelt Once the social center of old Hollywood, this 322-room establishment has LA-Spanish charm and an essence of the not so distant past. Traces of Tinseltown still remain—photographs of movie celebrities grace the walls, the Hollywood sign is up the hill, and the star-studded Walk of Fame is right outside. A restaurant, as well as a pool, a Jacuzzi, and a weight room are on the premises. Room service is available from 6 AM to 11PM. Other amenities include a concierge desk and business services. 7000 Hollywood Blvd., Hollywood (phone: 213-466-7000; 800-333-3333; fax: 213-462-8056).

Le Réve With 80 suites, this is a small, modest hotel with European flair. The decor and atmosphere are country French. There is a rooftop swimming pool, a Jacuzzi, a self-service laundry, and full room service from early morning until 11 PM, but no restaurant. Business services are available. 8822 Cynthia St., W. Hollywood. (phone: 310-854-1114; 800-424-4443; fax: 310-657-2623).

INEXPENSIVE

Beverly Garland Holiday Inn Close to *Universal Studios,* this 258-room, California mission–style hotel offers pleasant rooms at very appealing rates (their weekend package features breakfast and free accommodations on Sunday night). Amenities include an outdoor pool, a sauna, a putting green, tennis, free parking, room service from 6 AM to 11 PM, and a restaurant. 4222 Vineland Ave., Studio City (phone: 818-980-8000; 800-HOLIDAY; fax: 818-766-5230).

Courtyard Marriott Formerly the *Chesterfield,* this is a charming find; the 133-room hotel provides guests with all the amenities of higher-priced hostelries such as a concierge, a fine restaurant, and afternoon tea. In the rooms, you'll find complimentary mineral water, bathrobes, hair dryers, and even potpourri sachets. 10320 W. Olympic Blvd., W. Los Angeles (phone: 310-556-2777; 800-321-2211; fax: 310-203-0563).

Safari Inn If you're planning to visit the studios in Burbank, this will be more convenient than Beverly Hills or downtown LA hotels. The spacious valley environment also provides more of a sense of being in the open. There are 85 rooms and 20 suites, as well as a restaurant and room service. Business services are available. 1911 W. Olive Ave., Burbank (phone: 818-845-8586; 800-STAHERE; fax: 818-845-0054).

EATING OUT

These days, Los Angeles may be the country's most exciting restaurant town. Only the purest of purists still look to *L'Escoffier.* Ethnic places abound in all price ranges, and imaginative chefs meld superb raw materials, international accents, and good nutrition into pots of culinary gold. Though popularity with the show-biz crowd is often inversely proportional to the quality of a kitchen and the maître d's treatment of non-celeb guests, good food and good manners are creeping back at the hot spots. Regrettably, dining in din is still in, even when the food is exquisite, but some new restaurants have rediscovered the joy of calm. Los Angeles has banned smoking in all restaurants in the city proper (alfresco dining places, bars, and nightclubs are exempt, however). For dinner for two, expect to pay $100 or more at those places we've listed as very expensive; $75 to $90 at places in the expensive category; $40 to $70 at moderate places; and less than $30 at restaurants described as inexpensive. Prices do not include drinks, wine, or tips. Note that all restaurants serve lunch and dinner, unless otherwise noted. All telephone numbers below include area codes.

For an unforgettable dining experience, we begin with our culinary favorites, followed by our recommendations of cost and quality choices listed by price category.

INCREDIBLE EDIBLES

Arnie Morton's of Chicago, the Steakhouse Direct from the Windy City comes this steakhouse franchise where beef is the name of the game. Porterhouse, New York strip, and rib eye steaks—served in man-size portions—are the raison d'étre for eating here. Many confirmed carnivores claim the steaks are the best in town. The veal and lamb chops and the Maine lobsters are also scrumptious, and the side dishes—especially the hash browns and giant mushroom caps—are almost meals in themselves. Open daily. Reservations necessary. Major credit cards accepted. 435 S. La Cienega Blvd. (phone: 310-246-1501) and several other locations around LA.

Chinois on Main At *Spago,* Wolfgang Puck makes pizza topped with goat cheese and grills tuna to perfection. At *Chinois,* Puck's cooking leans more toward French-Chinese cuisine—goose liver with marinated pineapple and ginger-cinnamon sauce, barbecued squab with scallion noodles, and charcoal-grilled Szechuan beef in a cilantro-shallot sauce. The upscale, contemporary dining room has track lighting and pastel-colored walls covered with modern art. It's lovely, but as noisy as most in LA. If you show up without a reservation (they're impossible to get, anyway), you wait at a counter in front of the kitchen and watch the chefs at work. Open daily for dinner, Wednesdays through Fridays for lunch. Reservations advised. Major credit cards accepted. 2709 Main St., Santa Monica (phone: 310-392-9025).

David Slay's La Veranda Owner David Slay is a talented chef and a gracious host who has won a place in the hearts of all who have discovered this Beverly Hills spot. Decorated in soft cream tones, the dining room is comfortable and inviting. The menu offers contemporary California-Italian fare, such as a robust roasted garlic soup, roast veal loin, and salmon tartare with waffle-cut potatoes. Save room for one (or two or three) of the homemade pastries—our favorites are the tiny puffs filled with vanilla cream and caramel sauce. For social nibblers, the new Sunday night "grazing" menu features delightful samples of grilled Japanese eggplant, salmon tartare, and quesadillas with grilled chicken and cheddar cheese. Closed weekends for lunch. Reservations advised. Major credit cards accepted. 225 S. Beverly Dr., Beverly Hills (310-274-7246).

Le Dôme This Art Deco setting in the heart of the Sunset Strip is great for star watching, especially at lunch on Saturdays and after midnight at the magnificent bar. The rooms up front are stylish and casual, but the superagents, with their star clientele, negotiate contracts with big-name directors in the back. These rooms are more formal—velvet upholstery and candlelight—with magnificent views of the city. The food is French-continental; there's also an extensive wine list. Closed Saturday lunch and Sundays. Reservations necessary. Major credit cards accepted. 8720 Sunset Blvd. (phone: 310-659-6919).

Maple Drive From the folks who brought you Venice's own *72 Market St.,* Dudley Moore, Tony Bill, and Julia Stone have combined their talents once again to create this trendy restaurant—often loud, but always fun. You'll taste the best meat loaf you've ever had *and* the best chili. The roast turkey, bouillabaisse, and Caesar salad (made without eggs) have their fans too. There's live entertainment nightly, and the piano-playing Moore might even stop by to tickle the ivories. Closed Saturday lunch and Sundays. Reservations necessary. Major credit cards accepted. 345 N. Maple Dr. (phone: 310-274-9800).

Morton's Relocated last year in a spanking new building, set on the site where *Trumps* once reigned, *Morton's* is still the place of choice for tinseltown moguls, mavens, and anyone else seeking to dine on good food while basking in the social spotlight. The menu has undergone a few small changes, but still offers the standards that made *Morton's* famous—pasta, pizza, salads, and grilled dishes. Closed Sundays. Reservations necessary. Major credit cards accepted. 8764 Melrose Ave. (phone: 310-276-5205).

L'Orangerie One of LA's truly elegant French restaurants, this posh, flower-filled, special-occasion spot is among the most beautiful dining places in town. Pastel furnishings, flickering candlelight, stunning mirrors, and high-arched windows add to the romance. The delicacies served here include coddled eggs with caviar, rack of lamb, roasted squab, lobster fricassee, and scrumptious desserts. Closed Mondays and weekends for lunch. Reservations necessary. Major credit cards accepted. 903 N. La Cienega Blvd. (phone: 213-652-9770).

Patina Superchef Joachim Splichal has really pulled out all the stops with a whimsical menu that includes a corn *blini* "sandwich" filled with marinated salmon; a soufflé (how French) of grits (how American) with Herkimer cheddar and an apple-smoked bacon sauce; or New York duck liver with blueberry pancakes and blueberry sauce. Closed weekends for lunch. Reservations necessary. Major credit cards accepted. 5955 Melrose Ave., W. Hollywood (phone: 213-467-1108).

Spago When you're hot, you're hot. Famed chef Wolfgang Puck turned pizza making into an art form. His are baked in wood-burning brick ovens and topped with shrimp, duck, sausage, and goat cheese. Celebrity diners also munch on Sonoma lamb, Washington oysters, North Pacific salmon, and grilled free-range chicken. Be sure to leave room for one of the incredible desserts. Open daily for dinner only. Since this still is one of the most popular spots in town, make reservations weeks in advance. Major credit cards accepted. Also see *Quintessential Los Angeles* in DIVERSIONS. 1114 Horn Ave., W. Hollywood (phone: 310-652-4025).

VERY EXPENSIVE

Citrus Owner Michel Richard's French-Provençal–California fare uses delicate seasonings and creative touches to turn ordinary entrées into masterpieces. Among the highlights are grilled swordfish with lentils, pepper tuna steaks, roast veal, and rack of lamb. Don't miss the tasty fish specialties or his famous signature desserts. Closed Saturday lunch and Sundays. Reservations necessary. Major credit cards accepted. 6703 Melrose Ave. (phone: 213-857-0034).

Geoffrey's The wings of Eros beat here, and whether you fall in love with the views of the Pacific, the tasty food, or your dinner companion, it's nigh impossible not to find contentment here. Rich, roasted garlic soup topped with parmesan cheese, addictive rosemary muffins, and hearty braised veal ribs are the stars of the menu. The gallant service continues through the end of the meal, when ladies are offered a rose. Open daily. Reservations advised. Major credit cards accepted. 27400 Pacific Coast Hwy. (phone: 310-457-1519).

Rex II Ristorante Filled with Lalique, oak paneling, and brass, this downtown eatery in an Art Deco building duplicates the dining room of the *Rex,* an Italian passenger liner popular during the 1920s. Each evening there's a six-course special dinner or à la carte dining. There's a full bar featuring soft dance music on the mezzanine level. Closed Sundays and at lunch Mondays through Wednesdays, and Saturdays. Reservations necessary. Major credit cards accepted. 617 S. Olive St. (phone: 213-627-2300).

EXPENSIVE

Adriano's High atop the Hollywood hills is this picturesque restaurant decorated with a vaulted ceiling and a brass-trimmed sculpture surrounded by flowers. A favorite with celebrities, it offers tasty northern Italian fare, with perfect pasta and a superb Caesar salad. Open daily. Reservations advised. Major credit cards accepted. 2930 Beverly Glen Blvd. (phone: 310-475-9807).

Babylon Supermodel and actress Tia Carrere's interpretation of an Arabian-style restaurant draws celebs in limos (Tom Cruise, Cher, k. d. lang), some eager to feast on Middle Eastern dishes, others on filet mignon. Closed Sundays; open from 7 PM until the wee hours the rest of the week. Reservations necessary (dress trendy if you don't know any celebrities). Major credit cards accepted. 616 N. Robertson Blvd. (phone: 310-277-6200).

Bikini The young, the hip, and the beautiful squeeze into this stunning, Japanese-style eating emporium. The eclectic, health-conscious menu offers everything from East Indies enchiladas to dim sum dumplings. The high-tech Japanese decor spreads over two stories with a rooftop garden patio. Closed Saturday lunch and Sunday dinner. Reservations advised. Major credit cards accepted. 1413 Fifth St. (phone: 310-395-8611).

Bistro 45 Just a short drive from the city, this splendid Pasadena dining place with pale pink walls, skylights, and a separate trellised outdoor dining area excels in California-French fare. Menu items include fish stews and Hawaiian tuna *sashimi* with lemon-Dijon vinaigrette. Desserts are just as tempting, especially the chocolate hazelnut torte. Closed Sunday lunch and Mondays. Reservations advised. Major credit cards accepted. 45 S. Mentor Ave., Pasadena (phone: 818-795-2478).

Café Four Oaks One of LA's loveliest cafés, this indoor/outdoor spot is unabashedly romantic. Indoors, there's a roaring fireplace. Outdoors, a fabulous garden with lush flora and bubbling fountains that make you feel you're no longer in the city. The food here is a visual treat and a pleasure to eat; especially appealing are the gorgeous salads (such as Belgian white and California red endive with walnuts), and the lightly sauced grilled fish selections (such as farm-raised catfish with a lobster-orange-ginger infusion). There are fabulous goodies for dessert and the service is friendly and unobtrusive. It's one of the prettiest places in LA for a leisurely Sunday brunch. Closed Mondays. Reservations suggested. Major credit cards accepted. 2181 N. Beverly Glen Blvd., Bel-Air (phone: 310-470-2265).

Campanile Named for the tower that crowns this landmark built in 1928 by Charlie Chaplin, this stunning place is run by the husband and wife team of Mark Peel and Nancy Silverton, veterans of *Michael's* and *Spago*. Enter through a delightful, skylit café and walk through a long, cloister-like room with tables on one side and the kitchen on the other to get to the balcony-rimmed dining room in the rear. The food is California-Italian, with other Mediterranean influences. The tastes of Tuscany—like antipasto and poached mozzarella—abound; other specialties include all-American grilled prime ribs and sinfully delicious desserts. Open weekdays for all three meals, Saturdays for dinner only; closed Sundays. Reservations necessary (the farther in advance the better). Major credit cards accepted. 524 S. La Brea Ave. (phone: 213-938-1447).

Champagne Bis The owner/chef is American, but the food is French—traditional, contemporary, and spa. The crispy Norwegian salmon and the veal shanks are the most popular choices. The restaurant itself is simple, elegant, and blissfully quiet. Closed Mondays and weekends for lunch. Reservations advised. Major credit cards accepted. 10506 Little Santa Monica Blvd. (phone: 310-470-8446).

Le Chardonnay In an unlikely setting on bustling Melrose Avenue, this Belle Epoque dining place is reminiscent of a 1920s Left Bank bistro. Owners Robert Bigonnet and Claude Alrivi have combined beautiful decor (rich mahogany, mirrored walls, hand-painted French tile) and first-rate food (roast venison, terrine of squab and sweetbreads, and goat cheese–filled ravioli with Italian parsley sauce) to create an extraordinary dining experience in the heart of Los Angeles. Open for dinner only; closed Mondays. Reservations advised. Major credit cards accepted. 8284 Melrose Ave. (phone: 213-655-8880).

Chasen's A somewhat stuffy LA institution for decades, this celebrity favorite has shed its former image for a more casual atmosphere. There's a new, more budget-friendly, prix fixe menu. Specialties include scampi maison, signature chili, and chicken pot pie. Frank Sinatra, Rosemary Clooney, and Jimmy Stewart are regular patrons. Closed Sunday lunch and Mondays. Reservations advised. American Express accepted. 9039 Beverly Blvd. (phone: 310-271-2168).

La Chaumière Despite its location—the fifth floor of the tower at the *Century Plaza* hotel in a bustling area off Santa Monica Boulevard—this dining room evokes the charm of a French country manor. Diners can look out over the city while enjoying such California-French inspirations as Dungeness crab chowder with cheddar cheese, or roast rack of Sonoma lamb with a parsley, garlic, and herb crust. In addition to some of the best California vintages, the wine list offers fine French and German selections. There is dancing and entertainment at the adjacent bar. Closed weekends for lunch. Reservations advised. Major credit cards accepted. 2055 Ave. of the Stars (phone: 213-551-3360).

Chianti Tasty Italian and continental fare are served in a romantic, old-fashioned room with cozy banquettes and extremely professional service. Some favorites are veal *piccata* and angel-hair pasta with shrimp and crabmeat. Open daily for dinner only. Reservations necessary. Major credit cards accepted. 7383 Melrose Ave., W. Hollywood (phone: 213-653-8333).

Cicada Former *L'Orangerie* chef Jean François Meteigner has created a menu to delight all palates in this charming, auberge-like dining room. The Norwegian smoked salmon melts in your mouth; other menu highlights are large, grilled Santa Barbara shrimp, *penne* with *porcini* mushrooms, and linguine with scallops. Plan on a long, leisurely evening of fine food, and some serious "star-gazing." Closed Saturday lunch and Sundays. Reservations necessary. Major credit cards accepted. 8478 Melrose Ave., W. Hollywood (phone: 213-655-5559).

Drago One of Santa Monica's trendy spots. Chef-owner Celestino Drago demonstrates his culinary talents with such stylish Sicilian dishes as *cannellini* beans and tuna and *tramezzino di polenta* with wild mushrooms. The cheesecake accompanied by an espresso ends the meal on just the right note. Closed weekends for lunch. Reservations necessary. Major credit cards accepted. 2628 Wilshire Blvd., Santa Monica (phone: 310-828-1585).

Drai's Chanel-clad women and Armani-draped men drive up to Victor Drai's hot new bistro in Rolls Royces, Mercedes, and BMWs. They come for the fantastic creations of chef Claude Segal: impeccably prepared whitefish wrapped in phyllo, crabmeat-stuffed pasta, grilled Spencer steaks coated with rich cream, and his signature potatoes *boulangere*. For dessert, there's divine *crème brûlée* and or an equally celestial chocolate hazelnut cake. Adding to the dining experience are Villeroy & Boch china with Christofle silver amid an elegantly whimsical setting of mismatched furnishings. Open daily for dinner only. Reservations necessary. Major credit cards accepted. 730 N. La Cienega Blvd. (phone: 310-358-8585).

Dynasty Room California-French food is served in a dining room that showcases original artwork and artifacts from China's T'ang Dynasty. The creative fare coupled with an eye-opening Sunday brunch are among the reasons it's remained one of the most popular dining spots in town. Baby abalone and pink-lip scallops on green beans with sauce *citronette* is just one of several winning combinations. Open daily for dinner. Reservations advised. Major credit cards accepted. In the *Westwood Marquis Hotel*, 930 Hilgard Ave., Westwood (phone: 310-208-8765).

L'Escoffier This once formal and somewhat snobby local landmark now boasts a brighter, more casual look and is under the direction of the celebrated culinary genius Michel Blanchet. The inviting room, high atop the *Hilton*, offers a spectacular view of Beverly Hills and an equally wonderful menu of such Blanchet specialties as tartlet of shrimp with asparagus, Maine lobster in lemon and vegetable broth on couscous, and *côte de boeuf* with grilled vegetables and *choron* sauce. For dessert, the chocolate and Grand Marnier soufflés are to die for. Open for dinner Tuesdays through Saturdays. Reservations necessary. Major credit cards accepted. In the *Beverly Hilton Hotel*, 9876 Wilshire Blvd., Beverly Hills (phone: 310-274-7777).

Georgia A dark, brooding supper club, it features hand-painted upholstered canvas walls, rich mahogany furnishings and a très chic celebrity clientele (the latter is not too surprising considering the owners: Debbie Allen, Eddie Murphy, Norm Nixon, Denzel Washington, and Connie Stevens). The food's terrific, too: "Southern comfort" dishes such as charred tomato okra stew, grits, catfish, and hushpuppies. Open for dinner only; closed Mondays. Reservations necessary. Major credit cards accepted. 7315 Melrose Ave. (phone: 213-933-8410).

Granita Wolfgang Puck's Malibu entry. Designed by his wife, Barbara Lazaroff, the restaurant has an aquarium theme: mosaics, shells, and a *koi* fishpond. Puck's designer pizza still ranks among the best, and the seafood is superb. But the star-struck staff tends to ignore anybody less famous than the local celebrities who flock from their nearby beachfront homes. Closed Monday and Tuesday lunch. Reservations necessary. Major credit cards accepted. 23725 W. Malibu Rd., Malibu (phone: 310-456-0488).

Ivy A favorite venue for lunchtime power deals, it is an anomaly—an old brick farmhouse on bustling Robertson Boulevard, bordering Beverly Hills. Its rustic decor is the perfect setting for the eclectic (with a Southern accent) American menu; it's also a great place for outdoor dining. Corn chowder with fresh tarragon, salad with mesquite-grilled chicken or shrimp, and twice-cooked Cajun prime ribs—first oven-seared and then grilled—are standouts on the changing menu. Then there are the desserts—the likes of which mama could only dream of making. Open daily. Reservations necessary (during evening hours, expect at least an hour's wait even with reservations). Major credit cards accepted. 113 N. Robertson Blvd. (phone: 310-274-8303).

Jimmy's Popular with the Beverly Hills set, this elegant dining place is unbeatable for a romantic dinner or a late-night supper. Try the peppered salmon on a bed of spinach or grilled veal chop with chanterelles. Leave room for the delicious chocolate truffle cake with espresso sauce; insulin shock aside, it's a knockout. Closed Saturday lunch and Sundays. Reservations advised. Major credit cards accepted. 201 Moreno Dr., Beverly Hills (phone: 310-879-2394).

Locanda del Lago A spunky Italian trattoria–style eatery situated on Santa Monica's Third Street Promenade, it has oversize windows that afford a great view of the crowd strolling by. Favorite menu selections include wild mushroom polenta, grilled eggplant, *osso buco con risotto alla milanese,* and just about any pasta. Closed weekends for lunch. Reservations advised. 231 Arizona Ave., Santa Monica (phone: 310-451-3525).

Locanda Veneta A tiny trattoria offering some of the most sophisticated Italian food this side of Rome. Try the arugula, mushroom, and parmesan salad; the veal chop is nearly perfect, juicy and charred just so. For dessert, the *tiramisù* is a must. Closed Saturday lunch and Sundays. Major credit cards accepted. Reservations necessary. 8638 W. Third St. (phone: 310-274-1893).

Michael's Now that prices have dropped closer to the level of LA's other high-priced restaurants, this pioneer eatery—where California nouvelle was first new—just may be accessible to a few more diners. The gorgeous garden and contemporary art add visual pleasure to the gustatory feats. Try the wild mushroom salad and the grilled Norwegian salmon filet with *beurre blanc* sauce and steamed vegetables. Closed Mondays, Saturday lunch, and Sunday dinner. Reservations advised. Major credit cards accepted. 1147 Third St., Santa Monica (phone: 310-451-0843).

Orso Although the outside decor is extremely unassuming, this popular northern Italian trattoria more than compensates with its interior ambience and its charming patio framed by ficus trees and candlelit tables. Earthy country salads, pizza with all-but-transparent crusts, grilled meat, and delicious calf's liver are served on attractive Italian pottery plates. There is an extensive wine list as well. Well-known actors frequent this spot, and the bar becomes lively after theater hours. Open daily. Reservations advised. MasterCard and Visa accepted. 8706 W. Third St. (phone: 310-274-7144).

Pacific Dining Car Steaks—cut on the premises from aged, corn-fed beef—are the house specialty, although the menu also offers four types of fresh fish every day. The restaurant is set in a real dining car (plus an additional building) that's been at the same downtown location since 1921. This is a good place for early dinner or late supper when you have tickets for a show at the *Music Center*. Open daily, around the clock. Reservations necessary. Major credit cards accepted. 1310 W. Sixth St. (phone: 213-483-6000).

Pinot Housed in a charming yellow brick building, *Patina*'s bistro sister offers many of the same culinary delights as its sibling, but in a more casual atmosphere. The menu features a salad of wild greens with a poached egg, bacon, and toasted country bread; *blinis* topped with creamy goat cheese and ratatouille; and roasted duck *confit*. Dessert is a must—try the lemon tart with baked strawberries or the flourless chocolate cake with coffee sauce. This eatery is a favorite among the trendsetters and mega-stars—Warren Beatty is one of the regulars. Closed Sundays. Reservations necessary. Major credit cards accepted. 12969 Ventura Blvd., Studio City (phone: 818-990-0500).

Remi Evocative of a tony seaside Italian restaurant (even though it's three blocks from the sea), and named for Venetian gondoliers' oars, this eatery serves ambrosial Venetian fare in a casually elegant atmosphere. The rich wood, gleaming brass, and nautical theme provide an airy backdrop for enjoying such dishes as whole fish infused with herbs and the wonderful selection of grappas. The outdoor tables are ideal for people watching on Santa Monica's Third Street Promenade. Open daily. Reservations necessary. Major credit cards accepted. 1451 Third St. Promenade (phone: 310-393-6545).

Tatou This lavish, 1930s-style supper club, where the dressed-to-the-nines clientele dine under a 25-foot-high, tented ceiling accented with a crystal chandelier, is patterned after the legendary *Coconut Grove* nightclub. Plush banquettes line the ornate walls, and center stage tables are shaded by faux palm trees. Live entertainment accompanies chef Desi Szonntagh's traditional, hearty American–French-Provençal fare. A sampling of menu items might include Maine lobster, Caesar salad, crispy roast duck with ginger and black currants, and herb-packed red snapper with oven-dried tomatoes. Desserts are a chocolate lover's paradise. After dinner, go upstairs and dance off those calories (the club is open weekdays until 2 AM, Fridays and Saturdays until 4 AM). Jackets are required for men. Closed Sundays. Reservations necessary. Major credit cards accepted. 233 N. Beverly Dr., Beverly Hills (phone: 310-274-9955).

Valentino Devotees generally describe the food as Italian, and the homemade pasta certainly bears them out. But there's also a world of other choices on the eclectic menu—starters such as *timballo* (rolled baby eggplant) or *crespelle* (corn crêpes stuffed with seafood) and entrées like grilled fresh shrimp wrapped with swordfish and dressed with lime juice. This casually elegant spot boasts an impressive wine cellar: more than 50,000 bottles, including Italian, French, German, and California labels. Closed Sundays; lunch is served only on Fridays. Reservations necessary. Major credit cards accepted. 3115 Pico Blvd., Santa Monica (phone: 310-829-4313).

Val's Good food such as grilled calf's liver, fried shrimp, and all kinds of pasta are dished out to the crew of regulars who jam this popular spot. Closed Saturday lunch and Sundays. Reservations advised. Major credit cards accepted. 10130 Riverside Dr., Toluca Lake (phone: 818-508-6644).

Water Grill The only oyster bar in the downtown area is located in this handsome spot. Eight varieties of the mollusk are served along with a wide selection of fresh regional seafood: Atlantic soft-shell crabs with cranberries, northern pike with succotash, and California cioppino are just a hint of what you can experience. Closed weekends for lunch. Reservations advised. Major credit cards accepted. 523 W. Sixth St. (phone: 213-891-0900).

MODERATE

Benvenuto A tiny trattoria offering friendly service and exquisitely prepared Italian food. This cozy café is a popular hangout for celebs, artists, entertainers, and other assorted Hollywood types. Although chef Mustapha Sadd's menu is the main attraction—designer pizza, fresh fish, pasta, baked rabbit, *tiramisù*—lingering over an espresso in the candlelit dining room or on the patio overlooking Santa Monica Boulevard while watching the celebrity parade pass by makes this place hard to leave. Closed weekends for lunch. No reservations. Major credit cards accepted. 8512 Santa Monica Blvd., W. Hollywood (phone: 310-659-8635).

Bistro Garden The very same Beverly Hills celebrities who have parked their Rolls-Royces up the street at the *Bistro* for years have made its sister restaurant the "in" spot. Lunch is especially chic, with such fare as baked sea scallops with a muscat-ginger sauce. The garden-like patio is *the* place to be seen, and it's quite a pretty place at that. Closed Sundays. Reservations necessary. Major credit cards accepted. 176 N. Canon Dr., Beverly Hills (phone: 310-550-3900).

Ca'Brea Everything about this two-level restaurant owned by Antonio Tommassi and Jean Louis de Mori is earthy—from its ocher-walled dining area to a menu of simple Italian dishes at down-to-earth prices. Specialties include tortelloni filled with spinach and ricotta, and grilled lamb chops with a robust mustard sauce and truffles. Be sure to leave room for the *tiramisù*—it's worth every calorie. Yes, trivia fans, this is the same spot once occupied by the legendary eatery *Robaire's;* mementos of that past have been carefully preserved in the third-floor private dining room. Closed Saturday lunch and Sundays. Reservations advised. Major credit cards accepted. 346 S. La Brea (phone: 213-938-2863).

Café La Bohème This whimsical West Hollywood eatery attracts a lively crowd that comes mostly for the ambience: The high-ceilinged Nouveau Baroque dining room is draped in faded velvet and adorned with gilded mirrors. The menu has something for everybody—pizza, pasta, salads topped with garlic-seared beef, and filet mignon with shiitake mushrooms. Open daily. Reservations advised. Major credit cards accepted. 8400 Santa Monica Blvd., W. Hollywood (phone: 213-848-2360).

Celestino The young Italian chef draws on his Sicilian roots and Tuscan training for a limited menu with innovative twists, such as the highly praised seafood baked in a paper bag. The restaurant is airy and unpretentious. The art exhibit changes periodically, as does the menu. Closed weekends for lunch. Late-night suppers are served Fridays and Saturdays until 1 AM, with jazz until 2 AM. Reservations advised. Major credit cards accepted. 236 S. Beverly Dr. (phone: 310-859-8601).

Chaya Venice The family responsible for the *Chaya* (Japanese for tea house) chain has been operating tea houses in Japan for three centuries now. Their latest venture blends Japanese and American fare with such dishes as Hawaiian-tuna spring rolls accompanied by a spicy salsa, charred rare tuna *niçoise*, and broiled sea eel with julienned vegetables. The decor is very high-tech—an eclectic mix of chrome, copper, stone, and wood, reflecting the diversity of the menu. Open daily for dinner; closed Saturday lunch. Reservations necessary. Major credit cards accepted. 110 Navy St., Venice (phone: 310-396-1179).

Chez Mélange This South Bay eatery is true to its name, offering an international variety of victuals. There is a champagne bar, a wine bar with tastings on Tuesdays, and a dining room, all in a former coffee shop of a motor inn. Open daily for all three meals. Reservations advised. Major credit cards accepted. 1716 Pacific Coast Hwy., Redondo Beach (phone: 310-540-1222).

Il Cielo Set in a brick cottage, with several romantic dining rooms (a fireplace glows in the winter) and a heated patio, this place serves excellent northern Italian food. During quiet hours the staff treats guests as if they were at a family reunion. On a balmy evening, eating in the garden feels like dining in Tuscany. Closed Sundays. Reservations advised. Major credit cards accepted. 9018 Burton Way, Beverly Hills (phone: 310-276-9990).

Engine Co. No. 28 This converted firehouse re-creates an American grill of the 1940s, but serves what chef Naomi Serizawa calls old-fashioned comfort food with a health-conscious attitude. Popular dishes include seafood salad, turkey burgers on whole-wheat buns, a light "Firehouse" chili, and special pasta. Weekly specials feature recipes created by firehouse cooks from around the US. Open daily for dinner, weekdays only for breakfast and lunch. Reservations advised. Major credit cards accepted. 644 S. Figueroa St. (phone: 213-624-6996).

Epicentre Although some Angelenos fail to see the humor in the faux post-earthquake damage decor presented here, the place attracts a steady clientele. Gimmicky food names—"seismic entrées"—include quesadillas, crab cakes in corn chili sauce, curries, and homemade ice cream. Closed Saturday lunch, Sundays, and Monday dinner. Reservations advised. Major credit cards accepted. *Kawada Hotel,* 200 S. Hill St. (phone: 213-625-0000).

Gilliland's The owner is Irish but the fare is Californian—with Irish accents (such as soda bread on Sundays). Closed Saturday lunch. Reservations necessary on weekends. Major credit cards accepted. 2425 Main St. (phone: 310-392-3901).

Jackson's The decor is unpretentious, with wagon-wheel ceiling lights and a Western, ski-lodge feel; the mood is frisky; and both the home-style and more elaborate dishes are first-rate. Try the rabbit with polenta, roasted pork loin with crispy potato pancake, or crab- and leek-stuffed ravioli, with a fresh raspberry tart for dessert. Open daily. Reservations advised. Major credit cards accepted. 8908 Beverly Blvd. (phone: 310-550-8142).

Joss The austere decor makes this a high-style showcase for unfamiliar regional Chinese delicacies, such as glazed ginger venison with *quei hua* wine. The waiter shows off the whole perfectly crisped, golden brown Hong Kong Pin-Pei chicken before carving and preparing it in the style of Peking duck on a side table. Closed weekends for lunch. Reservations advised. Major credit cards accepted. 9255 Sunset Blvd. (phone: 310-276-1886).

Lawry's, the Prime Rib What's billed is what you get—delicious prime ribs with horseradish sauce—at this reliable eatery. Accompaniments include perfect Yorkshire pudding, mashed potatoes, and salad. The room is paneled but bright, the better to see the immense portions. Open daily for dinner. Reservations advised. Major credit cards accepted. 100 N. La Cienega Blvd., Beverly Hills (phone: 310-652-2827).

Mandarin Northern Chinese cooking is presented in elegant surroundings instead of the usual plastic, pseudo-Oriental decor. Not on the menu, but well worth requesting as an appetizer, is the minced squab wrapped in lettuce leaves; also be sure to try the spicy prawns. Closed weekends for lunch. Reservations advised. Major credit cards accepted. 430 N. Camden Dr., Beverly Hills (phone: 213-272-0267).

Matsuhisa The Japanese fare with Peruvian accents (honest!) is described by its chef as "New Wave seafood." The most popular dishes are squid cut like pasta, with an asparagus topping, and seafood with soy, *wasabi,* and garlic. Closed weekends for lunch. Reservations necessary two to three days in advance. Major credit cards accepted. 129 N. La Cienega Blvd. (phone: 310-659-9639).

Mon Kee's Amazing seafood combinations are the draw at this bustling Chinese dining spot, which caters to downtown LA's business crowd as well as to tourists. "Live" lobster, 15 squid dishes (try the crispy squid with special salt), and steamed or fried saltwater and freshwater fish are the mainstays of the seafood menu. For those not compelled by the above—or the conch, clams, or oysters—there are dozens of traditional pork, poultry, beef, and vegetable dishes which are sure to dazzle. Open daily. Reservations advised. Major credit cards accepted. 679 N. Spring St. (phone: 213-628-6717).

Musso & Frank Grill It really is a grill, operating in Hollywood since 1919, and apparently not redecorated once (not that its regulars—film people, journalists, the moiling LA middle class—want it to change one iota). The kind of place whose cachet is having none at all, it's fine if you like nostalgia and surly waiters. Traditional American food is served—try the short ribs, chicken pot pie, or macaroni and cheese. Closed Sundays. Reservations advised. Major credit cards accepted. 6667 Hollywood Blvd. (phone: 213-467-7788).

Pane Caldo Bistro An unpretentious Italian *ristorante* with a great view of the city's famed hills. What it lacks in fancy appointments, it more than makes up for with careful food preparation, generous portions, and reasonable prices. A complimentary appetizer and basket of *focaccia* arrive with the menu to ease the difficult task of choosing from among Tuscan specialties such as warm bell-pepper salad, risotto specials, tagliatelle with *porcini* mushrooms, spinach tortelloni with butter and sage, osso buco, and a selection of 14 kinds of individual pizza. Try the ultra-rich *tiramisù* for dessert. Closed Sunday lunch. Reservations advised. Major credit cards accepted. 8840 Beverly Blvd. (phone: 310-274-0916).

Parkway Grill California cooking is served in a cozy, informal Pasadena eatery without the glitz and prices of *Spago*. The innovative cuisine features mesquite-grilled fish and game, fresh pasta, and pizza lovingly baked in an oak-burning oven. Its late hours make it convenient for supper after the theater or a concert. Open daily for dinner, weekdays for lunch, and Sundays for brunch. Reservations advised. Major credit cards accepted. 510 S. Arroyo Pkwy. (phone: 818-795-1001).

Rockenwagner It's loud, even raucous, but the food's great at this Frank Gehry–designed, high-tech eatery. Set behind a glass façade, it features booths lighted by modern streetlamps and a huge German countryside mural. The creative menu features tasty appetizers such as garlic flan, goat cheese, and beet terrine with grilled radicchio; among the entrées is cilantro fettuccine with chicken, mild chilies, onion, and roasted jalapeño tomato sauce. Dessert highlights include caramelized pear Napoleon, crisp warm apple pizza, and scrumptious signature cookies. Open weekdays for all three meals; brunch and dinner on weekends. Reservations advised. Major credit cards accepted. 2435 Main St., Santa Monica (phone: 310-339-6504).

Rustica Brothers James and John Beriker's romantic restaurant offers two lovely settings for dinner: a gracious garden room/patio with real fruit trees and an Italian fountain under a retractable roof, and the elegant yet cozy front room with a striking bar and pretty tables nestled among live plants. The excellent fare suits the setting; choose from wood-fired pizza, homemade pasta, charbroiled fish, and specialties such as roasted eggplant and potato mousse with black Kalamata olives. Closed Sundays. Reservations necessary. Major credit cards accepted. 435 N. Beverly Dr. (phone: 310-247-9331).

Siamese Princess This Oriental eatery, which predates the Thai proliferation, looks like an antiques shop. European furniture and collectibles vie for space with Siamese gift items and photos of British, Thai, and show-biz royalty. The food, billed as "Royal Thai" and beautifully presented, ranks high above run-of-the-mill. For example, slivers of orange peel turn rice noodles into a delicacy. Closed Saturday through Wednesday lunch. Reservations necessary. Major credit cards accepted. 8048 W. Third St. (phone: 213-653-2643).

A Thousand Cranes Besides having such a beautiful name, this Japanese spot is well versed in the traditional art of serving beautiful food. It has several tatami rooms and a Western dining room. Go for Sunday brunch, a spectacular Japanese buffet accompanied by live music. Open daily. Reservations advised. Major credit cards accepted. In the *New Otani Hotel,* 120 S. Los Angeles St. (phone: 213-629-1200).

INEXPENSIVE

California Pizza Kitchen *Spago* for the masses, it's Beverly Hills's favorite pizza place. Upscale fast food is served in a sleek black-, white-, and yellow-tiled environment—this is not your average neighborhood pizzeria. Nouvelle cuisine pizza specialties, served straight from a wood-fired oven, include such delights as Original BBQ Chicken Pizza, Thai Chicken Pizza, Tandoori Chicken Pizza, Peking Duck Pizza, BLT Pizza, and Tuna-Melt Pizza. The menu also offers fresh pasta with interesting sauces, and yummy desserts. Open mid-morning to late evening daily. Unlike *Spago,* there's no need for a reservation here—but there'll probably be a line. Major credit cards accepted. 207 S. Beverly Dr., Beverly Hills (phone: 213-272-7878) and several other locations around LA.

Chianti Cucina Sister to the far pricier *Chianti* next door (see above), this casual trattoria specializes in great-tasting pasta and pizza. Open daily. Reservations necessary. Major credit cards accepted. 7383 Melrose Ave. (phone: 213-653-8333).

Chin Chin Delicious dim sum and traditional Chinese food, cooked without MSG, account for its ongoing popularity as do its quick service and low prices. Takeout also is available. Open daily. Reservations unnecessary. Major credit cards accepted. Five locations: 8618 Sunset Blvd., Sunset Plaza (phone: 213-652-1818); 11740 San Vicente Blvd., Brentwood (phone: 213-826-2525); 12215 Ventura Blvd., Studio City (phone: 213-985-9090); 16101 Ventura Blvd., Encino (phone: 818-783-1717); and 13455 Maxella Ave., Marina del Rey (phone: 213-823-9999).

El Cholo LA is glutted with places promising authentic south-of-the-border cooking, but this is the best, without question. Around since the 1920s, its burritos and combination plates are real knockouts. Open daily. Reservations advised—and you may have to wait anyway. Major credit cards accepted. 1121 S. Western Ave. (phone: 213-734-2773).

Chopstix A small chain turning out novel variations on Chinese themes, including Chinese pizza. Open daily. No reservations. Major credit cards accepted. 7229 Melrose Ave. (phone: 213-937-1111) and other locations.

DIVE! Yes, LA has another theme restaurant—this one, the brainchild of film director Steven Spielberg, is designed like a submarine and decorated with many of the appropriate sub parts and gadgets. A marine soundscape compliments underwater sights appearing on a 210-square-foot video wall. The menu offers more than 20 types of hot, cold, and "nuclear spicy" submarine sandwiches, including ones filled with soft-shell crab, Tuscan steak, and three vegetarian choices. Also on the menu are wood-oven–roasted shrimp and chicken, ribs, main course salads, home fries, and unusual desserts. Inventive drinks are served at the bar, and a retail window sells *DIVE!* T-shirts and the like. Though it looks more like a Hollywood set than a restaurant, the food rates star billing. Open daily (after-theater meals, takeout, and delivery are available). No reservations. Major credit cards accepted. *Century City Shopping Center,* 10250 Santa Monica Blvd. (phone: 310-203-0928).

Emporio Armani Express Café and Restaurant After busting your budget downstairs on Italian designer clothing, head for the balcony and the comfort of a glass of wine and a plate of ravioli *di zucca* (homemade pasta filled with pumpkin and mascarpone cheese) or risotto with artichoke hearts and duck prosciutto. There's also lighter fare, such as a salad of crisp greens tossed in lemon dressing over a bed of sliced oranges and fennel. Open daily for all three meals. Reservations unnecessary. Major credit cards accepted. 9533 Brighton Way (phone: 310-271-9440).

Gladstone's Malibu One of the best beachfront restaurants for casual dining, this funky fish house offers alfresco, picnic-style dining on wooden tables stationed on a floor rife with peanut shells and sawdust (or you can eat indoors, but you'll miss the fresh sea air). The menu offers a variety of seasonal seafood in soups, salads, and an assortment of appetizers and entrées. Bring a hearty appetite because portions are generous. Open daily for all three meals. Reservations unnecessary. Major credit cards accepted. 17300 Pacific Coast Hwy., Pacific Palisades (phone: 310-454-3474).

Hugo's This charming, country-style café with attentive waiters and great coffee is the home of the "power breakfast" for studio heads and major stars (Julia Roberts, Bette Midler, and Geena Davis are regulars). Million-dollar deals are made over pumpkin pancakes, pasta *alla Mamma* (the house specialty: linguine, eggs, garlic, and Hugo's secret seasoning), and smoked salmon omelettes with tomatoes and sour cream. Get here early; window tables go fast. Lunch and dinner have a calmer atmosphere, but the food is equally first-rate: pasta carbonara, fresh fish, veal parmesan, and so forth. Open daily. No reservations. Major credit cards accepted. 8401 Santa Monica Blvd., W. Hollywood (phone: 213-654-3993).

Nosh of Beverly Hills Stop in for a quick, delicious bite of "authentic delicatessen" at this New York–style eatery, where the sizable portions would make any Jewish mother proud. It's all here—bagels and lox, chicken soup, and incredible cheesecake. Open daily. No reservations. Major credit cards accepted. 9689 Little Santa Monica Blvd., Beverly Hills (phone: 310-271-3730).

Old Town Bakery A real charmer. Chef-owner Amy Pressman's bakery-cum-restaurant caters to hefty appetites, offering giant country crêpes (filled with chicken, herb pesto, ratatouille, or ricotta), great rotisserie chicken tacos, crisp bow tie pasta, and home-style pan pizza. Leave room for delectable desserts—bittersweet chocolate terrine, orange poppyseed cake, and Amy's hand-spun ice cream. Open daily. No reservations. No credit cards accepted. 166 W. Colorado Blvd., Pasadena (phone: 818-792-7943).

Original Pantry The decor is early greasy spoon—the food, waiters, and prices ditto—yet long lines at lunch have forced the first expansion since its opening in the 1920s. A potful of raw vegetable sticks precedes big portions of basic food. If the mood for a big American breakfast strikes at 3 AM, one might even find a parking place outside. Open nonstop. Reservations unnecessary. No credit cards accepted. 877 S. Figueroa (phone: 213-972-9279).

Thunder Roadhouse The theme at this trendy bar/restaurant is motorcycles, with a decor that features antique bikes, iron sculptures, motorcycle memorabilia, and mementos of the Old West. The 30-foot brass and copper bar is thick with beer-drinkers after dark, while the restaurant dishes out just what you would expect: burgers, shakes, sandwiches, omelettes, Cajun catfish, grilled pork chops, and hot pecan or sweet potato pie for dessert. Open daily for all three meals. Reservations unnecessary. Major credit cards accepted. 8363 Sunset Blvd. (phone: 213-650-6011).

Whitney's A special little place where chef/owner Whitney Werner and wife, Cheryl Kunitake Werner, work their culinary wonders. Seafood lovers should sample the seared sea bass with tomatillo and black bean salsa or the peppered tuna with crispy wontons and *ponsu* sauce. If pasta's your passion, try the linguine with Norwegian smoked salmon or *arrabbiata penne* (fresh parsley and tomato sauce over quill-shape pasta) with Japanese eggplant smothered with warm goat cheese. Open daily. Reservations unnecessary. Major credit cards accepted. 1518 Montana Ave., Santa Monica (phone: 310-458-4114).

TAKING TEA

The ritual of afternoon tea has become quite popular in Los Angeles in recent years. Even the "ladies who lunch" pause for a mid-afternoon break from their shopping sprees. Visitors to the city should consider doing the same. It's a very Los Angeles thing to do—and it's done at some of the very best places.

Checkers Kempinski A fine addition to the downtown hotel scene, *Checkers* is one of the city's more elegant tea stops. Afternoon tea, served daily from 3 to 5 PM in the lounge, features wonderful baked goods made fresh on the premises every day. 535 S. Grand Ave. (phone: 213-624-0000).

Lobby Lounge The elegantly furnished *Regent Beverly Wilshire* hotel has become quite the place for tea; at peak hours, expect a bit of a wait. And no wonder: The *Lounge* is lovely, and the feeling very cosmopolitan. The exemplary afternoon tea served daily here from 3 to 5 PM consists of an infused pot, tiny sandwiches, excellent scones with rich Devonshire cream and jam, and a selection of pastry. A pianist plays tunes ranging from Cole Porter to Chopin, and you feel as though you've been transported from tacky old LA to a plush European salon. 9500 Wilshire Blvd., Beverly Hills (phone: 310-275-5200).

Paddington's Tea Room A charming little tearoom/curio shop that's an homage to Paddington Bear. Owned by an expatriate Australian, the tea served here daily from 2 to 5 PM consists of a pot of one of Fortnum & Mason's various blends, a platter of the usual finger sandwiches (cucumber and cream cheese, ham, curried egg), crackers, crudités with a very good spinach dip, and finally, a plate of butter cookies. The shop is filled with tea-brewing paraphernalia, kitchen gadgets, and packaged Australian foodstuffs. 729 N. La Cienega Blvd., W. Hollywood (phone: 310-652-0624).

Rose Tree Cottage Owners Edmund and Mary Fry have created a wonderful English cottage ambience in their Pasadena tearoom. (After tea, enjoy browsing in the on-premises curio shop.) In addition to serving their own specially blended tea—which took some six years to perfect—the Frys pride themselves on their scones, homemade jams, Scottish shortbread, and finger sandwiches. There are three tea sittings, which begin at 2, 3:15, and 4:30 PM; reservations are taken one day in advance. 824 E. California Blvd., Pasadena (phone: 818-793-3337).

THE FINAL TOUCH

For dessert, try the luscious ice cream made by *Robin Rose* and sold in the *Robin Rose* shops located in Venice (215 Rose Ave.; phone: 310-399-1774) and downtown in the Wells Fargo Center (333 S. Grand Ave.; phone: 310-687-8815).

Diversions

Exceptional Pleasures and Treasures

Quintessential Los Angeles

Rarely, if ever, does a native Angeleno step out onto the deserted sidewalk in front of his or her well-manicured home and start walking somewhere. The joke about Los Angeles consisting of 72 suburbs in search of a city sometimes seems more truth than parody. Just look around: It seems almost impossible to find the essence of the place amidst so much diversity and distracting clutter.

In addition, stereotypes abound. Yes, it seems that most of the people who live here are under 25 and blond. Yes, jogging (never walking) is the local religion. And yes, everyone seems to be either seeking or giving autographs. But look beyond those trim bronzed bodies running along the Esplanade (you're probably green with envy anyhow) and immerse yourself, even just for a while, in the magic that is Los Angeles. The truth is that quintessential Los Angeles is found in all kinds of places—from a chichi restaurant to a funky beach town to a day at an amusement park to watching a whale blow its top. Wild, weird, wacky, wonderful—it's all that and much, much more.

A DAY AT DISNEYLAND The original dream of Walt Disney, celebrating its 40th anniversary this year, is as irresistible as you've probably heard, as magical as Tinker Bell's fairy dust, and perfect to the last detail. Thrill rides aren't the big deal. Instead, there are "adventures"—you get bombarded by cannonballs fired by *Pirates of the Caribbean,* visit a haunted mansion, explore the frontier, or fly through outer space. During summer evenings, the *Main Street Electrical Parade*—floats and creatures outlined in thousands of tiny white lights—is supercalifragilisticexpialidocious, and the fireworks are stupendous. Ditto for *Fantasmic!,* a high-tech battle between the forces of good (led by Mickey Mouse) and several classic Disney villains; and *Fantasyland,* whose old-fashioned kiddie attractions have been treated to some $55 million of Disney's most magical special effects.

Speaking of special effects, George Lucas designed a few for one of the park's most popular attractions, *Star Tours,* a flight simulator in which riders experience a *Star Wars*–type journey to the moon of Endor, home of the Ewoks. *Mickey's Toontown,* the latest addition to the park's many neighborhoods, is "home" to many of the Disney characters. And then there is *Splash Mountain,* the ultimate flume ride. Not to be overlooked is the techno-spectacular *Imagination,* where classic animated Disney films and live performers are staged in an after-dark show on *Tom Sawyer's Island.*

Future plans include *WESTCOT Center,* inspired by Florida's *EPCOT,* which showcases foreign lands and theme pavilions. (*Birnbaum's Disneyland 95,* published by Hyperion at $10.95, provides complete details about this still-expanding wonderland.) And if you can't get enough Disney, you can stay at the adjacent *Disneyland* hotel. For information, contact the *Guest Relations Office, Disneyland,* 1313 Harbor Blvd., Anaheim, CA 92803 (phone: 714-999-4565). For a list of nearby lodgings, an area map, and other vacation aids, contact the *Anaheim Area Visitor and Convention Bureau,* PO Box 4270, Anaheim, CA 92803 (phone: 714-999-8999).

AN AFTERNOON AT THE MALL Los Angeles is the "Land of Malls," and no wonder: In a city that spreads over 464 square miles, the mall holds it all together. It's not only a shopper's lifeline but a social hub at which otherwise isolated Angelenos can mingle.

Near the center of the mall zone (which includes the *Sherman Oaks Galleria, South Coast Plaza,* and *Woodland Hills Promenade*), on the border between West Hollywood and Beverly Hills, stands the mother of all malls: the *Beverly Center.* This massive bunker is home to an impressive assortment of upscale shops and restaurants, as well as a multiplex movie theater. Here you can shop till you drop at more than 200 stores, then revive yourself with a meal at the *Hard Rock Café* (a brat-pack hangout with great burgers) or the *California Pizza Kitchen* (18 different toppings). Just for the fun of it, do some fancy food shopping at the *Irvine Ranch Market* and then treat yourself to a movie—all without losing your parking space.

SHOPPING THE FARMERS' MARKET With its giddy assortment of shops and restaurants, this is like a hokey country fair, with European sidewalk-café overtones and some Ghirardelli Square know-how thrown in for good measure. Some people say it's too touristy; we say don't leave LA without seeing it. Started as a cooperative during the Depression years, the market has evolved into quite an attraction.

Don't just walk through the market—become a part of it. Enjoy the people watching, buy some overpriced souvenirs, soak up the sunshine, snack on an ice-cream cone. Instead of charging through the aisles, mill around; nibble on goodies from the various food stalls (Chinese, Japanese, French, Italian, and Spanish); relax at one of the colorful umbrella-shaded tables; and shop! Here are clothes, jewelry, toys, art, and, yes, even fresh produce. It's comforting to know that in the the midst of this star-struck world, there's still a down-to-earth place to spend the afternoon. The market is at 6333 W. Third, at Fairfax (phone: 213-933-9211); also see *Tour 3: Fairfax/Farmers' Market* in DIRECTIONS.

DINNER AT SPAGO When Wolfgang Puck first opened his celebrity restaurant back in the early 1980s, he said he just wanted to create a pleasant pizza and pasta shop where friends could come by for a late-night snack. Puck got more than he bargained for. The hottest restaurant in LA (even if you call six months in advance, you may be told reservations are available only at 6 AM and 11 PM), this is a regular haunt of Sylvester Stallone, Arnold Schwarzenegger, Tom Cruise, Meryl Streep—and just about everyone else who's anyone in this image-conscious town.

If you do manage to secure a table, you'll have a chance to sample the *Spago* magic. The paparazzi outside will clue you in to who's inside munching away on Puck's legendary goat cheese–topped pizza, cooked in a wood-burning oven. *Spago* has also earned the reputation for serving the best grilled fish and fowl in town. The noise level is astounding, the bustle (thanks in part to the open kitchen) is maddening, and the waving and air-kissing is right out of a scene penned by Jackie Collins (who also happens to be a regular). A far cry from a simple pasta shop, it's the place everyone goes to see or be seen. 1114 Horn Ave. at Sunset Blvd. (phone: 310-652-4025).

SATURDAY ON MELROSE AVENUE Like wow, man. Awesome. Fer sure, you're in LA. Melrose Avenue is SoHo West, only more so. It's Main Street with a dose of California weird. It's the hippest stores, the hottest restaurants, the coolest street scene. If it's true that the West Coast is the birthplace of the way-out and radical in food, fashion, and art, then Melrose Avenue is its spawning grounds. Even if you don't go into a single shop (but please do), just walking down Melrose is a perfect way to experience this very LA shoppers' row. Enjoy it. Groove on the consumer madness. Take in the sights. Sip a cappuccino at a sidewalk café and watch the madding crowds. Step into *Soap Plant* or *Wacko* and pick up some things you really need—like an inflatable Japanese monster or a book on the history of miniature golf. Pick up a basket handwoven of telephone wire at *New Stone Age*. Stop in at one of the local eateries—we recommend *Citrus* or *Patina*—or grab a chili dog at *Pink's*. With tourists, trendies, and punks alike patronizing this shoppers' paradise, the hottest club-and-café center in the city, it's LA at its zaniest. Sample the flavor. Cowabunga! Melrose Avenue is interesting for the three miles from Highland east to Doheny, but if you want to focus on a smaller stretch, you should find plenty of local color between La Brea and Fairfax. Also see *Tour 2: Melrose Avenue* in DIRECTIONS.

SUNDAY ON THE VENICE PROMENADE This 300-ring circus that spins into high gear on the weekends typifies what most people believe all of Southern California is like—complete with performing daredevils juggling chain saws, rappers, bikini-clad roller skaters, and jocks flexing their pectorals on Muscle Beach (an exercise zone in the center of it all). Add to this street vendors selling sunglasses of every imaginable hue, T-shirts from the sublime to the ridiculously obscene, and beachwear so minuscule it's a wonder anyone bothers to put it on, and you've got a scene that amazes even jaded locals.

Venice originally was the dream of tobacco heir Abbot Kinney, who (in 1905) created an American version of his favorite Italian city. In its heyday, Kinney's Venice was replete with gondoliers, swank seaside hotels, bathhouses, bazaars, honky-tonk entertainment, and an amusement park. Today, only a few of the old canals remain (most of the original 16 miles of waterways were filled in by the city in 1929), but the original carnival atmosphere reigns supreme. Fast-food stands line the 3-mile strip: For the best hot dogs in Southern California, head over to *Jody Maroni's Sausage Kingdom* (2011 Ocean Front Walk), and try the Yucatán chicken dogs and sausages made with bacon and maple syrup. Since the roller-skating craze started in Venice, you might want to work off your lunch by renting a pair of Rollerblades and becoming part of the liveliest sideshow in Los Angeles. Though it bears no resemblance to the Piazza San Marco, this Venice is as memorable in its own way.

WHALE WATCHING Every year (between December and mid-April) hundreds of humpback whales migrate south from Alaska to their spawning waters off the coast of Baja, California. And every year, thousands of tourists stand along the piers or go out on boats to try and spot them. Actually, when they're in the area, the whales are pretty hard to miss: Measuring from 40 to 50 feet long and weighing about 40 tons, they are agile and even graceful swimmers. In one incredible display known as "breaching," the whale will propel its entire body up out of the water and then land on its back or side, sending up a wall of spray. Whether it breaches to communicate its location, to dislodge the many barnacles and lice that cling to its ample body, or simply to express a natural exuberance, no one knows for certain. But the display is undeniably impressive.

Best whale watching times are early in the morning or late in the afternoon. Be patient. Scan the horizon till you see what looks like an explosion of smoke about 18 feet high. That's the blow of the humpback. Don't forget your binoculars—or your camera. This is one sight you'll want to preserve in your memory and your scrapbook. Whale watching cruises are offered by *Buccaneer-Mardi Gras Cruises* (Ports O' Call Village, Berth 76, San Pedro; phone: 310-548-1085), *Redondo Sport Fishing* (Sport Fishing Pier, 233 N. Harbor Dr., Redondo Beach; phone: 310-772-2064), *Cabrillo Whale Watch* (3720 Stephen White Dr., San Pedro; phone: 310-548-7563), and *Whale Watch Cruises* (Sport Fishing Pier, 233 N. Harbor Dr., Redondo Beach; phone: 310-372-3566).

To learn more about the humpback and the Pacific gray whale, visit the *American Cetacean Society Library* (807 Paseo del Mar, San Pedro; phone: 310-548-6279), open weekdays by appointment only; no admission charge.

HIKING MALIBU CREEK STATE PARK Driving into this 4,000-acre sylvan hideaway, just minutes off the freeway, you'll be struck by the resemblance of the California hills to the mountains of Korea: For nearly a decade, this was the location for the filming of the popular TV series "M*A*S*H." In fact, over the years, this well-maintained park has been the setting for many a movie memory, including *How Green Was My Valley* (1941), *Love Is a Many-*

Splendored Thing (1955), *Love Me Tender* (1956), *Planet of the Apes* (1968), *Butch Cassidy and the Sundance Kid* (1969), and *The Towering Inferno* (1974), to name a few.

There are more than 15 miles of trails to be explored here, with a wide variety of flora and fauna. Rabbits, coyotes, foxes, and bobcats inhabit the richly adorned Southern California hills, and it's possible to spot great blue herons, violet-green swallows, hawks, woodpeckers, and red-wing blackbirds. Stay alert: You might even get a glimpse of a movie star bird watching.

If you're interested in seeing the former "M*A*S*H" set, you can take a memorable 5-mile round-trip hike past Rock Pool (used in many a Western and jungle adventure), past Century Lake (a great picnic spot) and right up to the edge of Malibu Lake. At the end of the trail there's a wide clearing—an open-air museum of "M*A*S*H" memorabilia: the helicopter landing pad, a rusted jeep, and what remains of the 4077.

On Sundays, the nearby *Saddle Peak Lodge* (419 Cold Canyon Rd., Calabasas; phone: 818-340-6029) serves an excellent brunch. As you look out over the rolling hills, it's hard to imagine that the burgeoning population of Los Angeles is just minutes away. To get to *Malibu Creek State Park,* take the Ventura Freeway west from Los Angeles through the San Fernando Valley to the Las Virgenes exit, and make a left. (For a more scenic trip, take Malibu Canyon Road up from the Pacific Coast Highway.)

A DAY AT THE BEACH: MALIBU One of Southern California's most famous stretches of sand, Malibu is a favorite haven of celebrities and surfers, and the place where movie stars have been frolicking in the surf since the 1920s. Today, the likes of Johnny Carson, Jack Lemmon, Goldie Hawn, Kenny Rogers, Linda Ronstadt, Barbra Streisand, and Steven Spielberg call this 27-mile-long strand of pearly beaches home.

Although local residents act as if theirs is a private beach community, the state of California thinks otherwise, and there are now several clearly marked public accessways along the Pacific Coast Highway, Malibu Road, and Broad Beach Road. Even in Malibu Colony—where the "in" crowd lives—ownership extends only to the mean high-tide line, so stick to the hard-packed sand down by the water and you'll be okay. If you need some incentive, consider the fact that Alexis Maas—Johnny Carson's current wife—met him as she walked by his Malibu house wearing a bikini.

Start your surfside sojourn with a bite to eat on the Malibu Pier. At *Alice's Restaurant* (23000 Pacific Coast Hwy.; phone: 310-456-6646) there are magnificent views extending up the beach and out across the ocean. The Malibu Surf Riders State Beach just north of the pier is very popular with the hang-ten crowd; the *Pro Surfing Tour* (phone: 310-372-0414) is held here in August. Up the coast, just shy of Point Dume, is Paradise Cove, a wonderful spot with a sheltered white beach, sandstone cliffs, and fishing and boating facilities (also see *Best Beaches,* below).

If you're ready for some celebrity gazing, stop in at *Granita* (23725 W. Malibu Rd.; phone: 310-456-0488), the hottest spot in Malibu, for Wolfgang Puck's designer pizza. Or, if you prefer, try *La Salsa* (22800 Pacific Coast Hwy.; phone: 310-456-6299) for good Mexican food. Local luminaries often can be found at *Saint Honoré* (22943 Pacific Coast Hwy.; phone: 310-456-2651); the lure here is the fabulous French pastries. *Geoffrey's* (27400 Pacific Coast Hwy.; phone: 310-457-1519), a cliffside restaurant overlooking the ocean, is a longtime favorite.

Zuma Beach County Park, on the other side of Point Dume, is one of Malibu's largest beaches, and the recreational possibilities—playgrounds, volleyball courts, and surfing—attract large crowds. As you wander along these beaches lined with the "cottages" of the rich and famous, you might decide to stay a while. Try the *Casa Malibu* motel (22752 Pacific Coast Hwy.; phone: 310-456-2219), right in the middle of Malibu, or the *Malibu Beach Inn* (22878 Pacific Coast Hwy.; phone: 310-456-6444) on the beach one block from the Malibu Pier. Sit out on your private balcony and pretend you're one of the locals—even if only for a little while.

A Few of Our Favorite Things

Los Angeles has no shortage of luxurious hotels and divine restaurants; however, we've singled out a few select choices that are guaranteed to delight. Follow our lead; we promise you won't be disappointed.

Each place listed below is described in detail in THE CITY.

GRAND HOTELS AND SPECIAL HAVENS

The following are our particular favorites for a stay in Los Angeles. Some are large and palatial, others are small and intimate, but each offers its own particular combination of impeccable service, gorgeous scenery, and plenty of amenities. (You might even get a peek at a celebrity or two during your stay.) Complete information about our choices can be found on pages 61 to 63 in THE CITY.

> *Bel-Air*
> *Four Seasons*
> *Peninsula Beverly Hills*
> *Regent Beverly Wiltshire*
> *St. James's Club*
> *San Ysidro Ranch*

INCREDIBLE EDIBLES

Contrary to the stereotype of oh-so-trendy "California cuisine" dished out in ludicrously small quantities, LA's food scene is lively, sophisticated, and always intriguing. The city's best restaurants combine the freshest ingredients, culinary imagination, and exciting (if a bit noisy) ambience. Our top choices are listed below; complete information about them can be found on pages 71 to 73 in THE CITY.

> *Arnie Morton's of Chicago, the Steakhouse*
> *Chinois on Main*
> *David Slay's La Veranda*
> *Le Dôme*
> *Maple Drive*
> *Morton's*
> *L'Orangerie*
> *Patina*
> *Spago*

Performing Arts

One of the most delightful things to do in LA is to spend an evening listening to fabulous music under the stars. Seeing movie stars on stage is another cultural draw; excellent stage productions thrive here. In addition, the West Coast has come into its own in the rock world, while classical music has always been a major passion in LA. As you will see from the listings below, there are countless ways to take in drama, musicals, and music, as well as television sitcoms and game shows during your stay.

THE MUSIC SCENE

With grunge, the blues, hip-hop, and the symphony, Los Angeles is rarely without a musical moment. Below are some of the larger listening venues; also see *Music* and *Nightclubs and Nightlife* in the THE CITY.

GREEK THEATRE This beautiful outdoor theater has featured such eclectic musical talents as *Spin Doctors,* Michael Bolton, Michael Feinstein, and James Brown. It's just a few steps south of *Griffith Park,* a wooded, hilly retreat in Los Angeles, so make an evening of it—enjoy a picnic dinner and listen to some great music outdoors. Information: *Greek Theatre,* 2700 N. Vermont Ave. (phone: 213-665-1927 for a recorded listing of upcoming performances; 213-665-3125 from 3 to 6 PM for further information; 213-480-3232 for tickets).

HOLLYWOOD BOWL One of the loveliest places to spend an evening in all Los Angeles, this natural amphitheater seats 17,000 and is the summer home of the *Los Angeles Philharmonic.* Have a pre-concert picnic on the park-like grounds or an alfresco supper on the patio of the *Bowl's* restaurant (phone: 213-851-3588). The musical program (held from July to mid-September) ranges from jazz to pop to classical. Actor and pianist Dudley Moore has been a popular performer. It gets chilly in the evenings, so remember to bring a sweater and a blanket (and a cushion for the hard wooden seats). Parking can be difficult, so inquire about the park-and-ride service from several LA locations. Information: *Hollywood Bowl,* 2301 N. Highland Ave. (phone: 213-850-2000).

PALOMINO Originally opened in 1951 exclusively as a country-and-western music venue, it has featured most of country's top performers: Waylon Jennings, Johnny Cash, Linda Ronstadt, and Dwight Yoakam. To this day Jerry Lee Lewis stops by to tickle the ivories. Over the last few years the club has expanded its musical horizons and now features a variety of groups playing country, jazz, rock 'n' roll, and bluegrass. Information: *Palomino,* 6907 Lankershim Blvd., North Hollywood (phone: 818-764-4010).

ROXY A very hip club/music hall with atmosphere. It's dark, sometimes crowded, a lot of fun, and a great place to go for the evening—you'll feel like you're part of the "in" crowd (even though it's too dark to see who's "in"). Entertainment is offered by up-and-coming local and national groups; about 60% of the music is rock 'n' roll and progressive, the other 40% ranges from jazz to country. The *Roxy* has a history of having showcased talents like Bruce Springsteen, Whitney Houston, and Bob Marley before they hit the big time. David Bowie also is among those who cut his teeth here, and he still stops by to play when he's in town. Information: *Roxy,* 9009 Sunset Blvd., West Hollywood (phone: 310-276-2222).

UNIVERSAL AMPHITHEATRE Built in 1973, this enclosed amphitheater on the grounds of *Universal Studios* features a wide array of talent (this is the place to see Linda Ronstadt, Barry Manilow, Diana Ross, and Julio Iglesias), although it shies away from heavy metal. It's a nice place to take the whole family. Stroll along the quaint walks and visit one of the pleasant restaurants on the grounds. Information: *Universal Amphitheatre,* 100 Universal Plaza (Hollywood Fwy. and Lankershim Blvd.), Universal City (phone: 818-980-9421).

WILTERN The name is a combination of Wilshire Boulevard and Western Avenue, and the *Wiltern* is located on the corner of those two streets. Built in 1931, this is one of LA's favorite music venues, as well as one of the best examples of Art Deco architecture in the city. The tall, green building showcases a wide range of musical talents from rock 'n' roll to bluegrass and jazz. The Art Deco interior is a show in itself. Information: *Wiltern Theatre,* 3790 Wilshire Blvd. (phone: 213-380-5005).

THEATERS

Between projects, big-name film stars and your favorite television actors like to take a turn on the boards. You might even get to brag about seeing future superstars when they were unknowns.

AHMANSON Part of the world-famous *Music Center* in downtown LA, the *Ahmanson* has been host to such musical hits as *Phantom of the Opera* and a cadre of Neil Simon comedies—*California Suite, Brighton Beach Memoirs,* and *Biloxi Blues.* Among the many great talents who have performed on its stage are

Ingrid Bergman, Richard Chamberlain, Faye Dunaway, Katharine Hepburn, and Elizabeth Taylor. The *Ahmanson*'s bold design and dramatic, plush interior make it the gem of the *Music Center* and an enchanting place to spend the evening. Information: *Ahmanson Theater,* 135 N. Grand Ave. (phone: 213-972-7211).

MARK TAPER FORUM Also in the *Music Center* is one of the nation's most respected theaters, offering many premieres and an occasional revival; the subject matter tends toward the timely, the currently problematic. The *Mark Taper* production of *Jelly's Last Jam* went on to win Broadway's Tony Awards for best actor, actress, and lighting design in 1991, and in 1993 and 1994 *Angels in America* (parts I and II) won in the best play, director, actor, and featured actor categories. Also under the *Taper* wing are *P.L.A.Y. (Performing for Los Angeles Youth)* and the intimate *Taper, Too* for special readings, workshops, and new work festivals. Others might want to check out the *Improvisational Theatre Project* (phone: 213-972-7622). Information: *Mark Taper Forum,* 135 N. Grand Ave. (phone: 213-972-0700).

PASADENA PLAYHOUSE Founded in 1925, this lovely, 700-seat theater is on the National Registry of Historic Places; its Spanish-Baroque architecture is just one of its appeals. The theater offers a wide variety of musicals and plays (it was the first American theater to stage the entire 37-play Shakespearean cycle). An added incentive is that celebrities such as Dustin Hoffman and Gene Hackman often grace the stage. Since Pasadena is evolving into one of LA's most popular nightspots, make an evening out of your visit to the playhouse and dine in one of the many fine restaurants in the area. Information: *Pasadena Playhouse,* 39 S. El Molino Ave., Pasadena (phone: 818-356-7529).

SHUBERT THEATRE A wonderful, modern space that is especially good for musicals because of its fine acoustics and unobstructed views. The large (1,830-seat) theater is in the very contemporary *ABC Entertainment Center,* which also houses a movie theater, shops, and restaurants. This is the perfect place for a special evening out—enjoy a good musical and relax afterward in the outdoor mall. Information: *Shubert Theatre,* 2020 Ave. of the Stars, Century City (phone: 310-201-1500; 800-233-3123 for information and credit card reservations).

WESTWOOD PLAYHOUSE A charming, 498-seat theater housed in a historic Spanish Colonial Revival building, it presents a wide variety of Broadway and off-Broadway productions, often with celebrity headliners. Information: *Westwood Playhouse,* 10886 Le Conte Ave., Westwood (phone: 310-208-5454).

Audience Participation: Getting into the Act

If you didn't make it as a star of stage and screen, there's still hope for you—as a member of the audience. It's a tough job, but somebody's got to do it. Tickets are free, and it's a fun way to experience the glamour of Hollywood.

Pick up tickets at the TV stations' ticket counters or write for them. (Tickets are not sent out of state. You will receive a "guest" letter or card redeemable for tickets.) But having a ticket or a guest letter doesn't necessarily guarantee a seat. Generally, you'll still have to wait in a long, first-come, first-served line to get in. If you're traveling with young children, remember there are minimum-age requirements that vary from show to show, so be sure to check. Studio hotline numbers are provided below.

IN THE AUDIENCE

ABC TV Ticket information hotline: 310-557-7777. Write to: ABC Tickets, 4151 Prospect Ave., Los Angeles, CA 90027. Requests should be sent at least a month in advance. Enclose a self-addressed, stamped envelope. Indicate the name of the show, number of tickets, and date.

ABC does not have a ticket counter. When you call the hotline number, your name will be put on the list for the show and date you want. Show up at least an hour ahead of taping time.

CBS TV Ticket information hotline: 213-852-2458. Write to: CBS Tickets, 7800 Beverly Blvd., Los Angeles, CA 90036. Requests should be sent at least a month in advance. Enclose a self-addressed, stamped envelope. Indicate the name of the show, number of tickets, and date.

For day-of-the-show tickets: CBS Information Window, CBS Television City, address above (near the *Farmers' Market*). Hours are 9 AM to 5 PM weekdays; weekend times vary depending on taping schedule. Arrive early.

FOX TV Ticket information hotlines: 818-506-0067 or 213-856-1520. Write to: Fox Tickets, 5746 Sunset Blvd., Hollywood, CA 91608. Requests should be sent two weeks in advance. Enclose a self-addressed, stamped envelope. Indicate the name of the show, number of tickets, and date. Or simply show up at the studio (same address) on Wednesday, a week before scheduled taping.

NBC TV Ticket information hotline: 818-840-3537. Write to: NBC Tickets, 3000 W. Alameda Ave., Burbank, CA 91523. Requests should be sent at least a month in advance. Enclose a self-addressed, stamped envelope. Indicate the name of the show, number of tickets, and date. There is a limit on tickets for some shows (four per request for "The Tonight Show").

For day-of-the-show tickets: NBC-TV Ticket Counter, address above. Hours are 8 AM to 5 PM weekdays; weekend times vary according to taping schedules. Tickets are distributed on a first-come, first-served basis, so arrive early. Tours of *Studio 1* (home of "The Tonight Show") are also available.

ON STAGE

So, you wanna be a game-show contestant—here's your chance. You don't have to make a special trip to Hollywood to audition for these shows, because they often hold tryouts in major cities around the country throughout the year. If you're planning to be in town, it's worth a shot while you are here. Be aware that while the shows need people to audition, only a very small percentage are chosen to be on the air. If you decide to try out, do it just for the fun of it. (And if you *are* selected, think of all the great prizes you could win!)

Although game shows appear on network television, most are produced by independent production companies. Contact each show for details on auditioning.

FAMILY FEUD Contestant hotline: 213-965-9999. Call three months in advance with the dates of your visit. You will receive an information sheet detailing the audition procedure. All five family members (related by blood or marriage) who hope to participate must be present. Each family plays a mock version of the game and is auditioned twice, so make sure you will be in LA long enough to do this—and make sure it's during a time when the show is being taped.

JEOPARDY Contestant hotline: 213-466-3931. Call a month in advance to check the production schedule and to make an appointment. At the audition you will be given a written test; if you pass, you will be asked to perform a mock version of the game. Your name will then be placed in a contestant pool for up to six months—but there is no guarantee you will be chosen.

WHEEL OF FORTUNE Contestant hotline: 818-972-8088. Call three weeks in advance for an appointment. At the audition you'll take a five-minute written test and play an hour-long, mock version of the game, followed by a very brief interview. If you pass, you'll be called back within a week to play a longer version of the mock game (two and a half hours). Out-of-towners chosen as contestants are notified within two weeks.

Oddities, Insanities, and Just Plain Fun

This is soooo California! If you're into oddball architectural wonders or just fun places to visit, Southern California is the place to be. For those who want to experience the offbeat side of LA, these are places to write home about.

DONUT HOLE This doughnut-shaped doughnut shop is one of America's classic roadside attractions. They say it's good luck for newlyweds to drive through the hole. The doughnuts are pretty good, too. Take the Pomona Freeway No. 60 to the Hacienda Boulevard exit, turn left (north), and drive about 2 miles until you come to Amar Road. Make a right (east), and the giant confection will be right in front of you. Open 24 hours. Information: *Donut Hole*, 15300 E. Amar Rd., La Puente (phone: 818-968-2912).

EXOTIC FELINE BREEDING COMPOUND Lovers of big cats will enjoy this place, where the focus is on research and breeding of endangered felines, including the Siberian tiger, puma, snow leopard, and other wild animals. This decade-old habitat also offers visitors informative slide shows and lectures. To get here, take Highway 14, exit at Rosemond Boulevard, and follow signs to the compound. Information: *Exotic Feline Breeding Compound,* Mohave-Tropico Rd., Rosamond (phone: 805-256-3332).

FINLEY & GIBBONS FASHION FLOWERS Even if you're not in the market to send flowers, it's well worth coming here just for a glimpse of Elizabeth Taylor's favorite sterling silver roses (yes, they're the real thing!). This is also the place that furnished floral arrangements for Roseanne and Tom Arnold's splash wedding, and where Hollywood types such as Kevin Costner, Barbra Streisand, and Cher pick their blooms. Also deserving a look are the animal creations artistically fashioned from chicken wire and covered entirely in ivy and flower petals. Pick up a few for your stars back home. Information: *Finley & Gibbons Fashion Flowers, Inc.,* 9960 Santa Monica Blvd. (phone: 310-275-0159; 800-356-1325).

PETITE ELITE MINIATURE MUSEUM & GALLERY Less is certainly more at this museum. Its collection of hand-crafted miniatures includes tiny figurines of contemporary personalities such as Count Basie, Nancy Reagan, and Michael Jackson; detailed historic rooms, each no larger than a matchbox; and minute mansions, palaces, and castles. Open Mondays through Saturdays by appointment only. Admission charge. Information: *Petite Elite Miniature Museum & Gallery,* 5900 Wilshire Blvd., East Wing (phone: 310-277-8108).

PHOTO EXPRESS An architectural curiosity that is pure Americana, this is a photo shop in the shape of an old-time box camera. One picture is worth a thousand cocktail-party conversations—have a friend snap a shot of you getting film developed here. Take the San Diego Freeway No. 405 south and get off at the Golden West Street/Bolsa exit. Head south toward the beach; it's in the *S&S* parking lot. Information: *Photo Express,* 15336 Golden West St., Westminster (phone: 714-897-4777).

SPORT WALK OF FAME Unlike the Hollywood version devoted to screen celebrities past and present, this walk of fame—complete with handprints and signatures—is dedicated strictly to professional athletes, *Olympic* medalists, and collegians who have made outstanding contributions to their respective sport. Notable honorees include Mark Spitz, Fred Dryer, Wilt Chamberlain, Ron Cey, and Jackie Joyner-Kersee. Information: *Sport Walk of Fame,* located along Sixth St., San Pedro.

SILENT MOVIE Not just another movie house, this historic 1942 theater showcases classic films from days gone by (when admission was a mere 10¢). Former owners John and Dorothy Hampton accumulated a vast number of screen favorites; now the property of Larry Austin, a film historian and lover of silent films, the library ranks as the largest private collection of its kind in the world. Fans can enjoy vintage footage to the sound of live organ music. Open Wednesday, Friday, and Saturday evenings. Admission charge. Information: *Silent Movie,* 611 N. Fairfax Ave. (phone: 213-653-2389).

Grave Matters

Movie stars are an elusive bunch—slipping in and out of chauffeured limousines, traveling incognito. If you're getting frustrated trying to spot them, consider going someplace from which they can't escape: the cemetery. Although the idea may seem a little macabre, the cemeteries in Los Angeles are a fascinating microcosm of Hollywood lore. Anybody who was anybody is buried here, from Marilyn Monroe to Rudolph Valentino.

FOREST LAWN HOLLYWOOD HILLS The sister cemetery to the very famous one in Glendale (see below) is sort of a theme park. The subject: America and the ideal of liberty. A 60-foot statue of George Washington and a replica of the *Liberty Bell* set the tone. There are reproductions of historic American places of worship and a huge mosaic depicting major events in American history. Interestingly enough, in keeping with the theme, D. W. Griffith filmed scenes for *The Birth of a Nation* on this site in 1915. Buster Keaton, Stan Laurel, Liberace, Ozzie Nelson, and Andy Gibb enjoy a patriotic rest here. Take the Hollywood Freeway No. 101 to the Ventura Freeway No. 134 and go east to Forest Lawn Drive; the cemetery is on your right. 6300 Forest Lawn Dr., Burbank (phone: 213-254-7251).

FOREST LAWN MEMORIAL PARK The list of those buried here reads like a *Who's Who* of Hollywood—Humphrey Bogart, Spencer Tracy, Clark Gable, Carole Lombard, Errol Flynn, Jean Harlow, Mary Pickford, W. C. Fields, Nat King Cole, and Walt Disney, to name just a few.

Disney should be resting in peace, because this place is as Disneyesque as a cemetery could get: Sections are named *Slumberland, Lullabyland, Everlasting Love,* and *Inspiration Slope.* The 300-acre expanse was designed as an "enchanting park with sparkling lawns, shaded arborways, garden retreats, and noble statuary." This is almost an understatement. On the grounds are copies of Michelangelo statues (including his *David*), a stained-glass interpretation of Leonardo da Vinci's *Last Supper,* churches modeled after 10th-century English and 14th-century Scottish ones (popular for weddings, as well as funerals), and a swan lake. This is an incredible place around which to wander—but be aware that several of the areas are private, so go to see the setting, not necessarily the graves. Take the Golden State Freeway No. 5 north, exit east at Glendale Boulevard, then turn right onto Forest and left onto Glendale Avenue. 1712 S. Glendale Ave., Glendale (phone: 818-241-4151).

HILLSIDE MEMORIAL PARK This is a resting place for those of the Jewish faith, and Al Jolson, one of the more famous entertainers interred here, does death proud. His tomb, a Greek temple–like structure with a cascading waterfall, is visible from the freeway. There's also a statue of the Jazz Singer down on one knee with arms outstreched in his classic "Mammy" pose. Keeping him company are the likes of George Jessel, Eddie Cantor, and Jack Benny. Take the San Diego Freeway No. 405, exit at Sepulveda-Centinela, go south on Sepulveda Boulevard, then turn left and proceed to the cemetery. 6001 Centinela Ave. (phone: 310-641-0707; 800-576-1994).

HOLLYWOOD MEMORIAL PARK It is fitting that Cecil B. De Mille is buried here: The place looks like one of the elaborate sets in *The Ten Commandments*. Egyptian, Greek, and Roman temples, incredible statues and obelisks, grand old tombstones, a small lake, and breathtaking mausoleums are ringed by majestic palms. The final resting places of De Mille, director John Huston, actor Tyrone Power, and actress Marion Davies (William Randolph Hearst's mistress) are around the lake, along with a Jayne Mansfield memorial.

Rudolph Valentino, the cemetery's most famous permanent guest, rests in the *Cathedral Mausoleum* (No. 1205). Peter Lorre and Peter Finch are neighbors. A stone staircase leads to the magnificent *Sunken Garden* and Douglas Fairbanks's reflecting pool and monument (reportedly paid for by Mary Pickford, his first wife). Also interred here is mobster Benjamin "Bugsy" Siegel, whose dream of a resort in the desert grew into a reality called Las Vegas. The famed "Hollywood" sign is visible from the cemetery, which is right next door to *Paramount Studios*—bittersweet reminders that life goes on. Take the Hollywood Freeway No. 101 north to the Santa Monica Boulevard exit, then follow Santa Monica west a few blocks; the cemetery is on the left between Gower Street and Van Ness Avenue. 6000 Santa Monica Blvd. (phone: 213-469-1181).

HOLY CROSS CEMETERY In Europe grottoes are believed to be favorable settings for miracles. This cemetery, the permanent home of some of Hollywood's most famous Roman Catholic stars, has an absolutely stunning one. The *Grotto of the Holy Cross* shelters a graceful statue of the Virgin Mary in prayer. Resting in its tranquil shadows are Rita Hayworth, Charles Boyer, Bing Crosby, Jack Haley, and Jimmy Durante. Rosalind Russell has her own impressive memorial farther on. On a truly tragic note, Sharon Tate Polanski and her unborn child, victims of the Manson family massacre of 1969, are laid to rest here. Take the San Diego Freeway No. 405 to the Slauson Avenue exit going east; the cemetery will be on your left. 5835 W. Slauson Ave., Culver City (phone: 213-670-7697).

PIERCE BROTHERS WESTWOOD VILLAGE MEMORIAL PARK Dwarfed by tall buildings, *Westwood* is a small, tranquil spot within the boundaries of LA. Office workers and students from nearby *UCLA* use the exquisitely planted grounds as a lunchtime retreat. The most famous crypt is Marilyn Monroe's, and she is in good company—Natalie Wood, Donna Reed, Oscar Levant, drummer Buddy Rich, producer Darryl F. Zanuck, and renowned industrialist Armand Hammer are all here.

Joe DiMaggio no longer sends roses to Marilyn's grave every week, but faithful fans keep up the tradition. Sugar cubes are left on Natalie Wood's grave. Before he died, Armand Hammer had a stereo system installed in the family mausoleum that plays classical music when the door is opened. (Maybe you *can* take it with you!) Take the San Diego Freeway No. 405 to the Wilshire Boulevard exit, go east on Wilshire about a half mile to Glendon Avenue, then turn right onto Glendon; the cemetery is straight ahead on the left. 1218 Glendon Ave. (phone: 310-474-1579).

> ### MACABRE LANDMARKS
> **If seeing where Janis Joplin overdosed, Marilyn Monroe bought her last prescription, and George Reeves (the star of TV's "Superman") put a "speeding bullet" through his head is your kind of thing, have we got a tour for you. On a *Grave Line Tour,* you'll be whisked around in a renovated hearse for a two-and-a-half-hour tour past 85 sites of celebrity scandal and tragedy. Reservations necessary. PO Box 931694, Hollywood, CA, 90093 (phone: 213-469-3127).**

Spas

After several days of hardcore sightseeing, come back to life with a rejuvenating visit to a spa—the ultimate indulgence. Unlike traditional European spas, which use mineral waters as therapy, the typical American spa considers a fully equipped gym its epicenter. Sophisticated equipment and specialized treatments are combined to relax the mind as well as strengthen the body. In addition to such standbys as massages, herbal wraps, and facials, many spas and wellness centers now offer such treatments as fruit showers (hot water scented with citrus), "sound massages" (where classical or New Age music is played in the background), and aromatherapy. Most have a beauty salon, where guests can change nail color, have their hair cut, dyed, or curled, and enjoy a professional makeup session. Most programs emphasize exercise sessions, hikes, and nutritious diets.

BURKE WILLIAMS DAY SPA & MASSAGE CENTRE, Santa Monica This elegant, 7,000-square-foot facility draws a celebrity crowd, including Amy Irving, Goldie Hawn, Annette Bening, Darryl Hannah, and Oliver Stone. You may choose from a variety of à la carte treatments or purchase a package such as "BW Bliss"—five and a half hours of ecstasy starting with a private herbal or marine whirlpool bath and followed by a massage, a scalp treatment, an aromatherapy facial, a full-body mud masque, a manicure and pedicure, and lunch. Other options include "Stress Therapy," "Aromatherapy Escape," and "Gentlemen's Choice." Amenities include lockers, showers, a full supply of toiletries, all the purified water you can drink, and conference rooms for business meetings. Limousine transportation from anywhere in the greater Los Angeles area is available. Information: *Burke Williams Day Spa & Massage Centre,* 1460 Fourth St., Santa Monica, CA 90401 (phone: 310-587-3366).

LA COSTA, Carlsbad Just 90 minutes from Los Angeles, this immensely popular spa offers a variety of beauty and health treatments, including Swiss showers, herbal wraps, and a hydrotherapy tub; the massage rooms are often crowded, which may hamper one's ability to relax. Other activities and facilities include aerobics, jogging trails, outdoor heated pools, and two fine 18-hole golf courses. The 23 tennis courts (13 lighted) include grass, clay, and hard surfaces. The *Spa Dining Room* serves nutritionally balanced, surprisingly good-tasting, low-calorie meals. Celebrities typically laud *La Costa,* but be forewarned that not everyone receives the obsequious Tinseltown treatment. Information: *La Costa Resort and Spa,* Costa del Mar Rd., Carlsbad, CA 92009 (phone: 619-438-9111; 800-854-5000 for reservations).

GLEN IVY HOT SPRINGS, Corona The perfect one-day getaway, this is a Mediterranean-style, natural hot springs spa about 90 minutes south of Los Angeles. Relax in the natural mineral water pools and red-clay mud bath, pamper yourself with a massage or beauty treatment, and enjoy the aqua-aerobics class, delightful gardens, wholesome food, and friendly staff. Tucked away in a hidden canyon, these hot springs have been popular with the Hollywood set since the 1930s, when W. C. Fields, Paul Muni, and Ronald Reagan rolled around in the mud. In recent years Reggie Jackson and Dan Aykroyd have followed in the footsteps of the ancient Indians who believed the soothing waters had spiritual powers to heal illnesses of the body, mind, and spirit.

No miracle cures are promised, but you'll certainly be in a better mood by the end of the day. Admission charge includes use of the pools, spas, sauna, and mud bath (massage and salon services are extra and require reservations in advance); there is no charge for children two and under. There are no overnight accommodations, but the management can recommend nearby inns if you want to indulge for more than a day. Information: *Glen Ivy Hot Springs,* 25000 Glen Ivy Rd., Corona, CA 91719 (phone: 909-277-3529).

THE OAKS AT OJAI, Ojai Ninety minutes north of Los Angeles, owner Sheila Cluff has created a spa that practices fitness with fervor. Evening programs and special-interest theme weeks—such as high-energy workshops and celebrity chefs who prepare spa fare—are so numerous that Cluff publishes a quarterly magazine to update guests on the latest spa news. Classes include high- and low-impact aerobics, toning, and stretching; there also are programs to help guests stop smoking or learn how to cook low-calorie dishes. The

44 guestrooms are simply decorated yet very comfortable. Fishing, tennis, and golf are nearby—and you can always embark on an 8-mile hike if you feel a need to commune with nature. Information: *The Oaks at Ojai,* 122 E. Ojai Ave., Ojai, CA 93203 (phone: 805-646-5573).

TWO BUNCH PALMS, Desert Hot Springs A world away from the glitzy image promoted by neighboring Palm Springs, this 44-room mineral water spa prides itself on pampering its guests in privacy. Film stars who wish to remain almost anonymous come to be rubbed at this highly touted center for massage therapy. From shiatsu (Japanese acupressure) to *watsu* (yoga-like movement in the mineral pool, supported by a massage therapist) and esoteric massage (integrating and harmonizing the physical, emotional, and spiritual)—sometimes accompanied by enriching oils, the reverberation of gongs, and the flicker of candlelight—this spa concentrates seriously on the release of body energy. You can do as much or as little as you please; schedules, evening programs, and crash courses on counting calories do not exist at this sanctuary. There is no room service, no gift shop, and no valet parking, and no children are allowed. If you've been dreaming about dropping out for a few days, by all means sample the curative powers on tap here. Information: *Two Bunch Palms Resort,* 67-425 Two Bunch Palms Trail, Desert Hot Springs, CA 92240 (phone: 619-329-8791; 800-472-4334 in Southern California).

WHEELER HOT SPRINGS, Ojai This spot, an hour and a half north of LA, has drawn people to its therapeutic waters since the early 1800s. Today the waters can be taken in private redwood rooms, outfitted with hot and cold tubs and a skylight view of towering oak trees. Follow this up with a massage and a meal in the health-food restaurant and be born again. Located in a canyon this desert oasis is surrounded by a grove of tall palms fed by the natural springs. In addition to the hot tubs, there is an outdoor pool filled with mountain spring water. The excellent *Wheeler* restaurant (which serves dinner and Sunday brunch) is closed Mondays through Wednesdays; at those times, bring fixings for a picnic—the grounds are lovely. There are no guestrooms, but if you'd like to spend more time in Ojai, the staff can recommend nearby overnight accommodations. The spa is closed Tuesdays. Information: *Wheeler Hot Springs,* 16825 Maricopa Hwy., Ojai, CA 93024 (phone: 805-646-8131).

Best Beaches

Along the 60 miles of California coastline that curve by Los Angeles are more than 20 beaches—some best suited for swimming, others for catching a wave, still others just for sunning. Most Angelenos pick their turf according to proximity, so "best" beach has as much to do with convenience as wonderful waves and superb sand. Below are some of our favorite strands.

CABRILLO Known as *the* windsurfing place, this popular San Pedro strand is about 21 miles due south of Los Angeles. It's hard to miss: Nearby are docks harboring huge cruise ships bound for Alaska and the Mexican Riviera. Even if you're not into windsurfing, there's lots more to do here: Try jet skiing, swimming, or simply sunning. Parking is available. For more information, call the *San Pedro Peninsula Chamber of Commerce* (phone: 310-832-7272).

LAGUNA This artsy beachside community, framed by graceful hills and valleys sloping toward the jagged coastline, is well worth the two-hour drive south on Highway No. 1 from Los Angeles. The popular resort was once the residence of John Steinbeck (he wrote *Tortilla Flat* here) and home to Bette Davis during the 1940s. The action primarily is limited to the 3-mile stretch of beach, where volleyball players of every description play hard and fast. Join them for a turn or, if you prefer, browse along the avenues lined with small craft shops.

MALIBU Although residents like to give the impression that it's off-limits to the public, the state of California says ownership extends only to the mean high-tide line (wherever that is), and there are now several clearly marked access-ways along the Pacific Coast Highway, Malibu Road, and Broad Beach Road. The beaches are quiet and pristine, most of the homes along the shore are pretty spectacular, and celebrities often wander by. The following are some of the truly wonderful spots along this stretch.

Leo Carillo State Beach Named after the actor who played Pancho in *The Cisco Kid,* this incredibly scenic, mile-long stretch is much more rustic than the beaches closer to the city (it's about 40 minutes from Santa Monica). There are tide pools, interesting rock formations, nature trails, and campsites. Also here are lifeguards, and facilities include parking (for a fee), restrooms, showers, and public barbecue grills (but no food vendors). On the Pacific Coast Hwy., about 14 miles west of Malibu.

Paradise Cove A lovely, sheltered beach with a scenic fishing pier. The *Sand Castle* restaurant (phone: 310-275-2503) attracts big crowds for the fabulous ocean views. Facilities include parking (for a fee), restrooms, a lifeguard (summer only), and food vendors. Off the Pacific Coast Hwy. on Paradise Cove Rd., just east of Point Dume.

Robert H. Meyer Memorial State Beaches This complex comprises three hidden beaches—El Matador, La Piedra, and El Pescador—which are among the nicest along this strand. Long walkways lead down to these little-known, deserted beauties. There are no lifeguards, so be careful swimming. Along El Matador are fabulous rock formations and magnificent Malibu mansions to admire. There are parking spots (for a fee), but no other amenities. On the Pacific Coast Hwy., about 11 miles west of Malibu. Signs lead the way a mile west of Trancas Canyon.

WILL ROGERS STATE BEACH At the bottom of Santa Monica Canyon, this is a wide, sandy beach with even surf and the dramatic cliffs of the Pacific Palisades rising in the background. Different groups—families, surfers, teens, gays—stake out their own territory. There's good swimming and surfing, as well as ample parking (for a fee), restrooms, and a lifeguard. Located along the Pacific Coast Hwy. at Sunset Blvd. in Pacific Palisades.

Temescal Beach, at the bottom of Temescal Canyon, is part of Will Rogers. This wide, sandy strand is one of the area's hidden treasures. Just a short drive from LA, it's practically unknown, but there are convenience stands and a play area for kids. It adjoins *Temescal Canyon Park,* so beach-goers can picnic on the grass if they choose. Pacific Palisades.

Great Sailing and Cruising

The Los Angeles coastline is so sail-happy that it seems like everybody here owns a boat; if you don't, you usually can charter one. Expect to be asked about your sailing experience; most boats are handled by brokers for private owners. Your experience will determine which craft you get, and which one you select also will depend on how long you plan to cruise, since boats under 26 feet can be a little too cozy for a week on the water. We've singled out a few places that are both scenic and have boats to rent.

LONG BEACH It may not be Italy, but California's version of Venice is the next best thing. There are canal-like waters, ideal for gondola rides; *Gondola Getaway* (phone: 310-433-9595) offers a one-hour tour through the canals with a basket of bread, salami, and cheese. Bring your own wine.

MARINA DEL REY Ever since this marina, the largest manmade recreational-boat harbor in the world, was built in the 1960s, pleasure boaters have been passing through in droves; there are 6,000 slips and plenty of docks and sailing schools. Transient boat rentals are available for periods ranging from overnight to a week. You can even rent the *Wild Goose* (phone: 310-574-6611), John Wayne's 36-foot yacht, for a sail on the bay; the vessel boasts a fireplace, a helicopter landing pad, a wet bar, and an entertainment center. The *Sunset Sail Charter Company* (phone: 310-578-9248) offers romantic sails aboard 120-foot luxury yachts and 34-foot sloops, including candlelit dinner and wine or champagne. *Hornblower Dining Yachts* (phone: 310-519-9400) features a fun-filled sail around Marina del Rey Harbor and Newport Beach Harbor with food, drink, and dancing. Information: *Department of Beaches and Harbors,* 13837 Fiji Way, Marina del Rey, CA 90292 (phone: 310-305-9545).

NEWPORT BEACH Local celebs and some 10,000 others keep boats in this big, beautiful, busy Southern California harbor; an hour to the south of LA, it's the largest pleasure-boat harbor in the world. There are dozens of marinas.

Information: *Newport Harbor Area Chamber of Commerce,* 1470 Jamboree Rd., Newport Beach, CA 92660 (phone: 714-644-8211).

Best Golf Outside the City

While many of the golf courses in the Los Angeles area are part of private clubs, some of the most spectacular allow public access. These three have been rated highly by *Golf* magazine.

MONARCH BEACH This excellent golfing spot is located about halfway between San Diego and Los Angeles in the city of Dana Point. Much of the course is on the water, so only the most diligent duffer will be able to ignore the fabulous scenery and concentrate on the game. Designed by Robert Trent Jones Jr., the course is a true "links" (sandy, undulating, turf-covered ground on a seacoast) bordering the Pacific Ocean. The elevated bent-grass greens and ocean breezes add to the challenge. Rates (which include a golf cart) vary depending on the day you play. 33080 Niguel Rd., Dana Point (phone: 714-240-8247).

MORENO VALLEY RANCH This 27-hole property, designed by Pete Dye, is set on hilly terrain. The views are somewhat stark, but it's the best deal around price-wise. All greens fees include a golf cart. About an hour's drive from Los Angeles. 28095 John F. Kennedy Ave., Moreno Valley (phone: 714-924-4444).

OJAI VALLEY COUNTRY CLUB A 90-minute drive from LA, it features one of the most lavish golf courses in the US—the waiting list attests to it—so be sure to make reservations well in advance. When you do get onto the fairway, don't forget to raise your head every now and again to appreciate the panoramic views of the mountain-capped valley. A favorite of pros Jimmy Demaret and Doug Sanders, as well as a host of Hollywood stars, the course was originally designed by George Thomas Jr., then got a face-lift from golf architect Jay Morrish. Country Club Rd., Ojai (phone: 805-646-5511).

A Shutterbug's Los Angeles

With all its pastels, seascapes, and picturesque neighborhoods, Los Angeles is a very photogenic city. There is architectural variety: Art Deco is juxtaposed with modern, ornate with ordinary, and a skyline bristling with temples of modern commerce meets the seashore. There also is natural variety: Flowers embroider a park footpath, a palm tree waves in the breeze, and a sunrise sparks the horizon over the ocean. Immigrants exchange the latest news from the old country in Korean, Spanish, and Vietnamese; ruddy fishermen return with their catch; and beachcombers flaunt their tans on a boardwalk. The thriving city, the shimmering sea, the parks, the people, and most of all, the views make Los Angeles a fertile stomping ground for shutterbugs. Even a beginner can achieve remarkable results with a surprisingly basic set of lenses and filters. Equipment is, in fact, only as valuable as the imagination that puts it to use.

LANDSCAPES, SEASCAPES, AND CITYSCAPES Los Angeles's populated beaches and chrome and glass skyscrapers are most often visiting photographers' favorite subjects. But the city's green spaces and waterways provide numerous photo possibilities as well. Be sure to look for natural beauty: the tropical gardens, the well-manicured plots of flowers in the public parks, the San Gabriel mountains in the background, and the rolling waves of the Pacific.

Although a standard 50mm to 55mm lens may work well in some landscape situations, most will benefit from a 20mm to 28mm wide-angle. The Los Angeles skyline from the top of the *Westin Bonaventure* hotel, for example, is the type of panorama that fits beautifully into a wide-angle format, allowing not only the overview, but the opportunity to include people or other points of interest in the foreground. A fruit stand, for instance, may be used to set off a view of the *Farmers' Market;* or people can provide a sense of perspective in a shot of a café on Melrose Avenue.

To isolate specific elements of any scene, use your telephoto lens. Perhaps there's a particular carving in a historic theater that would make a lovely shot, or it might be the interplay of light and shadow on the façade of an old Spanish church. The successful use of a telephoto means developing your eye for detail.

PEOPLE As with taking pictures of people anywhere, there are going to be times in Los Angeles when a camera is an intrusion. Consider your own reaction under similar circumstances, and you have an idea as to what would make others comfortable enough to be willing subjects. People are often sensitive to having a camera suddenly pointed at them, but a polite request, while getting you a share of refusals, may provide a chance to shoot some wonderful portraits that capture the spirit of the area as surely as the scenery does. For candids, an excellent lens is a zoom telephoto in the 70mm to 210mm range; it allows you to remain unobtrusive while the telephoto lens draws the subject closer. And for portraits, a telephoto can be used effectively as close as five to seven feet.

For authenticity and variety, select a place likely to produce interesting subjects. *Knott's Berry Farm* is an obvious spot for visitors, but if it's local color you're after, try to capture the fitness scene on the boardwalk in Venice or at the Esplanade in Redondo Beach. Aim for shots that tell what's different about Los Angeles. In portraiture, there are several factors to keep in mind. Morning or afternoon light will add richness to skin tones, emphasizing tans. To avoid the harsh facial shadows cast by direct sunlight, shoot in the shade or in an area where the light is diffused.

SUNSETS When shooting sunsets, keep in mind that the brightness will distort meter readings. When composing a shot directly into the sun, frame the picture in the viewfinder so that only half of the sun is included. Read the meter, set, reframe the sunset as you want it to appear in the photo, and shoot. Whenever there is this kind of unusual lighting, shoot a few frames in half-step increments, both over and under the meter reading. Bracketing, as this is called, can provide a range of images, the best of which may well be other than the one shot at the meter's recommended setting.

Use any lens for sunsets. A wide-angle is good when the sky is filled with color-streaked clouds, when the sun is partially hidden, or when you're close to an object that silhouettes dramatically against the sky.

Telephotos also produce wonderful silhouettes, either with the sun as a backdrop or against the palette of a brilliant sunset sky. Bracket again here. For the best silhouettes, wait 10 to 15 minutes after sunset. Unless using a very fast film, a tripod is recommended.

Red and orange filters are often used to accentuate a sunset's picture potential. Orange will help turn even a gray sky into something approaching a photogenic finale to the day, and can provide particularly beautiful shots linking the sky with the sun reflected on the ocean. If the sunset is already bold in hue, however, the orange will overwhelm the natural colors. A red filter will produce dramatic, highly unrealistic results.

NIGHT If you think that picture possibilities end at sunset, you're presuming that night photography is the exclusive domain of the professional. If you've got a tripod, all you'll need is a cable release to attach to your camera to assure a steady exposure (which is often timed in minutes rather than fractions of a second).

For situations such as evening concerts or nighttime cruises, a strobe does the trick, but beware: Flash units are often used improperly. You can't take a view of the skyline with a flash. It may reach out as far as 30 feet, but that's it. On the other hand, a flash used too close to a subject may result in overexposure, resulting in a "blown out" effect. With most cameras, strobes will work with a maximum shutter speed of 1/125 or 1/250 of a second. If you set the exposure properly and shoot within range, you should come up with pretty sharp results.

CLOSE-UPS Whether of people or of objects such as antique door knockers, close-ups can add another dimension to your photography. There are a number of shooting options, one of which is to use a 70mm or a 210mm lens at its closest focusable distance. Unless you're working in bright sunlight, a tripod will be worthwhile. If you are very near your subject and there is a good deal of reflective light, it may pay to underexpose a bit in relation to the meter reading.

If you do not have a telephoto lens, you can still shoot close-ups using a set of magnification filters. Filter packs of one-, two-, and three-time magnification are available, converting your lens into a close-up lens. Even better is a special macro lens designed for close-up photography.

A SHORT PHOTOGRAPHIC TOUR

Here are a few of Los Angeles's most photogenic places.

EL PUEBLO DE LOS ANGELES Juxtaposing the old with the new always makes for an interesting shot. In the heart of downtown Los Angeles, towering skyscrapers form the backdrop to the sights and sounds of an old-time, Mexican marketplace. *El Pueblo* is as close as you can get to what Los Angeles was like in the very early days. The structures in *El Pueblo de Los Angeles Historic Park* date from the 1800s and look quite striking against the modern-day skyline. Be sure to get the buildings on the Old Plaza into the shot—the *Old Plaza Church,* built in 1818; the Italianate *Pico House,* built in 1870; and the *Firehouse,* built in 1884. As you snap away, imagine how startled the original 44 settlers, who came from Sonora, Mexico, in 1781, would be to see the old town now! On Olvera Street, you also can get some great "people" shots of folks browsing through the colorful, hand-crafted Mexican wares and stopping for a taco or burrito at the outdoor cafés. When you look at the slides back home, make sure you have mariachi music playing in the background.

VENICE BEACH Should your friends and relations doubt you went to California, just show them your way-out, wacky shots of a day in the life of Venice Beach. The heart of the scene runs from about Windward Avenue, at the *Venice Pavilion,* south to the *Venice Pier* at Washington Street. The weekend is the best time to capture the outrageous sights at this open-air carnival. You can get clowns, jugglers, panhandlers, and bikini-clad beauties all in one shot. For some real-life art forms, walk north to 18th Avenue and capture the modern-day strongmen flexing their pecs at Muscle Beach.

Another of the town's artistic manifestations are the outdoor murals. Check out Rip Cronk's *Venice Reconstituted* (Venus on roller skates) at 25 Windward Avenue, his van Gogh–esque *Homage to a Starry Knight* on Ocean Front Walk, Christina Schlesinger's *Marc Chagall Comes to Venice Beach* at 201 Ocean Front Walk at Ozone, and Emily Winters's *Endangered Species* at Ocean Front Walk and Park. To get more details on the murals, contact the *Social and Public Arts Resource Center (SPARC),* 685 Venice Blvd. (phone: 310-822-9560).

ARCHITECTURAL WONDERS Los Angeles has an incredible collection of architectural gems sprinkled throughout its many neighborhoods, so take that camera with you at all times. Lovingly restored examples of Spanish Colonial, Spanish Baroque, Art Deco, and Italianate structures from the 1920s and 1930s can be found all over town. In Hollywood, aim your camera at the theater façades of the *Pantages, Hollywood Egyptian, El Capitan,* and *Mann's Chinese.* In Beverly Hills the "Maya Deco" *Civic Center* is a nice architectural counterpoint to some of the city's more renowned hotels, like the Italian Renaissance–Beaux Arts *Regent Beverly Wilshire* and the Mission Revival *Beverly Hills.* In Westwood you'll be dazzled by the Spanish colonial sights—*Mann's Village Theatre, Mann's Bruin Theatre,* and the temple-like *Contempo Casuals.*

WHALES FOR POSTERITY Whether you try to catch a glimpse of them by standing on your tiptoes along the shoreline or go out on a whale watching cruise, it's a great thrill to bring home some snapshots of Moby Dick's friends and relatives. During the winter months, these fascinating creatures head south along the coastline from Alaska to Baja, California. Watch for rolling humps, a slapping tail, or a spuming spout of water. Early morning or late afternoon is the best time to spot them. If you're really lucky, you might capture a breach on film. That's when the whale (all 40 tons of it) leaps out of the water and dives back in with a thunderous splash.

STAR-STRUCK In a city where stars come out at all times of day and night, a sharp eye and an instant-focus lens can yield all manner of candid shots of those people you're accustomed to viewing only in the movies. And keep your flash handy: Some LA stars like to act like their heavenly counterparts and shine only at night. Happy hunting.

Directions

Introduction

Walking—except for power walking, which is an entirely different animal—is a relatively alien concept in Los Angeles. People here worship at the shrine of the internal combustion engine and genuflect at the sight of a Mercedes-Benz hood ornament. Walking occurs only because, as yet, Angelenos can't be "beamed" straight from their bedrooms to the garage, and after the car has been valet-parked, they still have to get from the curb to the restaurant. But it's really too bad that Los Angeles has bought the myth of itself as a freeway society, because there are some pretty places within the city limits to be discovered on foot.

Because so many people's experience of Los Angeles is through a car window, Gertrude Stein's lament that "There's no there there" seems appropriate. But the truth is that there is a "there"—or, rather, there are many. You have to drive and park to get to them, but they're quite fascinating once you arrive. In addition, there is so much focus on the LA of today—the hot, chic, hip, burgeoning metropolis—that compelling historical sites and early architectural gems often get lost in the shuffle.

To break this ugly cycle of neglect and misunderstanding, it helps to know that this city is really a collection of neighborhoods—little "villages," if you will. Downtown, Hollywood, West Hollywood, Beverly Hills, and Westwood are just some of these enclaves, each with its own distinct flavor. The most rewarding way to explore the city, therefore, is one neighborhood at a time. It's also wise to note that a lot of what you'll see can be credited to a man named De Mille. For apart from early Spanish and Mexican influences, Los Angeles was shaped most by the affluence and vision of an emerging motion-picture elite.

Back in 1913, the great Cecil B. De Mille shot one of the first movies ever made in Hollywood. Things would never be the same again. As De Mille and nascent stars such as Mary Pickford and Douglas Fairbanks gained popularity and financial position, they began to build homes, offices, and studios. Their style of unprecedented opulence was a hybrid of fantasy and royalty: to the manor born à la Hollywood. Around the same time, other people with equally grandiose real-estate visions began breaking new ground: Beverly Hills started as a sort of high-minded subdivision, the master plan for Westwood called for a Spanish Colonial shopping center, and so on.

As the salaries of stars such as Rudolph Valentino, Jean Harlow, and Gloria Swanson rose into the stratosphere, they too acquired lavish homes. Soon, whole neighborhoods of magnificent villas and private palaces sprang into being. It was as if fairy-tale characters (with lots of money) had come to life and designed a city.

In the late 1920s and early 1930s, as the building frenzy continued, Los Angeles became a town of architectural wonders. Truly spectacular, lovingly restored Spanish Baroque and Art Deco buildings from that period can be found all over town. Recently, Angelenos have taken an interest in the city's historic architecture, and several preservationist organizations have emerged. Two—the *Los Angeles Conservancy* (phone: 213-623-CITY) and *Hollywood Heritage* (phone: 213-874-4005)—offer fascinating walking tours focusing on the architecture and history of various sections of town.

So we invite you to join us. Our driving and walking tours will give you a view of Tinseltown that is off the beaten track.

Tour 1: Downtown

Any walking journey through Los Angeles should begin downtown, for this is where Los Angeles was born. On September 4, 1781, the Spanish colonial capital of El Pueblo de Nuestra Señora de Los Angeles (The Town of Our Lady, the Queen of the Angels), was founded here. The original site has now been turned into a state historic park, *El Pueblo de Los Angeles.*

EL PUEBLO DE LOS ANGELES

To reach the park, take the Hollywood Freeway No. 101. Exit at the Union Station–Alameda Street off-ramp, then follow the signs to *Union Station.* *El Pueblo de Los Angeles* is directly across the street. Park at *Union Station* or in the parking lots at *El Pueblo.*

It shouldn't take more than two hours to explore the park and visit the shops on Olvera Street. Enjoy your wanderings, but as in any big city, be mindful of your belongings and surroundings. There is a large directory in the middle of the park near the plaza to help you get your bearings. Start your visit at the *Visitor Information Center* (622 N. Main St.; phone: 213-628-1274); closed Sundays. If you want to learn about the colorful history of the area, free guided tours are given on the hour from 10 AM to 1 PM, Tuesdays through Saturdays; meet at the docent's office next door to *Firehouse No. 1.* For a self-guided tour pick up the *El Pueblo de Los Angeles* brochure with a detailed map and brief history of the area at the visitors' center.

El Pueblo de Los Angeles is bordered by Alameda Street to the east, Arcadia Street to the south, North Main Street to the west, and Cesar Chavez (Macy) Street to the north. A 44-acre, Mexican-style site, it contains 27 historic buildings dating from 1818 to 1926. At its center sits the Old Plaza, a lovely Spanish square with a gazebo in the center. An upward glance takes you from the past to the present, where the towers of downtown Los Angeles can be seen in the distance.

The park's main attraction is festive Olvera Street, which is closed to traffic, as is most of the park. With its cobblestone walkways and outdoor vendors selling all manner of food and trinkets, Olvera Street is the bright, bustling hub of activity in the park, a good place to pick up Mexican souvenirs, browse, or grab a snack. Lining the street are some of LA's oldest buildings, landmarks in the history of a city that belonged first to Spain (1781), then to Mexico (1822), and finally to the United States (1847).

The location of *Zanja Madre,* part of the pueblo's original irrigation system, dating from 1783, is indicated by a section of diagonal bricks on Olvera Street. The *Avila Adobe* (10 Olvera St.), the oldest house in Los Angeles, was built in 1818. It was home to Don Francisco Avila, the first mayor of the pueblo. It is closed Mondays; no admission charge. The *Pelanconi House*

Downtown

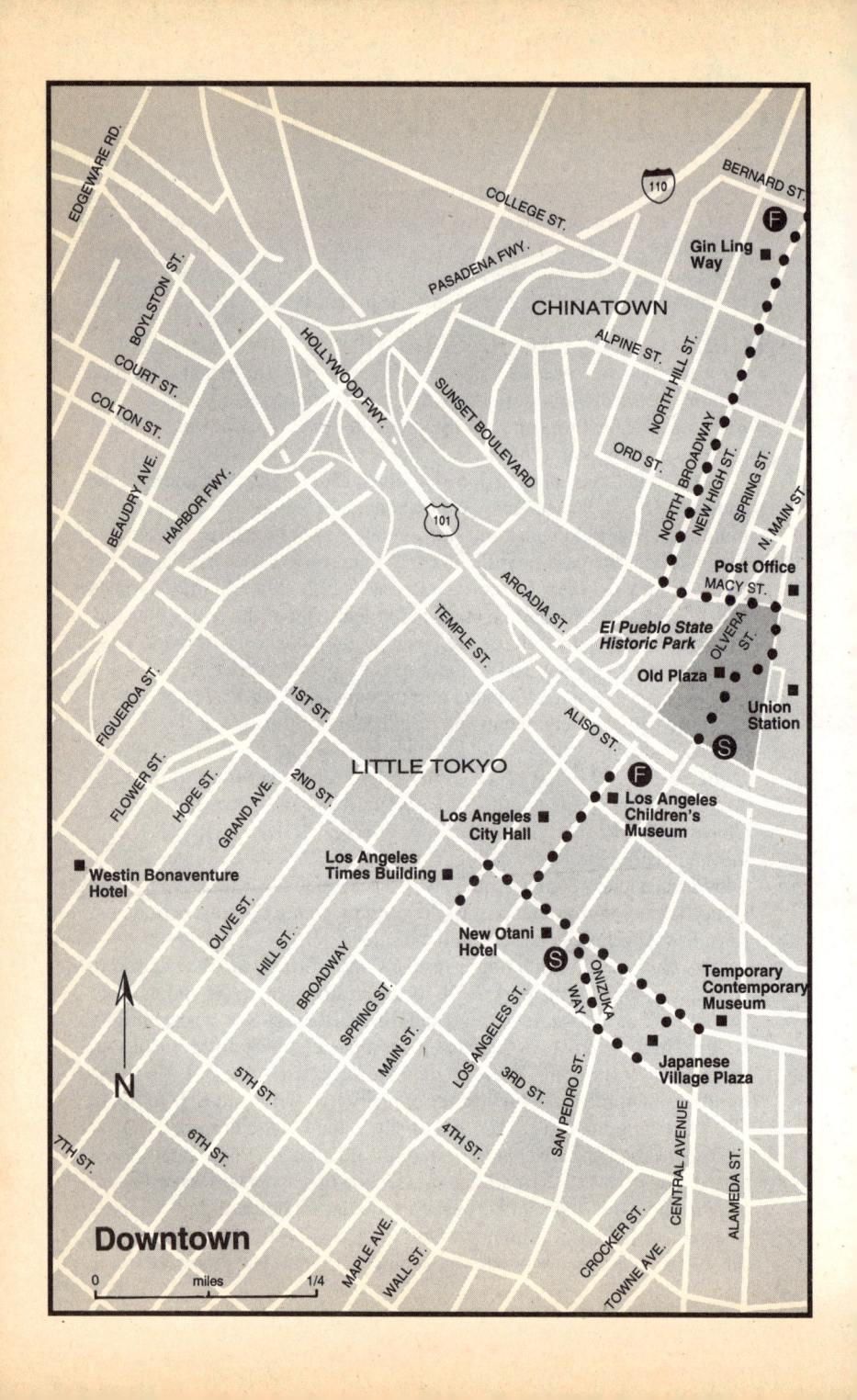

(17 W. Olvera St.), constructed in 1855, was one of Los Angeles's first brick buildings. (There's a mariachi show inside every evening at *La Golondrina* restaurant; phone: 213-628-4349). The *Sepulveda House* was constructed by Eliosa Martinez de Sepulveda in 1887 as a hotel/boarding house. Today it houses the *Visitor Information Center*.

The *Old Plaza Church* (100 W. Sunset), built in 1818, is the city's oldest Catholic church, and boasts California's largest Hispanic congregation. Also worth a look is *Firehouse No. 1* (134 Paseo de la Plaza), built in 1884. Although it's been a saloon, a store, and a boarding house, it is now a fascinating museum of late 19th-century fire-fighting equipment. It's closed Mondays; no admission charge. Behind the firehouse is the Victorian *Garnier Building*. Built in 1890, it was part of LA's original Chinatown, some of which was bulldozed in the late 1930s to make way for *Union Station*.

As you leave the park, be sure to stop across the street to admire mission-style *Union Station*. Built in 1939 as the western terminus for the *Southern Pacific, Union Pacific,* and *Santa Fe* lines and restored to its original splendor, it's one of the country's last great railroad cathedrals still in operation. The waiting room has a 52-foot ceiling, marble floor, and grand seating areas. The *LA Conservancy* runs guided tours focusing on its architecture (phone: 213-623-CITY).

Just north of *Union Station* on Alameda Street in the *Main Post Office–Terminal Annex* (900 Alameda St.) are a series of 1930s *Works Progress Administration (WPA)* murals depicting the history of communications. While you're in the neighborhood, stop for a cup of java and a snack at *Philippe's Original Sandwich Shop* (1001 N. Alameda St.; phone: 213-628-3781). Allegedly, the French dip sandwich was invented here in 1918. It's still a fine old spot, where a cup of coffee costs only a dime. But you might want to save your appetite for the culinary treats in Chinatown.

CHINATOWN

Continue north on Alameda until you reach Cesar Chavez (Macy) Street, then turn left (west) and walk a few blocks until you come to North Broadway. Make a right (north) onto North Broadway. This is the beginning of Chinatown. Exploring this area could take from two to four hours; there's lots to see. It's an easy walk, but some stretches are quite dull, and Los Angeles can get very hot and smoggy. If you choose to drive, there is ample parking along North Broadway and a nice garage on Bernard Street and North Broadway at the *Bamboo Plaza* mall.

Unlike the Chinatowns of New York and San Francisco, this neighborhood has broad streets lined with modern structures and boasts a sizable Vietnamese population as well. Vibrant, colorful, and crowded, it has dozens of terrific restaurants and hundreds of small shops; try to come here toward the evening, when the place really hums.

Chinatown is bounded by North Broadway to the east, North Hill Street to the west, Sunset Boulevard to the south, and Bernard Street to the north.

You can do some interesting shopping for Oriental goodies and eat very well at the *Empress Pavilion* (988 N. Hill St.; phone: 213-617-9898), *Ocean Seafood* (747 N. Broadway; phone: 213-687-3088), the *Mandarin Deli* (819 N. Broadway; phone: 213-625-0811), *Yang Chow* (819 N. Broadway; phone: 213-625-0811), or *Mon Kee's* (see *Eating Out* in THE CITY), where lobsters and crabs are plucked live from bubbling tanks.

The farther you walk up North Broadway, the closer you'll come to the heart of Chinatown. The area to which everybody flocks is between College and Bernard Streets. Just north of College Street are several pagoda-style buildings and the famous Oriental arches with "Chinatown" emblazoned on them. This is Gin Ling Way—the formal entrance to Chinatown.

North of Gin Ling Way on the corner of North Hill and Bernard Streets is *Bamboo Plaza,* a quiet, low-key mall with restaurants and shops. Just south of College Street is *Saigon Plaza,* an outdoor shopping area teeming with stores and eateries attesting to the large influx of Vietnamese. Another find in the heart of Chinatown is *Little Joe's* (900 N. Broadway; phone: 213-489-4900), one of Los Angeles's most popular Italian—yes, Italian—restaurants.

Once you have done the historic *El Pueblo de Los Angeles* area and Chinatown, you might want to call it a day. If you have any energy left, the next stop is Little Tokyo and the contemporary art museums. Otherwise, save this excursion through another interesting section of downtown for another time.

LITTLE TOKYO AND CITY HALL

To get to Little Tokyo, take the Hollywood Freeway No. 101 south to the Union Station–Alameda off ramp. At the end of the exit, make a right. At the first traffic signal, make a left (south) onto Alameda Street. Drive south for about a half mile to Second Street, then turn right (west). Park at any of the lots on Second Street between San Pedro and Los Angeles Streets. (The parking garage underneath Onizuka Way on Second Street is a very convenient place.)

This neighborhood of small plazas and gardens, dating back more than a century, contains a large segment of the city's Japanese community. No pagodas here, though; this is a stark, modern setting. Little Tokyo caters primarily to Japanese visitors and businesspeople, but if you want to spend an hour or two soaking up an Asian atmosphere, this is a good place to do it. The *LA Conservancy* (see above) brings this area to life on a walking tour that relays the history of the Japanese immigrant experience in Los Angeles.

The best place to begin an excursion into Little Tokyo is at *Weller Court,* a multilevel plaza on Los Angeles Street with a nice fountain in the middle. It houses a variety of shops, including a branch of *Matsuzakaya,* a Japanese department store. *Weller Court* connects to the ultramodern *New Otani* hotel (120 S. Los Angeles St.), which caters to Japanese tourists. The hotel's restaurant, *A Thousand Cranes,* has some of the best food in Little Tokyo (see *Eating Out* in THE CITY). Just off the restaurant level you'll find a serene, Japanese-style garden to soothe the spirit in the midst of the hustle and bustle of downtown Los Angeles. The hotel also houses *Kinokuniya,* a marvelous bookstore filled with excellent English-language guides to Japan and its culture.

Walk north on Los Angeles Street, then turn right onto First Street. On the right off First Street is Onizuka Way. Head south on Onizuka Way, where there are several stores in which to browse. (This is like a low-key Rodeo Drive with Japanese salespeople.) When you come to Second Street, make a left (east) and walk a few blocks down to *Japanese Village Plaza,* the heart of Little Tokyo. This mall is filled with a curious combination of inexpensive Japanese and American take-out eateries and stores. Across the street is the *Japanese American National Museum* (see *Museums* in THE CITY), which boasts the largest collection of Japanese-American artifacts ever assembled in the US. It is closed Mondays; admission charge.

From Little Tokyo you can walk or drive to several museums and city landmarks, starting with a quick trip to the *Temporary Contemporary Art Museum* (152 N. Central Ave.). Continue walking north along *Japanese Village Plaza* up to First Street. Turn right (east) and walk to Central Avenue. Make a left (north) at Central, and the museum will be right in front of you. (If you drive, be sure to take First Street to Central, as it's not possible to enter Central from the north. There's plenty of parking at the museum.)

The *Temporary Contemporary,* an annex of the *Museum of Contemporary Art* (250 S. Grand Ave.; phone: 213-621-2766), is itself a striking work of modern art. The building often is used to house oversize exhibits. (Note: At press time the *Temporary Contemporary* was undergoing renovation; call ahead to check on its reopening.) Both museums are closed Mondays; admission charge. There is a free shuttle service between the two museums; just show your admission ticket (also see *Special Places* in THE CITY).

For the motivated walker a trip to *Los Angeles City Hall* (200 N. Spring St.) and the *Los Angeles Times* building (First and Spring Sts.) is next. From the *Temporary Contemporary* walk back to First Street and head west. This is a fairly short walk, but it could be driven (and you'll probably want your car if you decide to continue with a visit to Pershing Square or the *Westin Bonaventure,* see below). *City Hall* is about a quarter of a mile down First Street on the right, between Main and Spring Streets. The *Times* building is across the street on the corner.

City Hall is a majestic structure. Viewers of the 1950s TV version of "Superman" might recognize it as the *Daily Planet* newspaper building, where Superman had his day job. An observation deck on the 27th floor is open to the public, and informative tours are given by appointment (phone: 213-485-4423 or 213-485-4424). If you want to see how a newspaper is put together, tour the "new" and "old" *Los Angeles Times* buildings. The original Art Deco plant (202 W. First St.) is a step back in history, while the ultramodern facility (2000 E. Eighth St.) features robotics and a streamlined interior (phone: 213-237-5757).

The next stop, one block north of *City Hall,* is for the young at heart. From the corner of First and Main Streets, head north on Main. Go one block past Temple Street to the *Los Angeles Children's Museum* (310 N. Main St.; phone: 213-687-8800). This place will fascinate even hard to please youngsters. The museum is part of Fletcher Bowron Square, whose shops and restaurants are frequented by downtown denizens. It is closed Mondays; no admission charge for children under two. (If you drive to the museum on a separate trip, take the Hollywood Freeway No. 101. Coming southbound, exit on Los Angeles Street and turn right. Northbound, take the Union Station–Alameda Street off ramp and continue west past Alameda to Los Angeles Street and turn left.)

OTHER CITY LANDMARKS

After one or all of these tours you may want to relax in a lovely garden or have drinks or a meal with a stunning view of the city. If so, get in your car and head for Pershing Square or the *Westin Bonaventure* hotel—or both. Should you prefer public transportation, hop aboard a *DASH* minibus (phone: 213-626-4455). Three *DASH* routes travel from the *Civic Center* district around *City Hall* to California Plaza, Broadway, or Pershing Square—downtown's most scenic areas—24 hours a day except on Sundays. The fare is a mere 25¢.

To reach Pershing Square, head down Main Street from the *Children's Museum* and turn right on Fifth Street, following it west to Grand Avenue. Here is recently renovated Pershing Square, located at the doorstep of the *Biltmore* hotel (at Fifth and Grand). LA's oldest park, it was first converted to a park in 1866 and later redesigned by noted landscape architect Laurie Olin. This place is a veritable feast for the eyes—its five acres feature two plazas dotted with bright yellow and pink kiosks, a café, a transit center, and a 125-foot purple campanile with a fuchsia bell (purely symbolic, it doesn't ring), as well as several pools, fountains, and stretches of green grass. It's a great place to picnic or simply to take a break from sightseeing.

One block west is the *Central Library* (630 W. Fifth St.; phone: 213-612-3383), another noteworthy piece of architecture. The historic building, erected in 1926, recently received a $214-million face-lift that restored its original Art Deco appearance. The country's third-largest public library, it's worth seeing just for its glorious gardens and impressive architectural details (both inside and out).

To reach the circular, silver towers of the *Westin Bonaventure,* go north on the Harbor Freeway No. 110. Take the Third Street off ramp and stay to the right. Turn right on Flower Street. The hotel's parking lot is on your right between Fourth and Fifth Streets. This is a tricky part of Los Angeles, with lots of one-way streets, so drive cautiously.

At night the skyline of downtown Los Angeles is magnificent. The lights on the imposing *First Interstate World Center* building on Hope Street illuminate the sky, and the pyramid-shaped towers of several Los Angeles landmarks can be seen in the distance. From the top of the *Westin Bonaventure* hotel (404 S. Figueroa St.; phone: 213-624-1000), you can see it all. The *Bonaventure* is definitely worth an evening out. There are eight levels of shopping and dining in this sleek, futuristic hotel. Enjoy stunning views of the city from the revolving bar and restaurant: Have drinks at the *Bonavista Lounge* on the 34th floor and dine at the elegant *Top of the Five* restaurant on the 35th floor. You also can get some spectacular views just riding up and down in the glass-enclosed elevators.

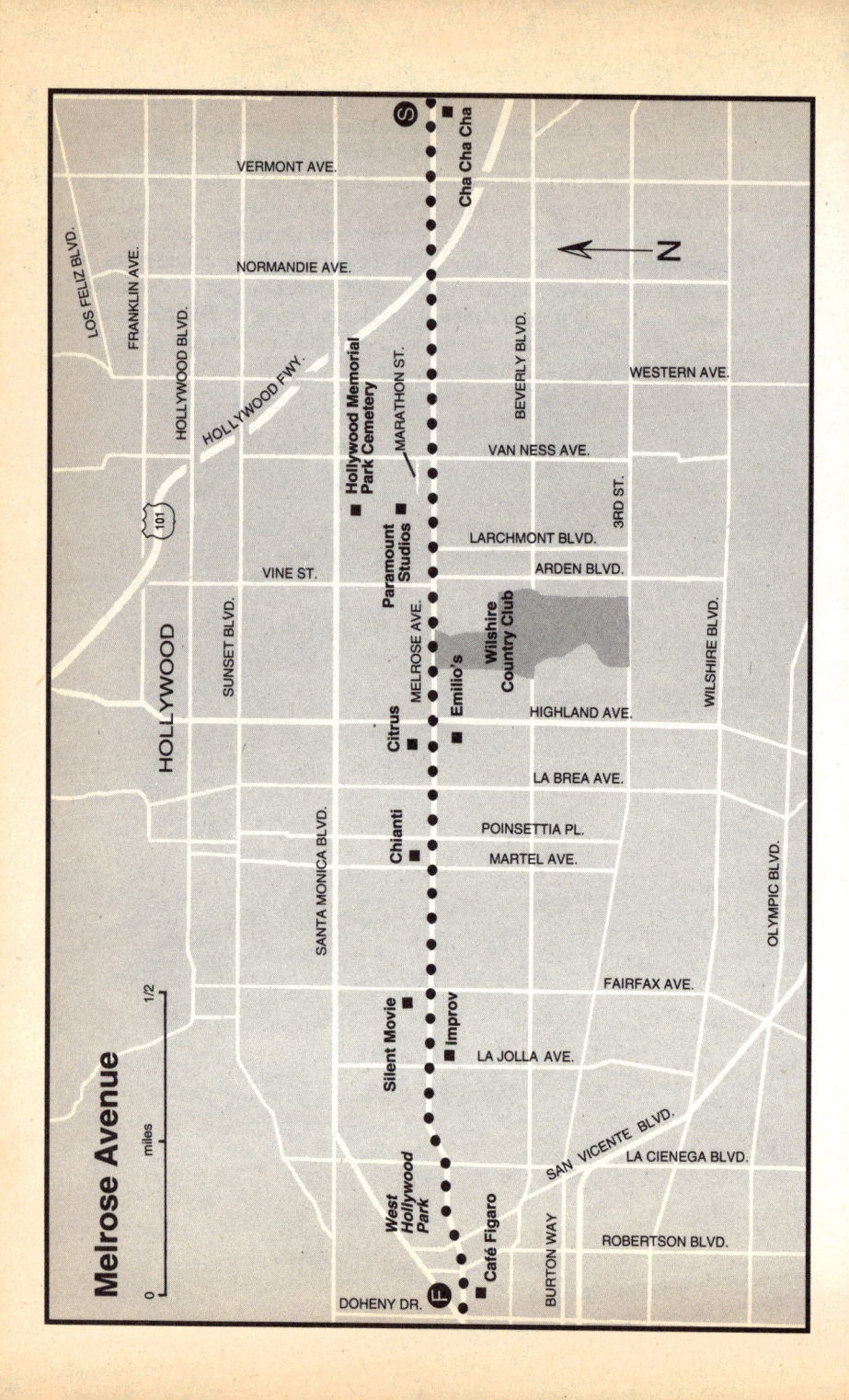

Melrose Avenue

Tour 2: Melrose Avenue

Melrose Avenue is where it's at. Everyone comes here to shop for the latest cutting-edge fashions, to see and be seen, to dine in ethnic restaurants, and to promenade down the avenue. On a warm weekend afternoon half the population of Los Angeles seems to be swarming through the stores and spilling out of the restaurants. Melrose has come to define hip and trendy, in a city where hip and trendy is a way of life.

Until the early 1980s Melrose was just another street lined with small shops and a few restaurants of no particular distinction—then something happened. The transformation began in 1979 when the owners of *LA Eyeworks* (outré eyeglass frames) opened a tiny restaurant and put fabulous food on its tables, contemporary art on the walls, and new-wave music in the air. Down the street *Ma Maison* (now in the *Sofitel Ma Maison* hotel) was giving *Chasen's* a run for its money as the latest celebrity hot spot. The decor was an exercise in reverse snobbism (astroturf and lawn furniture), but every star and power broker in town fought for a good table, and Wolfgang Puck became Southern California's first superstar chef. Around 1982 a cluster of new shops and restaurants catering to the yuppie crowd began to open nearby; within a few years Melrose became the single most interesting street in Los Angeles.

Popularity has its price, however. Parking here is often difficult; there is metered parking on Melrose, but that's tough to find. You have a better chance with off-street parking, though there's often a two-hour limit. Some streets may require a permit, so watch for signs. There are parking lots available, and some restaurants have valet parking.

Along with all the new places that have opened on Melrose, the avenue lays claim to the city's oldest continually operating restaurant, *Chianti*, which opened in 1939 (see *Eating Out* in THE CITY). It's also home to the famous and exclusive *Steak Pit* (7529 Melrose Ave.; 213-653-2011), where you have to know someone to get in.

Melrose begins at Hoover Street near downtown LA, goes through the Wilshire district, and ends in West Hollywood at Doheny Drive. Since it stretches on for miles and miles, it's best to tackle it in sections. First, an overview:

From Hoover Street to Highland Avenue is the least developed part of Melrose, with a few interesting sights and hip restaurants scattered along the way. This section has one distinct advantage: Unlike on other parts of Melrose, here you have at least a shot at parking close to your destination.

The stretch from Highland Avenue to Fairfax Avenue is the trendy section, with a colorful concentration of boutiques, specialty shops, and restaurants. Since this area is also the most popular, parking is next to impossible and you'll want to walk; wear comfortable shoes. Consider combining a visit here with a trip to Fairfax Avenue and the *Farmers' Market* (see *Tour 3* in DIRECTIONS). You could then park at the market and walk up Fairfax to Melrose.

From Fairfax Avenue to San Vicente Boulevard, Melrose shifts into higher gear. There are fewer stores, and they tend to be more expensive, from elegant clothiers, restaurants, and antiques shops to pricey home furnishings outlets.

The area from San Vicente Boulevard to Doheny Drive, known as "Decorators' Row," caters almost exclusively to professional decorators. There are some interesting bookstores and celebrity restaurants, however, for visitors to check out. Melrose ends at Doheny Drive.

Any journey down Melrose begins and ends with the restaurants along the street, with shopping in between. Start at the east end of Melrose, perhaps have lunch at *Cha Cha Cha* (656 N. Virgil Ave.; phone: 213-664-7723), and wind up at *Café Figaro* (see below), at the west end, for a cappuccino.

A funky, little blue-stucco bungalow, *Cha Cha Cha* is the hottest place in town for Cuban-Caribbean cuisine. Just across the street *Rincon Chileno* (4352 Melrose Ave.; phone: 213-666-6075) serves delicious seafood, empanadas, and *papas mayonesas* at affordable prices. This friendly little café is a favorite among Melrose's Latino population.

From here drive west to *Paramount Studios* beyond Van Ness Avenue. Although the studios are closed to the public, you can get a good feel for them by walking around the outside. There's an entrance on Melrose Avenue, but if you turn onto Marathon Street you'll come up to that imposing wrought-iron gate made famous in *Sunset Boulevard* and other films. The *Hollywood Memorial Park Cemetery*—resting place of Rudolph Valentino, Tyrone Power, and other heartthrobs—abuts *Paramount* and also is worth a detour (see *Grave Matters* in DIVERSIONS).

If hunger strikes, try *Patina* (see *Eating Out* in THE CITY), which some consider to be the best restaurant in Los Angeles. Although the menu is somewhat eccentric, the food is wonderful, the prices are high (but not outrageous), and the decor is very understated—a great dining experience.

Continue heading west to the corner of Highland and Melrose, where the truly trendy section begins. Once you find a parking spot, you'll want to walk this next stretch. The restaurant on the corner is *Emilio's* (6602 Melrose Ave.; phone: 213-935-4922), a wonderful Old World Italian eatery. Next door is the far more modern *Il Piccolino* (641 N. Highland Ave.; phone: 213-936-2996), run by Emilio's son. This reasonably priced spot serves good *nuova cucina*.

Perhaps the most famous restaurant on Melrose is *Citrus* (see *Eating Out* in THE CITY). Its gorgeous glassed-in kitchen presents one of the best culinary shows in town, turning out superb French-California cooking for a fashionable crowd. If you have time for only one meal on Melrose, this may well be the place to go.

Heading farther west, be sure to drop in at the *Rock Store* (6817 Melrose Ave.; phone: 213-930-2980). The memorabilia ranges from a silver sequined dress worn by Diana Ross in *Lady Sings the Blues* to one of Paul McCartney's guitars. It's a museum of rock history—and the exhibits are for sale!

As you cross La Brea Avenue, keep an eye out for *Pink's Famous Chili Dogs* (711 N. La Brea Ave.; phone: 213-931-4223), a Los Angeles institution fabled for its chili dogs—and the heartburn that goes with them. (If you have the energy, check out La Brea to the south. Due to the rising rents on Melrose, some of the more offbeat stores have moved here.)

At this point you're on the fashionable, boutique-lined side of Melrose, where most shops open about 11 AM. Madonna wannabes flock to *Retail Slut* (7264 Melrose Ave.; phone 213-934-1339); it's one of her favorite stores. *Unit 7301* (7301 Melrose Ave.; phone: 213-933-8391) sells reproduction Bauhaus furniture. *Vinyl Fetish* (7305 Melrose Ave.; 213-935-1300) carries a great selection of underground and alternative records—not for the easy listener. *Betsey Johnson* (7311 Melrose Ave.; phone: 213-931-4490) has striking hot-pink walls and a paisley decor, with campy women's wear to match. *Off the Wall Antiques* (7325 Melrose Ave.; phone: 213-930-1185) stocks bright, colorful collectibles, from gas pumps to jukeboxes to life-size horse, cow, and chicken statues.

If you need a little sustenance, pop into *Chopstix* (see *Eating Out* in THE CITY) for what they call "Really Risqué Rice" before moving on. A neon Indian head sign will direct you to *American Classics* (7368 Melrose Ave.; phone: 213-655-9375) for an excellent selection of westernwear—cowboy boots, suede jackets, Levi's, and fancy belt buckles.

Nearby, at the corner of Martel Avenue and Melrose, are a pair of stores, the *Soap Plant* (7400 Melrose Ave.; phone: 213-651-5587) and *Zulu* (7402 Melrose Ave.; phone: 213-651-4857), which many consider to be the apex of Melrose shopping. Housed in a brightly hand-painted building, these zany shops carry just about anything, as long as it's peculiar. The *Soap Plant* has offbeat sundries, and *Zulu* specializes in vividly colored spandex dresses and gaudy accessories.

The entranceway to *Wacko* (7416 Melrose Ave.; phone: 213-651-3811) takes you down a hallway of carnival mirrors. This place lives up to its name—inflatable sharks, books on loud ties, weird windup dolls, and Mexican *Day of the Dead* artifacts. If you've seen it in a dream, it's here in bold colors.

Farther along is *Antonio's* (7472 Melrose Ave.; phone: 213-655-0480), one of the oldest Mexican restaurants in the city, serving a variety of spicy, unusual dishes. And when Rob Lowe took Princess Stephanie of Monaco out for an evening on the town, they headed for *Johnny Rocket's* (7507 Melrose Ave.; phone: 213-651-3361), a spiffy 1950s-style diner serving great burgers, shakes, and fries.

Some of the interesting shops along the way are *Wasteland* (7428 Melrose Ave.; phone: 213-653-3028), for used clothing, jewelry, and trendy footwear; and *Leathers & Treasures* (7511 Melrose Ave.; phone: 213-655-7541), a popular clothing shop for rock stars (Bruce Springsteen has been sighted here).

Continuing west there's *Fantasies Come True* (8012 Melrose Ave.; phone: 213-655-2636), specializing in Walt Disney memorabilia, and *Fred Segal* (8100 Melrose Ave.; phone: 213-651-3342), an entire department store of interconnecting boutiques filled with trendy togs for kids and adults.

For entertainment try the *Matrix* (7657 Melrose Ave.; phone: 213-852-1445), one of the best Equity-waiver (99-seat) playhouses in Los Angeles, and the *Improv* (8162 Melrose Ave.; phone: 213-651-2583), where Robin Williams likes to pop in to try out new material. Just one block south of Melrose, on Fairfax Avenue, there's a special treat for silent-movie aficionados. According to its owner, *Silent Movie,* dating back to 1942, is now the only silent-movie theater in the world (see *The Performing Arts* in DIVERSIONS).

At the far end of Melrose is "Decorators' Row," just down the street from the *Pacific Design Center,* a big, blue behemoth. Although most of the stores here are for professional decorators only, the lavish window displays are reason enough for a visit. There are also several interesting shops open to the public. Be sure to browse in the specialized bookstores: *Heritage* (8540 Melrose Ave.; phone: 310-652-9486), for original manuscripts and first editions; *Elliott Katt* (8570 Melrose Ave.; phone: 310-652-5178), for books on the movies; and the *Bodhi Tree* (8585 Melrose Ave.; phone: 310-659-1733), one of Shirley MacLaine's favorite haunts, for arcana and esoterica.

One of LA's celebrity restaurants, *Morton's* (see *Eating Out* in THE CITY,) is at this end of town. The food served here is really beside the point; this power eatery is about movie muscle, mega-deals, who's hot, and who's not.

A bit farther west is *Maxfield* (8825 Melrose Ave.; phone: 310-274-8800), where you'll find an impressive collection of chic European and American designer fashions and perhaps spot some superstars—Jack Nicholson and Cher are regulars. Nearby is *Melrose Place* (650 N. La Cienega Blvd.; phone: 310-657-2227). Named for the hit TV show, this trendy eatery is a favorite watering hole for the cast of the nighttime soap.

At the end of your journey stop in at *Café Figaro* (9010 Melrose Ave.; phone: 310-274-7664), where the food is great and the prices low. Sit down, relax, and try to imagine the days when Melrose—this SoHo of the West Coast—was just a street lined with nothing but drab storefronts.

Tour 3: Fairfax/Farmers' Market

Fairfax Avenue has long been the heart of Jewish life in Los Angeles—a taste of the old shtetl in the midst of the City of Angels. It's as close as LA gets to the sights and sounds of New York's Lower East Side. The predominantly Jewish section of Fairfax runs approximately from Beverly Boulevard to Melrose Avenue. Along with the city's best delis, the area has half a dozen blocks of kosher butchers, Israeli restaurants, and shops selling Judaica—Hebrew books and Jewish religious artifacts.

Just south of the old Fairfax district is the *Farmers' Market* (6333 W. Third Street; phone: 213-933-9211), a Los Angeles institution dating back to the Depression. This lively, open-air market is normally swarming with activity, especially on weekends, when it's jam-packed. And although it's become a little too touristy, it's still a pleasant place to wander around. There are colorful awnings over the stalls, picnic tables hiding under umbrellas, tempting delicacies at the food stands, fresh produce galore, and shops selling everything from pet food to lottery tickets—clothing, jewelry, souvenirs, you name it.

To get to Fairfax, go west on Melrose and turn left (south) onto Fairfax Avenue. Or take the No. 10 Freeway west and get off at the Fairfax exit. Go 3 miles north to the *Farmers' Market,* park, and walk less than a mile north on Fairfax Avenue to Melrose.

A walk down Fairfax offers a fascinating glimpse into a vanishing world. Most of the businesses are mom-and-pop shops with Hebrew signs. Go into *Hatikvah Music International* (436 N. Fairfax Ave.; phone: 213-655-7083) for a wide selection of recordings by Jewish artists. If you've been searching for a particular book in Hebrew, try *Atara's Books and Gifts Center* (452 N. Fairfax Ave.; phone: 213-655-3050). For a good Israeli meal try *Shula & Esther's* (519 N. Fairfax Ave.; phone: 213-852-9154).

The smells of herring and corned beef waft from the center of life along Fairfax, legendary *Canter's Delicatessen* (419 N. Fairfax Ave.; phone: 213-651-2030). Known for its hearty breakfasts, triple-decker combination sandwiches, and sometimes surly waitresses, *Canter's* can give you heartburn any time of the day or night, as it's one of the few restaurants in Los Angeles open 24 hours a day.

The Jewish ghetto here is rapidly being replaced by a world of young professionals, happy to live close to CBS Television City (7800 Beverly Blvd.) in a quiet neighborhood adjacent to the hustle of Hollywood. The Fairfax district's younger residents hang out at the nearby *Nowhere Café* (8009 Beverly Blvd.; phone: 213-655-8895), a vegetarian dining spot two

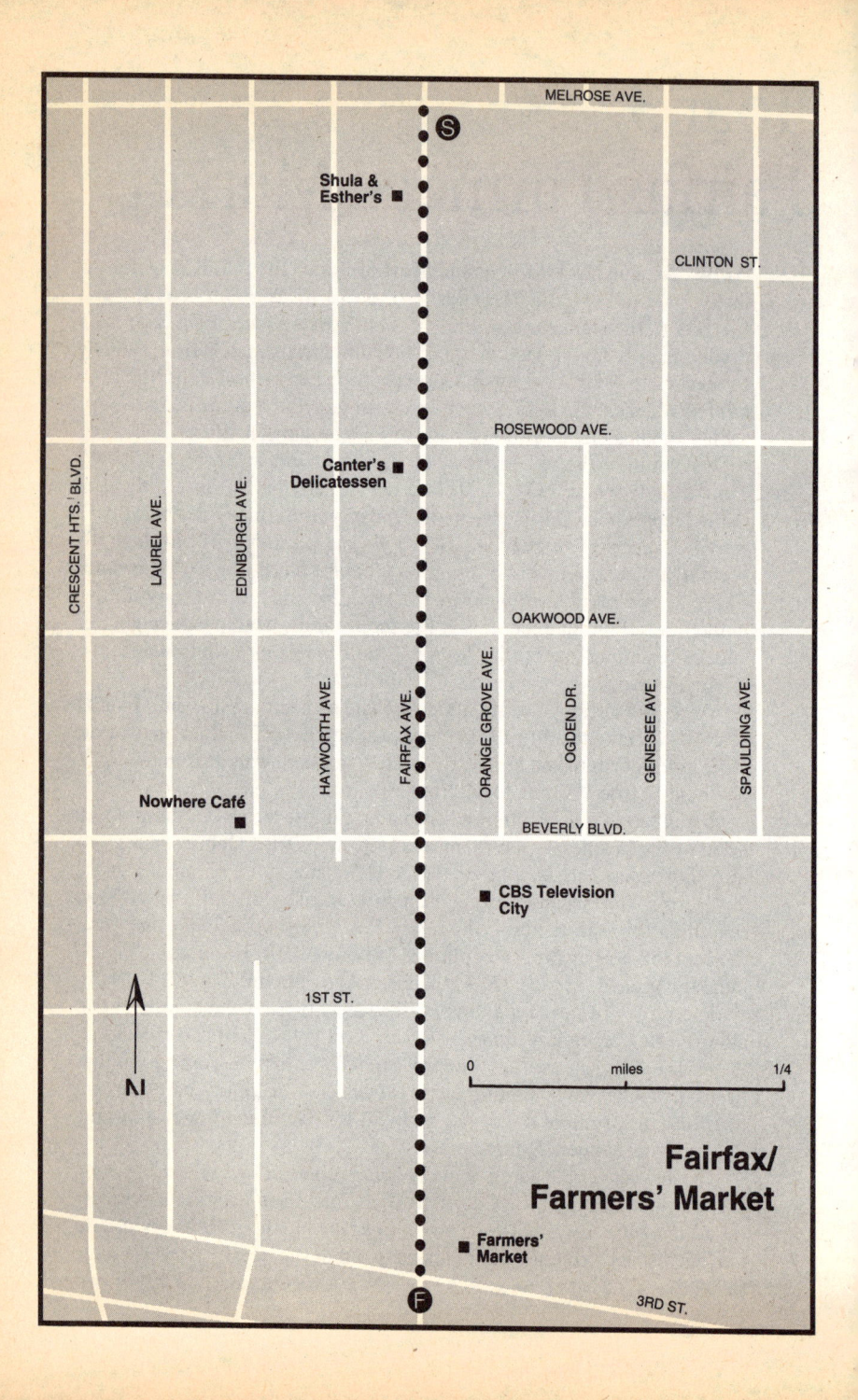

Fairfax/Farmers' Market

MELROSE AVE.
CLINTON ST.
Shula & Esther's
ROSEWOOD AVE.
Canter's Delicatessen
CRESCENT HTS. BLVD.
LAUREL AVE.
EDINBURGH AVE.
OAKWOOD AVE.
HAYWORTH AVE.
FAIRFAX AVE.
ORANGE GROVE AVE.
OGDEN DR.
GENESEE AVE.
SPAULDING AVE.
Nowhere Café
BEVERLY BLVD.
CBS Television City
1ST ST.
N
0 miles 1/4
Farmers' Market
3RD ST.

blocks west of the intersection of Fairfax and Beverly Boulevard, and at the *Authentic Café* (7605 Beverly Blvd.; phone: 213-939-4626), which serves Southwestern-style cooking. Drive by at any hour and you'll see a hipper-than-thou crowd waiting out front for tables.

To get to the *Farmers' Market* from these cafés, return to Fairfax via Beverly and turn right (south); the market is less than half a mile away at Fairfax and Third Street. (The market also can be reached from the Santa Monica Freeway No. 10. Just 3 miles north of the Fairfax exit, you'll spot the market's distinctive, white clock tower with a weather vane on top.)

Started in a vacant lot on the corner of Third Street and Fairfax Avenue, the *Farmers' Market* has been a major Los Angeles attraction for more than 60 years. In July 1934 a number of local farmers formed a cooperative to sell fresh produce at bargain prices. The original market had 18 stalls; today there are more than 160. (You can pick up a map at the *Farmers' Market* office, Gate 1.)

The *Farmers' Market* fell out of fashion during the 1970s, but it came back to life in the late 1980s, when writers from nearby CBS Television City started coming by in the mornings, stopping at *Bob's Coffee and Donut* (phone: 213-933-8929). They would then sit at the outdoor tables, exchanging gripes about actors and producers, and thumb through the "trades." You can pick up copies of *Variety* and the *Hollywood Reporter* at *Al's News* (Oakwood and Fairfax Aves.), one of the best newsstands in Los Angeles.

The writers gave the place an air of sophistication. Soon the casts and crews from the TV shows started coming by as well, and the area was back in vogue. A number of the restaurants became "in" spots. The *Gumbo Pot* (phone: 213-933-0358) became known for the best Cajun-creole food in town. *Kokomo* (phone: 213-933-0773), a New Age American café, won raves for great food (including the best BLT in town) dished up in a lively setting. And *326* (phone: 213-937-2337), named after its address on Fairfax, gained attention for serving fine California wines and beers made at small West Coast breweries such as Anchor Steam and Sierra Nevada.

Everyone has a favorite destination at the *Farmers' Market. Du-Par's* restaurant (phone: 213-933-8446) is known for scrumptious pies and brownies and delicious pancakes and French toast. *Tusquellas Fish & Oyster Bar* (phone: 213-939-2078) serves the best fresh fish and chowders in the market, and also runs a seafood store. Dozens of freshly squeezed fruit and vegetable juices can be had at *Paul's Juice and Salad Bar* (phone: 213-937-9360). Actor Corbin Bernsen has been seen buying the chocolate-covered marshmallow caramels at *Littlejohns English Toffee House* (phone: 213-936-5379), where the candy is made by hand, the way it was back in the 1940s. Various rock stars have been spotted sipping the fresh-squeezed limeades at *Gill's Old-Fashioned Ice Cream* (phone: 213-936-7986), which has been around since 1937.

And, yes, farmers still sell here as well. Try *Farmers' Market Fruit & Produce, Stone's Farm Fresh Produce,* or *Lopez Produce* for fruit and vegetables grown on nearby farms. The corn is picked and sold on the same day, but the prices are a little higher than they were in 1934. The market is closed on major holidays; admission and three-hour parking are free.

Tour 4: Beverly Hills

By all means—if you have the means—you should go to Rodeo Drive and shop till you drop. But don't stop there. Beverly Hills is a beautiful and historic area with stunning homes and parks. You would be remiss if you came here and left with nothing but bulging shopping bags.

Now one of the best-known neighborhoods in all the world, Beverly Hills had a tough time getting off the ground. Originally a Spanish land grant called Rodeo de las Aguas (Gathering of the Waters), the 4,500-acre property was owned by Maria Rita Valdez. In 1852, after repeated Indian attacks, Valdez sold it to two neighbors, who went bust trying to raise wheat on the land.

Several attempts to drill for oil on the property also were unsuccessful, so the land was used to grow lima beans. But at the turn of the century, the Amalgamated Oil Company struck another precious commodity—water. The firm changed its name to the Rodeo Land and Water Company and began an attempt at real-estate development in 1907. Burton E. Green, president of the company, envisioned a planned community of beautiful homes, tree-lined streets, and spacious parks. He called his utopia Beverly Hills after Beverly Farms, Massachusetts, where President Taft was vacationing. Unfortunately, the world didn't beat a path to his door—until 1912, when the ultra-posh *Beverly Hills* hotel (see below) opened. Beverly Hills was incorporated as a village in 1914.

The association of Beverly Hills with luxury and Hollywood magic really began in 1920, when Mary Pickford and Douglas Fairbanks moved in. *Pickfair,* their private estate, a refurbished hunting lodge, came to symbolize the glamour of Hollywood to the outside world. Soon movie moguls and the cream of the Hollywood crop—including Charlie Chaplin, Buster Keaton, Jeanette MacDonald, Gloria Swanson, and Rudolph Valentino—moved into this new playground for the rich, famous, and filmed.

Today, Beverly Hills is still home to movie stars and anyone with a high net worth—but it also has become one of the world's most conspicuous capitals of consumption, with some 300 boutiques, 160 restaurants, five major department stores, and seven luxury hotels. (There are also no less than 5,000 free parking spaces, so finding a place to leave your car shouldn't be a problem.) A stroll through the small commercial heart of the community will afford you many opportunities to dispose of your cash.

Begin your walking (and spending) tour of Beverly Hills at the northeast corner of Beverly Drive and Wilshire Boulevard. You can't miss the striking onion-shape dome of the *Israeli Discount Bank* (206 N. Beverly Dr.): Only in La-La Land would you find an Israeli bank inside something that looks like a mosque. Actually, the Moorish-style building was built in 1925 as a movie house. Called the *Beverly Theater,* it was known as the

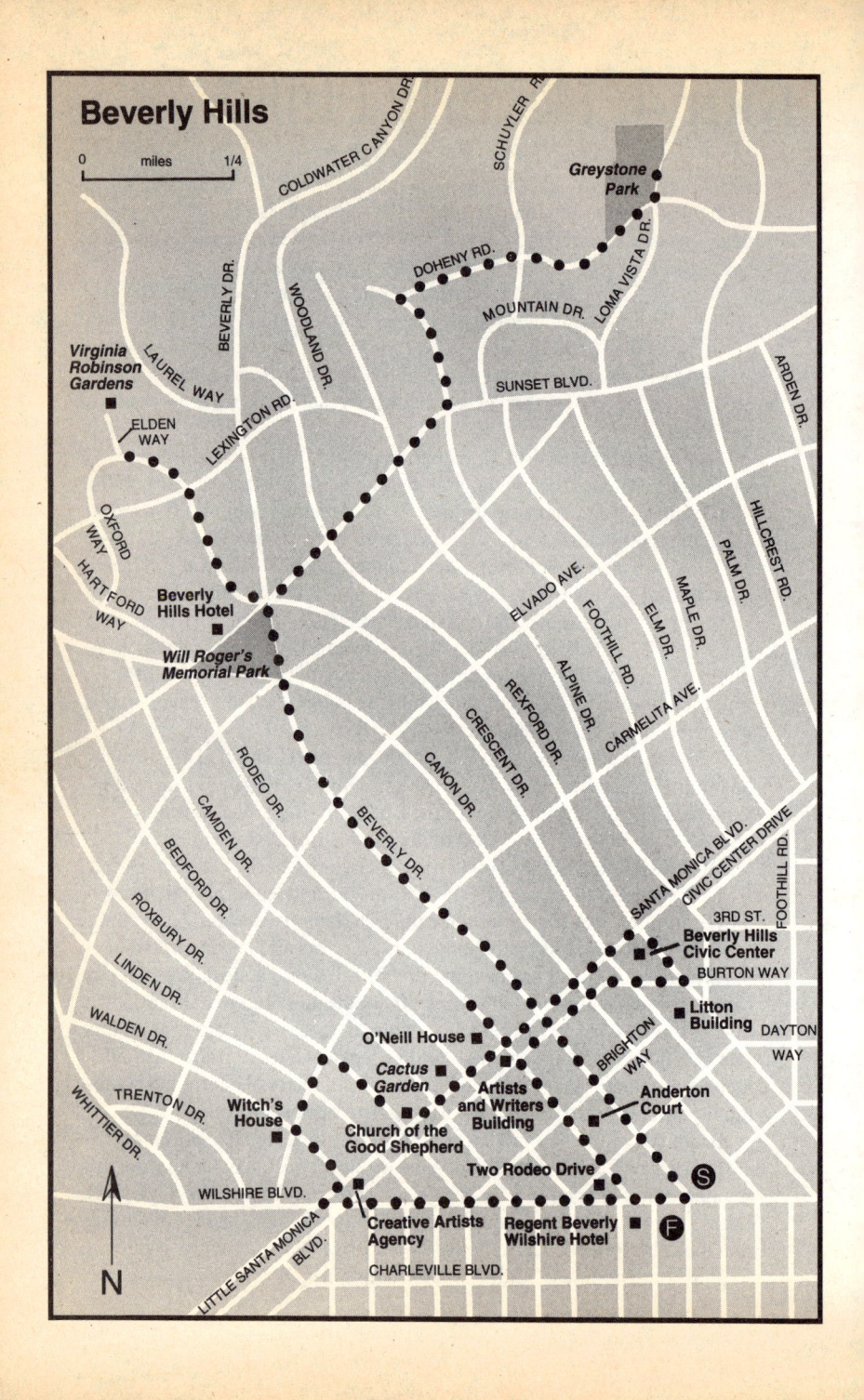

Beverly Hills

"Theater of the Stars" because so many world premieres were shown here from the 1920s to the 1940s. Right next door is *Sterling Plaza,* a handsome Art Deco office tower built in 1929 by Louis B. Mayer.

Go one block west (left) on Wilshire to Rodeo Drive. The magnificent Italian Renaissance–Beaux Arts structure on the south side of the street is the *Regent Beverly Wilshire* hotel (9500 Wilshire Blvd.), built in 1928. Stop in the *Lobby Lounge* for afternoon tea (see "Taking Tea" in *Eating Out,* THE CITY) and check out El Camino Real, the hotel's charming private street.

Now go north (right) on Rodeo Drive, and join the throng of determined shoppers swimming upstream. Saudi princes, Japanese tourists, and the monied international set will be sauntering along with you. On the north side of the intersection of Wilshire Boulevard and Rodeo Drive is *Two Rodeo Drive,* an upscale shopping complex incorporating Via Rodeo, a European-inspired, cobblestone shopping street. On Rodeo between Dayton Way and Brighton Way, stop and admire *Anderton Court* (332 N. Rodeo Dr.), an Art Deco–style shopping complex designed by Frank Lloyd Wright in 1953. Continuing north on Rodeo, between Brighton and Little Santa Monica Boulevard, note the opulent *Rodeo Collection* shopping plaza (421 N. Rodeo Dr.) and its upscale shops, including *Merletto* (425 $^1/_2$ N. Rodeo Dr.; phone: 310-273-1038), *the* place for Italian lingerie. For more on the stores of Rodeo Drive, see *Shopping* in THE CITY.

On the northwest corner of the intersection of Rodeo Drive and Little Santa Monica Boulevard is the *Artists and Writers Building* (9507 Little Santa Monica Blvd.), a small Spanish Colonial structure. Built in the early 1920s at the urging of humorist Will Rogers, it provides office space for creative artists. Billy Wilder, Jack Nicholson, and Ray Bradbury all have been tenants.

Turn right on Little Santa Monica Boulevard and head three blocks east to Crescent Drive. On the corner is a very futuristic gas station with a 1950s cantilevered canopy, the *Union 76.* Across the street is the *Litton Building* (360 N. Cresent Dr.), an office building that was formerly the headquarters of the Music Corporation of America (MCA). An elegant Federal Revival edifice with a grand portico, it was built in 1937. (MCA is now located in Universal City.)

Walk one more block east to Rexford Drive. Go north (left) on Rexford and you can't miss the *Beverly Hills Civic Center.* This ambitious "Maya Deco"-style project links the fire station, police department, and library to the original 1931 Spanish Baroque *Beverly Hills City Hall.* The graceful arches, central rotunda, and landscaped courtyards make this a very civil civic center.

Continue north to Santa Monica Boulevard and head west (left). Between Crescent and Canon Drives, notice the Italian Renaissance–style *US Post Office* (469 N. Crescent Dr.), built in 1933. Inside, this terra cotta and brick landmark has impressive vaulted ceilings covered with mosaics and murals depicting scenes of city street life.

Along Santa Monica Boulevard is a 2-mile stretch of greenery planted with a wide variety of trees, flowers, and shrubs. *Beverly Gardens* was created in 1911 to relieve the stark, barren look of the developing city. In the park, between Beverly and Rodeo Drives, is *Hunter and Hounds,* a statue from the *Château Thierry* in France. The work of Henri Alfred Marie Jacquemart, it was donated by former Beverly Hills residents as a memorial to their son, who was killed in World War I.

Stop on Rodeo Drive; half a block north of Santa Monica Boulevard is a private residence worth noting. Built in 1986, the *O'Neill House* (507 N. Rodeo Dr.) is a fine example of Gaudí-esque Art Nouveau architecture. The designer, Don Ramos, added elaborate mosaic tiles, art-glass windows, and skylights.

Walk back down to Santa Monica Boulevard and the park. Head west (right) one block to Camden Drive. Between Camden and Bedford Drives the *Cactus Garden* is a public space with an incredible collection of cacti and other succulents from around the world.

About one block south, between Bedford and Roxbury Drives, is the oldest church in Beverly Hills. Dedicated in 1925, the *Church of the Good Shepherd* (505 N. Bedford Dr.) has been the scene of some extravagant comings and goings. In 1950 Elizabeth Taylor said "till death do us part" for the first time here (to Conrad "Nicky" Hilton). In 1926 Rudolph Valentino got one of the world's greatest send-offs. Other spectacular funerals have been held here for Gary Cooper, Jimmy Durante, Peter Finch, Alfred Hitchcock, and Rosalind Russell.

Head northwest (right) on Roxbury Drive to Carmelita Avenue. Walk south (left) for two blocks to Walden Drive and follow the bread crumbs to the *Witch's House* (516 N. Walden Dr.). The storybook-style cottage, designed by Henry Oliver, is entered by an arched bridge over a moat. Built in 1920 as an office for a Culver City movie studio, it was moved to Beverly Hills in 1926 and has been a private residence ever since.

Go south, back to Santa Monica Boulevard, on Walden Drive. Walk west (right) one block on Santa Monica, and you'll be at the intersection of Santa Monica and Wilshire Boulevards. The *Electric Fountain,* built in 1930, represents the story of early California history; the statue on top symbolizes an Indian rain prayer.

If you're intrigued by modern architecture, walk one block east to Little Santa Monica Boulevard and stop by the *Creative Artists Agency Building* (9830 Little Santa Monica Blvd.). There's a gigantic Lichtenstein painting in the lobby of this curved marble, glass, and steel I. M. Pei creation. Less than half a block farther along is the stunning *Peninsula Beverly Hills* hotel (9882 Little Santa Monica Blvd.), with its lavish gardens and impressive palazzo-style architecture.

From Little Santa Monica Boulevard walk back east (left) on Wilshire Boulevard to Beverly Drive (where you started). Along with the palm trees, there's lively pedestrian traffic, a parade of snazzy cars, a mixture of new high-rises and older buildings, specialty shops, and some of Los Angeles's best department stores—including *Barneys New York* (9570 Wilshire Blvd.), *Neiman Marcus* (9700 Wilshire Blvd.), and *Saks Fifth Avenue* (9600 Wilshire Blvd.).

Back at Beverly Drive you'll need your car for the second half of the tour. Before heading out, grab a bite at *Nate 'n' Al* (414 N. Beverly Dr.; phone: 310-274-0101), one of the best delis in LA and a longtime favorite with big-name stars. For something a little more upscale dine alfresco at the *Bistro Garden* (176 N. Canon Dr.; phone: 310-550-3900).

This part of the tour takes you to some splendid old Beverly Hills locations. (You might actually want to do this part first or save it for another day's adventure.) Go north on Beverly Drive to Sunset Boulevard. Park and visit *Will Rogers Memorial Park* (9650 Sunset Blvd.). The Oklahoma humorist was sworn in as honorary Mayor of Beverly Hills at a 1926 ceremony held here.

Right behind the park is the renowned *Beverly Hills* hotel (9641 Sunset Blvd.). Referred to as the "Pink Palace," this sprawling, Mission Revival hotel opened in 1912 and quickly became a symbol of Hollywood glamour. Its *Polo Lounge,* a world-famous watering hole for celebrities, was the original home of the "power breakfast" on the West Coast. Both the hotel and restaurant have been undergoing extensive renovations for several years; at press time they were set to reopen this spring.

Because Rodeo Drive gets all the attention, two remarkable sites in the area—the *Virginia Robinson Gardens* and *Greystone Park*—are usually overlooked. Don't leave Beverly Hills without seeing them. To get to the *Virginia Robinson Gardens* (1008 Elden Way; phone: 310-276-5367) from the *Beverly Hills* hotel, go east on Sunset Boulevard, then make a left onto Crescent Drive and a right onto Elden Way. Planted with tropical flowers and palms, this six-acre estate is the oldest in Beverly Hills. It was originally the home of Mr. and Mrs. Harry Robinson (the department store heirs). Tours are given Tuesdays through Fridays. Reservations are necessary; there's an admission charge.

From here return to Sunset Boulevard and turn left. Take Sunset to Foothill Road, turn left, then go right on Doheny and continue east. Turn left on Loma Vista Drive and head to *Greystone Park* (905 Loma Vista Dr.; phone: 310-550-4796). Although the mansion, built in 1928, is now closed to the public, the panoramic view of Beverly Hills and the greater Los Angeles area is worth the trip. The 18 acres of landscaped gardens are open daily; no admission charge. Classical music concerts and other cultural events are often held at this park, a lovely place to end your tour of Beverly Hills.

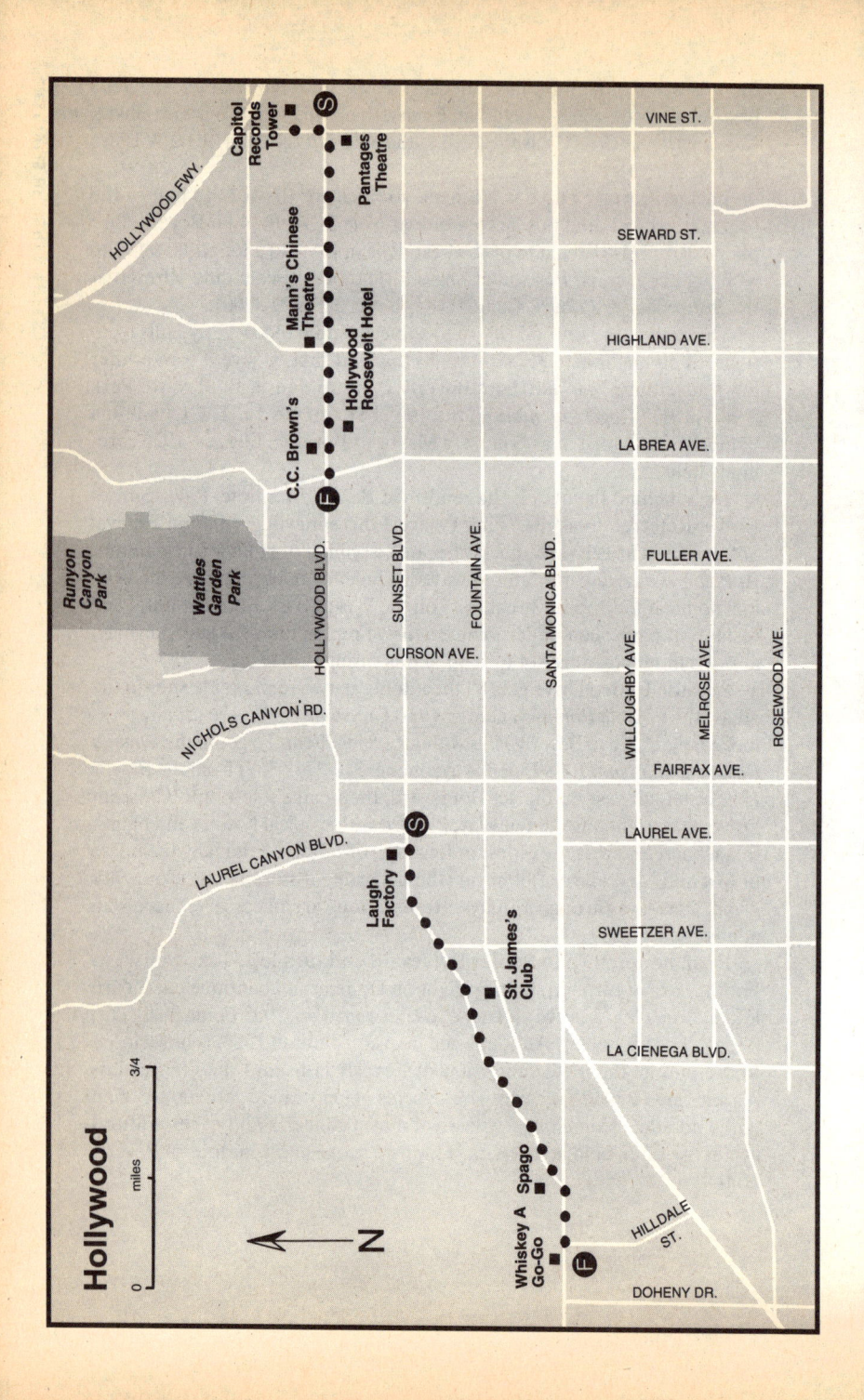

Hollywood

Tour 5: Hollywood

To most people Los Angeles is synonymous with Hollywood, where "California Dreaming" really began. Taking in the sights along Hollywood and Sunset Boulevards is easy to do on your own. These two walks cover a total of 1½ miles and last approximately two hours. There are parking lots throughout the area, and valet parking at many clubs and restaurants.

Start your Sunset Boulevard walk at the *Laugh Factory* comedy club (8001 W. Sunset Blvd.), where West Hollywood really starts. This part of Sunset is 100% LA, and the farther west you stroll, the more tony shops, chic cafés, and lovely hotels you'll see, many of which are favorite celebrity haunts. Though most of the original sights are gone, this still is one of LA's trendiest and most attractive streets.

Across the boulevard from the *Laugh Factory* is the 30,000-square-foot *8000 Sunset* mall (8000 Sunset Blvd.), home of the *Virgin Megastore* (phone: 213-650-8666), the first US outlet of the international music store chain, which carries everything from tapes and CDs to accessories and clothing; the *Westward Ho Market* (phone: 213-650-5591), a grocery with a coffee bar and one of the finest bakeries in town; and the five-screen *Laemmle Theatre* complex (phone: 213-848-3500). Nearby is the *St. James's Club* (8358 Sunset Blvd.), one of the best examples of Art Deco architecture in town. Once an apartment building to the stars, it is now an upper-crust, swank hotel. The *Comedy Store* (8433 Sunset Blvd.; phone: 213-656-6225), a bit farther on, is a hot comedy club.

The *Playboy* building (8560 Sunset Blvd.) is average looking except for the black-and-white bunny on the side. Hugh Hefner used to live in a penthouse here. *Spago* (see *Eating Out* in THE CITY) is *the* dining place for anyone who wants to see or be seen.

A bit farther west on Sunset, *Book Soup* (8818 Sunset Blvd.; phone: 310-659-3110) not only has one of the widest selections of books and magazines in the city but also is another place to be seen: Madonna and other superstars catch up on their reading by browsing the aisles here. *Whiskey á Go-Go* (8901 Sunset Blvd.; phone: 310-652-4202) has a place in music lore: In the 1960s and 1970s this club launched the careers of some of the country's best-known recording artists, including *The Doors*. Today bands still pack the club, hoping to be discovered.

To get to Hollywood Boulevard for the second walk, drive east along Santa Monica Boulevard to Vine Street, then turn left and continue north. Start at the *Capitol Records Tower* (1750 N. Vine St.). A futuristic, lavender building resembling a stack of records with a stylus on top, it can be seen from the Hollywood Freeway. (You're in Hollywood now, kids!)

Walk south down Vine Street and turn right (west) at the legendary corner of Hollywood and Vine. Though a bit disappointing in real life, the

Walk of Fame, with 2,029 stars embedded in the pavement to date, is at your feet. Stretching from here to La Brea Avenue, the *Walk* recently received a $4.4-million enhancement that includes rows of newly planted palm trees and special lighting at night.

Stroll along Hollywood Boulevard through the newly christened Cinema District—eight blocks of historic landmarks beginning with the *Pantages Theatre* (6233 Hollywood Blvd.; phone: 213-468-1700), a must-see example of Art Deco at its finest. It's one of LA's premier theaters, with an ornate exterior and a spectacular, plush interior. Opened in 1930, the theater hosted the Academy Awards from 1949 to 1959.

Hollywood's oldest restaurant, *Musso & Frank Grill* (see *Eating Out* in THE CITY) was opened in 1919 and remodeled in 1937. Many well-known wordsmiths—F. Scott Fitzgerald, Ernest Hemingway, William Faulkner, and Lowell Thomas among them—have drowned their sorrows at the mahogany bar here. Some say that the martinis served in this dark, wood-paneled refuge are the best in town.

Housed in a pink-on-gray building (you can't miss it), the *Fredericks of Hollywood Lingerie Museum* (6608 Hollywood Blvd.; phone: 213-466-8506) spotlights the "unmentionables" once worn by Madonna, Cher, Mae West, Judy Garland, Zsa Zsa Gabor, Tony Curtis—yes, Tony Curtis!—and others. It's open daily; no admission charge.

The *Hollywood Egyptian Theater* (6712 Hollywood Blvd.; phone: 213-467-6167) was once the quintessential expression of Hollywood glamour. The site of the first movie premiere in Tinseltown (*Robin Hood,* starring Douglas Fairbanks, in 1922), the theater has suffered from years of neglect and is no longer open to the public, but its exterior is still quite a sight.

Another stunning Hollywood Boulevard landmark is the *El Capitan Theatre* (6835 Hollywood Blvd.), opened in 1926 as a hall for song-and-dance variety shows. In 1941, when Orson Welles was unable to find a movie theater willing to screen *Citizen Kane,* his first feature film, he held the world premiere at *El Capitan.* The theater was remodeled as a movie house in 1942 and became the *Paramount.* (Cecil B. De Mille's *Reap the Wild Wind* was the feature presentation.) Today first-run movies can be seen in this gilded, Old World setting.

Built in 1927, *Mann's Chinese Theatre* (6925 Hollywood Blvd.), formerly *Grauman's,* remains one of Hollywood's most exciting—and crowded—spots; its Chinese-temple façade still is eye-catching after all these years. Compare your hands and feet to the celebrities' prints immortalized in cement. You can even see a movie here. (Also see *Special Places* in THE CITY.)

Also built in 1927, the *Radisson Hollywood Roosevelt* hotel (see *Checking In* in THE CITY) was the site of the first Academy Awards presentation and a favorite gathering place for Hollywood royalty. Today luxury and style are mostly absent (although the building currently is undergoing a complete restoration), but in 1987 David Hockney painted a free-form design in blue on the bottom of the pool. The hotel's *Cinegrille* has become one of the hottest spots for jazz (see *Music* in THE CITY).

Now it's time for a treat. Stop into *C. C. Brown's* (7007 Hollywood Blvd.; phone: 213-462-9262), a turn-of-the-century ice-cream parlor. Originally opened downtown in 1906, it moved to this location in 1929. Indulge in one of the best hot-fudge sundaes you've ever had in this old-fashioned soda shop. Not too far away is the *Hollywood Galaxy* (7201 Hollywood Blvd.)—a high-tech, trilevel entertainment complex with a broad multileveled walkway circling a courtyard. It's entertaining just to walk around this 148,000-square-foot funhouse; you also can enjoy ethnic food at its international food court, shop in its many stores, and take in a movie at its multiplex theater—the perfect way to end a Hollywood walk.

Westwood

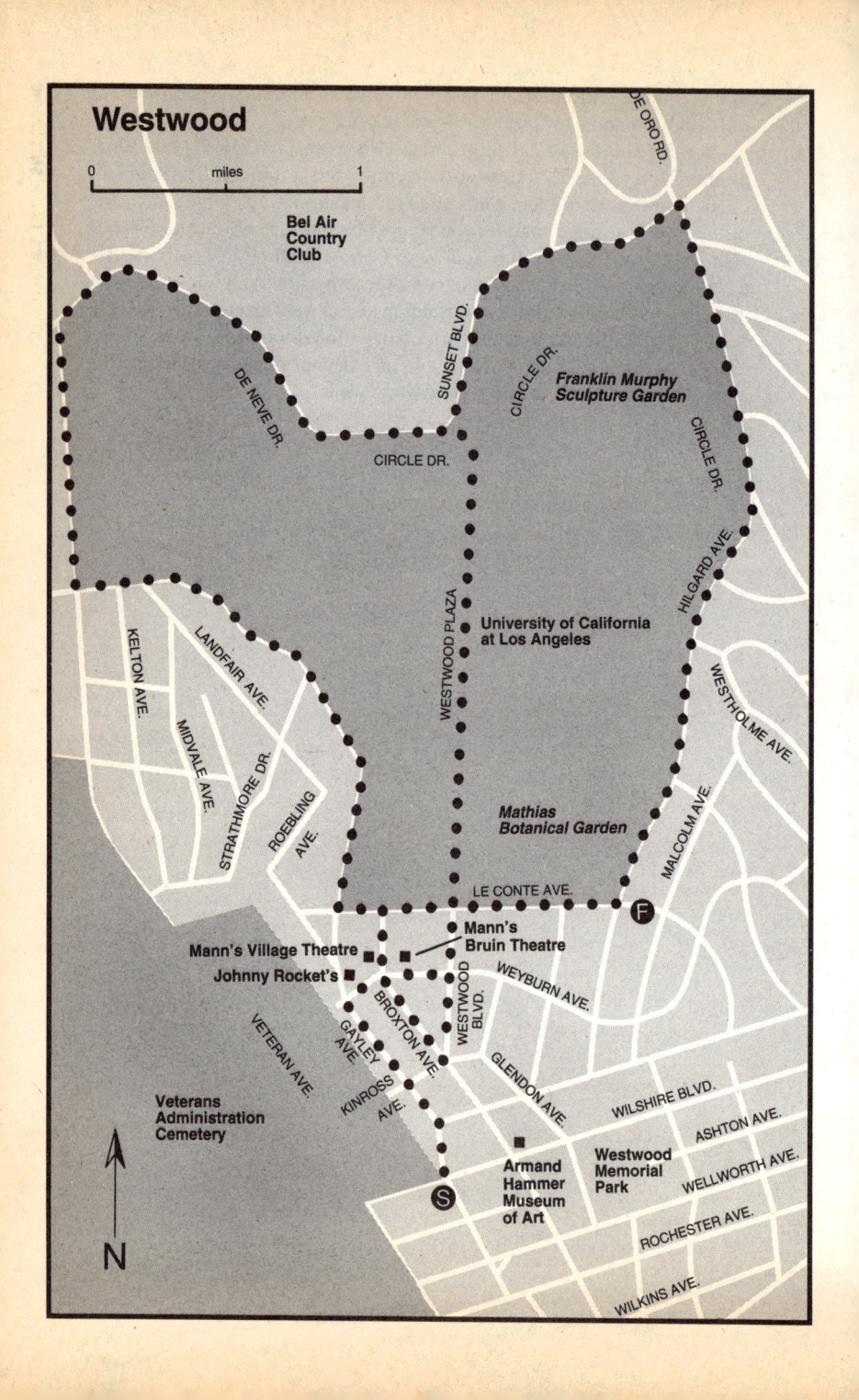

Tour 6: Westwood

The closest thing Los Angeles has to a college town, Westwood Village is affluent, clean-cut, and bustling with activity. Here are comfortable movie theaters, appealing restaurants, lots of clothing stores catering to the college crowd, and the beautifully landscaped *UCLA* campus to explore.

The area was developed in the 1920s as a Mediterranean-style shopping village, and all its buildings—homes, shops, banks—were to have a Spanish Colonial look. More recent development has eroded the spirit of the place, but, happily, a few examples of the original architecture remain.

Westwood is bounded by the fashionable neighborhoods of Brentwood, Bel-Air, and Beverly Hills. Its heart is between Wilshire Boulevard to the south (lined with skyscrapers and pricey high-rises), Le Conte Avenue to the north, Gayley Avenue to the west, and Westwood Boulevard to the east. To get there take the Santa Monica Freeway No. 10 west to the San Diego Freeway No. 405 north, and exit at Wilshire Boulevard East. When you get off the freeway, continue east for a half mile and make a left (north) onto Gayley Avenue. If this is your lucky day, you might find a parking spot on the street. If not, there are parking lots all over the neighborhood.

The neighborhood is fairly small and extremely easy to navigate. Before beginning the walking tour, there are two sites near the starting point that might capture your interest. The *Armand Hammer Museum of Art* (10899 Wilshire Blvd.; phone: 310-443-7000), on the northeast corner of Westwood and Wilshire Boulevards, houses the Rembrandts, van Goghs, Cézannes, Goyas and other masterpieces that the late industrialist collected during his lifetime. Closed Mondays; admission charge. *Pierce Brothers Westwood Village Memorial Park* (1218 Glendon Ave.; phone: 310-474-1579) is the cemetery where Marilyn Monroe, Natalie Wood, Armand Hammer, and other notables are buried (also see *Grave Matters* in DIVERSIONS).

To begin the walking tour, walk north on Gayley Avenue from the corner of Wilshire Boulevard. Along the way you'll pass *Light & Healthy* (1115 Gayley Ave.; phone: 310-208-1767), an inexpensive but very good sushi bar. Continue north on Gayley until you come to Weyburn Avenue. Turn right on Weyburn and stroll past the cafés and eateries such as *Johnny Rocket's* (10959 Weyburn Ave.; phone: 310-824-5656), an always-packed, 1950s-style diner famous for its burgers and shakes. If your thirst is more for knowledge, stop by the *Alexandria II Bookstore* (10944 Weyburn Ave.; phone: 310-824-7575), an enchanting haunt for New Age and metaphysical paraphernalia, books, and tapes.

Two of the most beautifully preserved movie theaters in Los Angeles are on the east and west corners of Weyburn and Broxton Avenues. *Mann's Village Theatre* (961 Broxton Ave.; phone: 310-208-5576), known as *The Fox,* opened in 1931 as part of the Fox Studios' theater chain. It was built in the Spanish Colonial style of early Westwood, and its snazzy exterior and plush interior made it a popular choice for big Hollywood premieres; its gleaming white tower dominates the village. Across the street, on the eastern corner, is the less spectacular, but still striking, 1930s Moderne *Mann's Bruin Theatre* (948 Broxton Ave.; phone: 310-208-8998).

Walk west along Weyburn and turn right (south) down Broxton Avenue to *Stratton's Grill* (1037 Broxton Ave.; phone: 310-208-0488), one of Westwood's most popular watering holes. The outdoor plaza on the western side of the street at the end of Broxton Avenue is another big draw. Silver jewelry, leather goods, and a variety of offbeat knickknacks can be purchased from the street vendors.

Broxton ends at the intersection of Westwood Boulevard and Kinross Avenue. At the end of Broxton note one of Westwood's first Spanish-style landmarks. This temple-like structure, built in 1929, now houses *Contempo Casuals* (1099 Westwood Blvd.; phone: 310-474-1485), which carries a collection of stylish women's clothing. Turn left (north) up Westwood Boulevard. Around the corner on Weyburn Avenue is *Butler/Gabriel Books* (10930 Weyburn Ave.; phone: 310-208-4424), one of LA's very best bookstores.

Make a left (west) at Le Conte Avenue and go one block to Broxton Avenue. Make a left (south) and stroll down the northern stretch of this shop-lined street until you come to Weyburn Avenue, then make another left. Wander past the T-shirt shops and cafés. When you come to Westwood Boulevard, turn left (north) and follow it to the *University of California, Los Angeles (UCLA)* campus. (Once you pass Le Conte Avenue, Westwood Boulevard becomes Westwood Plaza.) If you prefer not to walk, get on the free shuttle van that stops at Westwood parking lots and take it to the campus (phone: 310-825-4321 for shuttle information).

UCLA is a large and confusing campus. If you'd like a guide, free tours are offered weekdays. Led by students, the 90-minute tours emphasize the history of the university and take visitors through its noteworthy buildings. Reservations are required (phone: 310-825-4321). Otherwise, begin by picking up a map at the *Visitors' Center* in the *Uberroth Building* (phone: 310-206-8147). But be warned: Even with a map you might get confused.

Fortunately, this is a very pretty place in which to get lost. Over the years since *UCLA* moved to Westwood in 1929, this beautifully landscaped, 411-acre campus has become a city within a city. Allow plenty of time to wander the shady, tree-lined walks and appreciate the views, grassy knolls, gardens, and architecture.

Generally, the landscaping is more impressive than the buildings, but the first four, built in 1929 around the original quadrangle, are stunning. Known as the *Quad,* these four buildings—*Royce Hall, Haines Hall, Kinsey Hall,* and the *Powell Library*—are Italian Romanesque brick palazzi.

If you're dying for a *UCLA* sweatshirt—or haven't found a map yet—stop at the *UCLA* bookstore in the *Ackerman Student Union* by the *Bruin* bear statue. There's also a cafeteria in the building with a full selection at low prices. And don't miss the *Franklin Murphy Sculpture Garden* at the northeast end of the campus, where major works by Henry Moore, Joan Miró, Henri Matisse, Auguste Renoir, and others are displayed. This is a quiet spot to sit and contemplate the meaning of life—or to decide where to have dinner.

The northwest part of the campus is a lush, green, hilly paradise, best explored on foot. Take your time and enjoy the pleasant views and wooded areas. Sunset Boulevard, lined with sumptuous estates, is the northern border of the campus.

Hilgard Avenue, which forms the eastern border, is a stretch of well-tended sorority houses from Le Conte Avenue up to about Westholme Avenue. James Dean, one of *UCLA's* most famous dropouts, lived in the *Sigma Nu* house at 601 Gayley Avenue. As you head south from Sunset Boulevard, admire the houses. Then stop at the *Mathias Botanical Garden*, a woodsy retreat with exotic plants, right off Hilgard in the southeast part of the campus.

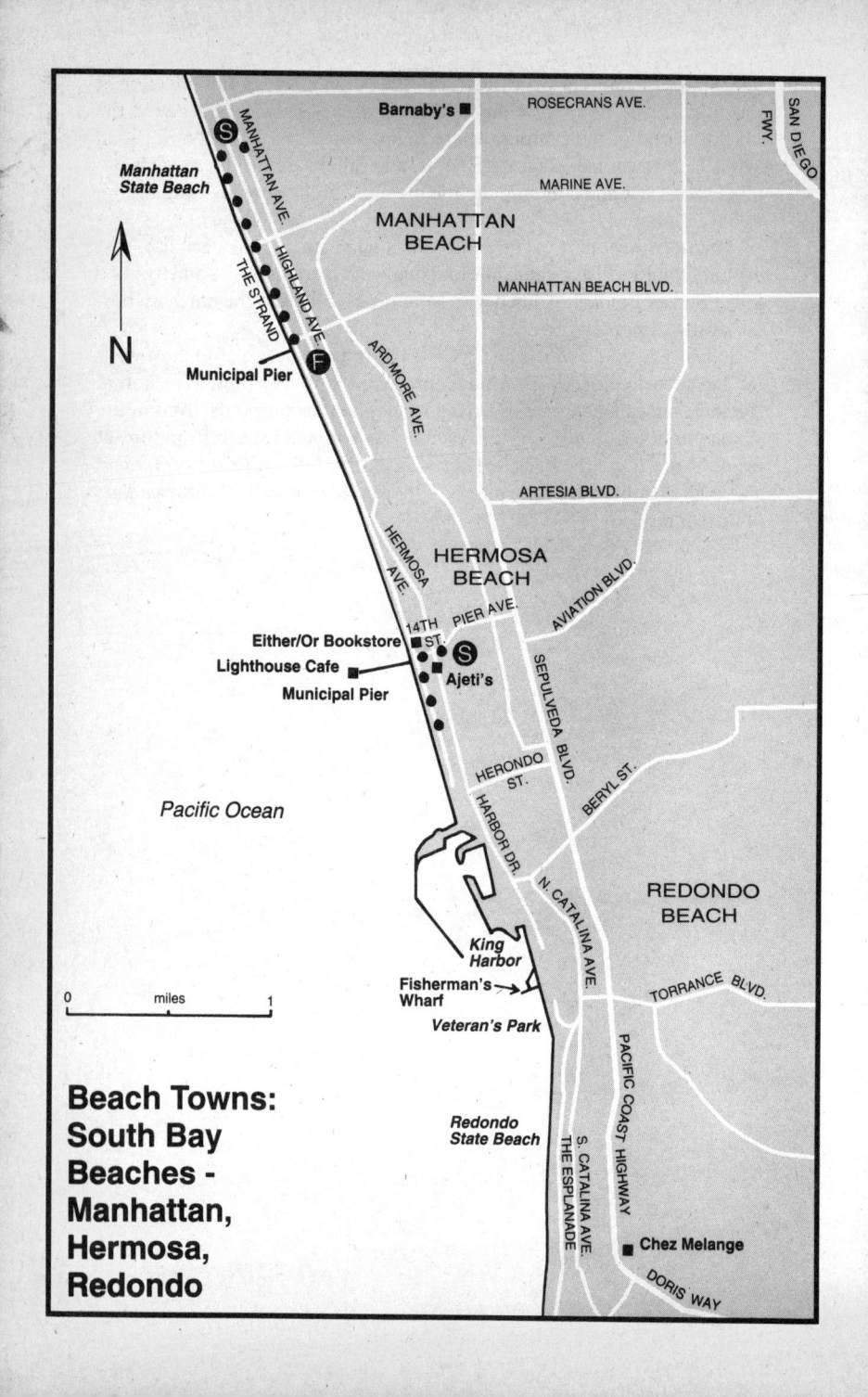

Beach Towns: South Bay Beaches - Manhattan, Hermosa, Redondo

Tour 7: Beach Towns
South Bay Beaches—
Manhattan, Hermosa, Redondo

South of Venice is a trio of beach towns—Manhattan Beach, Hermosa Beach, and Redondo Beach—that epitomize the Southern California "life's a beach" lifestyle. Originally just summer resorts, these beachfront oases have become thriving, year-round communities. Although California has other, more spectacular beaches, these towns offer a special taste of beach life.

Manhattan Beach is the trendiest of the beach towns—a yuppified, upscale, commuter community. Hermosa Beach is the quintessential laid-back beach town with run-down charm. Redondo Beach is more of a resort, with big oceanfront hotels and restaurants. In each the activity centers around the pier and in the shops and restaurants along the waterfront.

The development of the area dates back to 1907, when the owner of the *Redondo* hotel in what is now Redondo Beach was looking for an advertising gimmick to attract guests. While on vacation in Hawaii he saw a surfer named George Freeth riding the waves. Back in California, with Freeth as his star attraction, he set up surfing exhibitions. Every Sunday thousands flocked to the beach in front of the hotel to watch the new sport.

Over the years the popularity of the area—and the sport—continued to grow, creating a rich new vein of California culture. In the 1960s a group of local blond, blue-eyed surfers, who called themselves the *Beach Boys,* started singing, and the rest, as they say, is history. If you hold a Redondo Beach seashell to your ear, you can almost hear the strains of "Surfin' USA."

If you're interested in a good workout, the extremely popular *South Bay Bicycle Trail* runs along the water for 20 miles from the Santa Monica Pier down through Manhattan, Hermosa, and Redondo to the city of Torrance. You can pick it up at any point, and it's a great way to experience these towns. Bike rental shops to try are *Fun Bunns* (1144 Highland Ave., Manhattan Beach; phone: 310-545-3300) and *Jeffers* (1338 The Strand, Hermosa Beach; phone: 310-372-9492).

Our tour starts at Manhattan Beach, the first of the three that you encounter when traveling south from Los Angeles. To get there, take the San Diego Freeway No. 405 south, exit on Rosecrans Avenue, and go west. In a few miles Rosecrans ends at Highland Avenue in Manhattan Beach. Make a left (south) onto Highland Avenue and continue south. Park along the street.

A hotbed of funky chic, Manhattan Beach is the place where arbitrageurs and the smart young producer set live before making the big step up to Malibu. The steep streets and pastel-colored bungalows are reminiscent of

San Francisco (although these days a lot of the bungalows are being torn down to make way for ultramodern glass and metal structures). Walking along The Strand by the water here is a real treat; the magnificent homes, many costing upward of $3 million, are something out of the movies. The *Municipal Pier* is another good vantage point for gazing out to sea.

Start the day off right at *Bill's Pancake House* (1305 Highland Ave.; phone: 310-545-5177), where cheddar cheese–bacon waffles and Istanbul omelettes are the specialties. But prepare to wait: This funky little place is the most popular spot around.

Manhattan Avenue, two blocks up from The Strand, is a pretty street where the locals congregate nearby at such trendy restaurants as *Sunsets* (117 Manhattan Beach Blvd.; phone: 310-545-2523), an ideal place to watch the day end. Or, if you prefer an Italian feast, try *Mangiamo* (128 Manhattan Beach Blvd.; phone: 310-318-3434) or *Lido di Manhattan* (1550 Rosecrans Ave.; phone: 310-536-0730); two of the best restaurants in town, they're both owned by Ron Guidone. Shop for beach gear in chic boutiques like *Pete's Place* (1100 Manhattan Ave.; phone: 310-372-0900), with its string bikinis and outrageous swimwear designs.

Farther inland, near the *Manhattan Village Shopping Center* on Sepulveda Boulevard between Rosecrans and Marine, is *Barnaby's* (3501 Sepulveda Blvd.; phone: 310-545-8466), an 18th-century hostelry that puts up guests in style and offers English breakfasts and dinners. Head over to the delightful *Manhattan Market Place* (1570 Rosecrans Ave.), a plaza full of shops and restaurants. In the plaza is *Bristol Farms,* an upscale market stocked to the rafters with exotic wines, cheeses, and other food products.

Return to Highland Avenue in Manhattan and continue south on Highland, which turns into Hermosa Avenue and takes you to Hermosa Beach. Continue south on Hermosa Avenue until you come to 14th Street. You should have no trouble finding parking. (There are several metered municipal lots in town, so go armed with plenty of quarters; tourists are not exempt from parking fines.)

Hermosa is less affluent, and certainly less pretentious, than Manhattan Beach. Simple and easy to get around, the town shuns expensive boutiques and restaurants. There's a blue-collar feel about the place, and what it lacks in polish it makes up for in friendly, small-town atmosphere: The folks here are more concerned with welcoming visitors than impressing them.

As in Manhattan Beach, stroll along The Strand. Here are a number of inexpensive shops and small restaurants, such as the delightful *Good Stuff* (13th St. and The Strand; phone: 310-374-2334), which offers casual patio dining and healthy food. Nearby, on 22nd Street and Hermosa Avenue, is the *Bottle Inn* (26 22nd St.; phone: 310-376-9595), featuring solid Italian fare.

For more activity walk out on the pier and head up Pier Avenue. The *Lighthouse Café* (30 Pier Ave.; phone: 310-376-9833) is a music club that's been going strong since the 1950s. Make a point of stopping in at the

Either/Or Bookstore (124 Pier Ave.; phone: 310-374-2060). If you're really adventuresome, have dinner at *Ajeti's* (425 Pier Ave.; phone: 310-379-9012), an authentic Albanian restaurant. Or try *Casablanca* (53 Pier Ave.; phone: 310-379-4177), one of the area's most romantic eateries, with cozy booths and a lovely atmosphere.

The third town south of LA is Redondo Beach. To get here follow Hermosa Avenue south until it turns into Harbor Drive, then follow the signs to King Harbor. (There are several huge parking garages nearby.)

Although popular since the turn of the century, this beach community has a newer feel than Hermosa and Manhattan, and the large hotels and apartment buildings that line the coast make it more like a resort. Marinas dominate King Harbor—boats are everywhere, as are big-name restaurants and hotel chains. The area is family-oriented, and it caters to tourists in a big way.

In Redondo what was The Strand becomes The Esplanade. Go for a stroll, check out the beach activity, and enjoy great views of the ocean. Walk down to the water and kick off your shoes. For more browsing wander over to Catalina Avenue. *Chez Mélange* (1716 Pacific Coast Hwy.; phone: 310-540-1222), one of the hottest restaurants in the South Bay area, has a champagne bar and a menu that ranges from Cajun to Oriental.

The *Redondo Beach Marina,* the *International Boardwalk,* and the pier *(Fisherman's Wharf)* are lined with souvenir shops and seafood restaurants—the latter stay open late on summer evenings. The charming *Portofino Inn* (260 Portofino Way; phone 310-379-8481) is a good bet for overnight accommodations. Interesting dining choices include *Tony's on the Pier* (210 *Fisherman's Wharf;* phone: 310-374-9246), where the food is as good as the ocean view. Locals and tourists alike flock to retro-looking *Millie Riera's Seafood Grotto* (1700 The Esplanade; phone: 310-375-0531) for generous portions of home-style cooking (mostly seafood) and spectacular sunsets.

Catalina

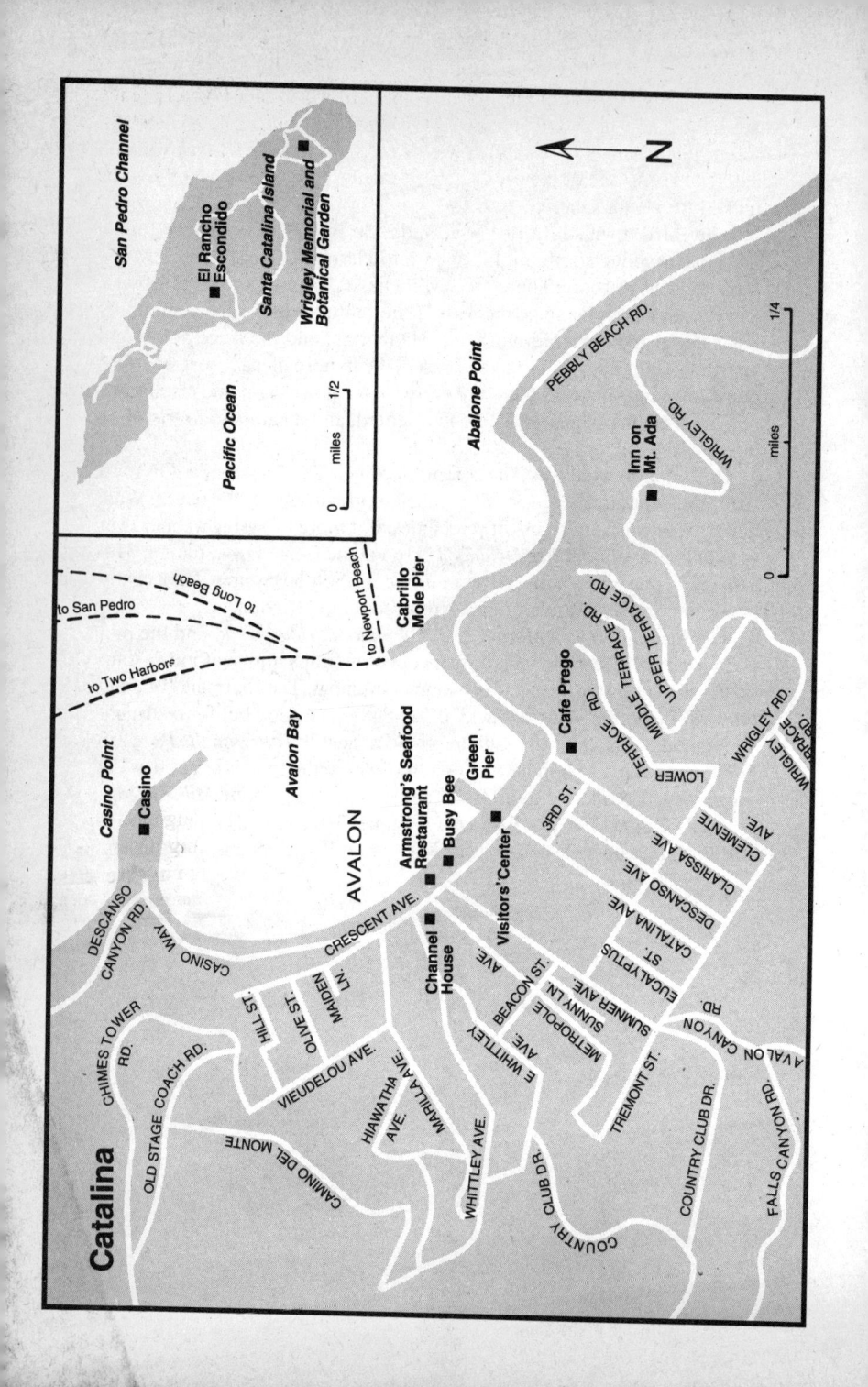

Tour 8: Catalina

To experience what California was like before the freeways, land booms, overbuilding, and smog, take a slow boat to Santa Catalina Island—referred to by one and all as Catalina. Don't be surprised when the ferry captain calls out: "We're docking in the town of Avalon, on the island of Catalina. Passengers are advised to set their watches back 50 years."

Indeed, Catalina Island, 22 miles from Los Angeles Harbor across the San Pedro Channel, is what the whole California coast once was like. The sleepy little town of Avalon is a charming, old-fashioned beach community, and the rest of the island is wilderness. Wild goats, boars, and a herd of bison (left by the film crew of *The Vanishing American* in 1924) roam free. From the moment you set foot in Avalon, you'll be caught up in the spirit of the place.

Today the *Santa Catalina Island Conservancy*—a nonprofit foundation—has title to 86% of this island; its goal is to preserve its natural resources. Until 1975 Catalina Island was the domain of the Wrigley family, chewing-gum tycoons and longtime owners of the Chicago *Cubs*. In 1919 William Wrigley Jr. purchased this 28-by-8-mile piece of paradise for use as a combination tourist attraction, private estate, and spring training camp for the *Cubs*. The town of Avalon already was there, built in the late 19th century by developer George Shatto. But it was Wrigley Jr. who turned the village into a major tourist destination, topping it off with the wonderful *Casino* (actually a theater) at the end of the harbor.

You can make this trip back in time by boat, helicopter, or small plane (for further information, see below). Flying is faster, but arriving by boat is part of the charm. As you dock, the ocean fog lifts, revealing the picturesque harbor of Avalon Bay and the mountain peaks rising in the distance. Come for the day or stay a while at one of the many lovely little hotels. There also are camping grounds for outdoors enthusiasts. Summertime is the high season here. Spring and fall actually are nicer, and the hotel rates are lower, but many of the shops and restaurants are closed.

The ferry boats to Catalina disembark at *Cabrillo Mole Pier*. Everything is within easy walking distance, but most of the activity is centered on Crescent Avenue. The town of Avalon, a delightful mix of Mediterranean and Victorian architecture, is small enough to find your way around easily. It takes about a half hour to walk from *Cabrillo Mole* to the other end of Crescent Avenue, where the *Casino* is.

Start your visit by walking west on Pebbly Beach Road to Crescent Avenue. Stop at the *Visitors' Center* on the corner of Crescent and Catalina Avenues, across from *Green Pier* (it's easy to find; the ferry boat's crew can direct you), for a map and other useful information. Rental cars are not allowed on the island, so if you're not in the mood to walk, ask about golf cart and bicycle rentals. The center also has lots of information on organized tours; it's closed weekends and holidays (phone: 310-510-2000).

From here follow Crescent Avenue. It's flat most of the way, although the side streets off it are fairly steep. Along the waterfront are plenty of stores, food stands, restaurants, and curio shops.

At the end of the avenue is the *Casino,* an eccentric bit of Spanish Mediterranean and Art Deco architecture. It's really a combination 1,000-seat movie theater and 20,000-square-foot grand ballroom, boasting what is supposedly the largest circular dance floor in the world. During the 1930s all the famous big bands—Glenn Miller, Benny Goodman, Tommy Dorsey—played the *Casino Ballroom,* and all of Los Angeles dreamed of spending a weekend on Catalina Island. Today you can still dance to big-band music on weekends, see first-run movies, or just go on a guided tour of this fabulous place (phone: 310-510-2000).

There are many other things to do on a trip to Catalina besides strolling through Avalon. Visit the *Wrigley Memorial and Botanical Garden* (1400 Avalon Canyon Rd.; phone: 310-510-2288), which is open daily and charges admission; go for a ride in a glass-bottom boat (the waters around Catalina are known for exquisite marine life); take a tour around the island to see the wildlife and the Arabian stallions at the Wrigley family's *El Rancho Escondido* on the west side of the island; or rent a golf cart and tootle around on your own.

If all that fresh air is making you hungry, the first restaurant you'll spot in Avalon is *Café Prego* (603 Crescent Ave.; phone: 310-510-1218); serving dinner only, it offers Old World charm and good pasta and seafood dishes. Another good choice is *Armstrong's Seafood* restaurant (306-A Crescent Ave.; phone: 310-510-0113), which features mesquite-grilled fish. Right next door is the *Busy Bee* (306-B Crescent Ave.; phone: 310-510-1983); this popular local hangout is one of the few places on the island open for breakfast, lunch, and dinner. Enjoy tasty salads, sandwiches, burgers, vegetable platters, and margaritas—and a picturesque view of the harbor, particularly at sunset. Other eateries with good food and great harbor views are *Pirrone's* (417 Crescent Ave.; phone: 310-510-0333) and the *Channel House* (205 Crescent Ave.; phone: 310-510-1617). For a quick snack try a delicious abalone burger from one of the food stands out on the pier. At the *Chi-Chi Club* (107 Sumner Ave.; phone: 310-510-2828) "happy hour" starts at 11 AM on weekdays, and performances of jazz and bluegrass are held in the evenings.

Chances are you'll want to stay on Catalina for more than a day. If so, there are a number of good hotels from which to choose. The gorgeous *Inn on Mt. Ada* (398 Wrigley Rd.; phone: 310-510-2030), built in 1921, is the former Wrigley mansion. There are six lavishly decorated rooms with spectacular views. The venerable *Zane Grey* hotel (199 Chimes Tower Rd.; phone: 310-510-0966) was originally built in 1926 as a summer home for the novelist. This 18-room Hopi-style pueblo sits high on a bluff above the harbor. (Even if you're just here on a day trip, these two places are worth looking at.) Down on Crescent Avenue, the *Vista del Mar* hotel (417 Crescent Ave.; phone: 310-510-1452) is right in the center of town. There are 14 Mediterranean-style rooms with fireplaces. The 72-room *Pavilion Lodge* (513 Crescent Ave.; phone: 310-510-1788) also is in the heart of Avalon. The *Hotel Catalina* (129 Whittley Ave.; phone: 310-510-0027 or 800-540-0184) is a renovated Victorian era building; built in 1892, the 32-unit facility offers rooms and cottages.

GETTING TO AND AROUND CATALINA

BY BOAT This is the most popular and least expensive way to go. Boats leave from the *Catalina Island Terminal* at Long Beach and San Pedro Harbors. Reservations are advised. Arrive early, especially during the summer season. The ride on *Catalina Cruises* (phone: 800-888-5939) takes about two hours. The boats are big (accommodating several hundred passengers) and comfortable, and snacks are served on board. *Catalina Express*'s (phone: 310-519-1212) airline-style 60-seaters make the trip in 90 minutes. It's a faster but, some say, less enjoyable trip.

BY AIR The helicopter ride from the *Catalina Island Terminal* at Long Beach or San Pedro takes about 15 minutes to the Pebbly Beach heliport. There also are several other departure points, so call for directions. Reservations must be made a week in advance. Helicopter companies include *Helitrans* (phone: 310-548-1314; 800-262-1472) and *Island Express* (phone: 310-491-5550).

TOURS Several firms offer tours of Catalina Island, including the *Santa Catalina Island Company* (phone: 310-510-2000), *Discovery Tours* (phone: 310-510-2500), and *Catalina Adventure Tours* (phone: 310-510-0409). Book tours at the boat terminal ticket booths in Long Beach or San Pedro or at the *Visitors' Center* (see above) when you arrive on the island.

Index

Index

ABC TV, 100
Accommodations
   bed and breakfast, 61
   hotels, 43, 60–70
      grand hotels and special havens, 61–63, 96
   on the Queen Mary, 41
   Relais & Châteaux, 63
   Santa Barbara, 43
African Marketplace & Cultural Fair, 47
Ahmanson Theater, 37, 58, 98–99
Airplane travel, 9–12
   charter flights, 10
   consumer protection, 12
   discounts on scheduled flights, 10–12
      bartered travel sources, 12
      consolidators and bucket shops, 11
      courier travel, 10–11
      generic air travel, 12
      last-minute travel clubs, 11–12
   insurance, 16
   scheduled flights, 9–10
      baggage, 10
      fares, 9
      reservations, 9
      seating, 9
      smoking, 10
      special meals, 10
   transportation from the airport to the city, 12–13

Armand Hammer Museum of Art, 47, 145
Audience participation (in television shows), 99–101
Automated teller machines (ATMs), 22
Automobiles. *See* Car, traveling by

Banking hours. *See* Business and shopping hours
Baseball, 56
Basketball, 56
Beaches, 40–41, 93–94, 95–96, 107–9, 113, 148–51
   See also specific beaches
Beach towns (Manhattan, Hermosa, Redondo)
   map, 148
   walking tour, 149–51
Bed and breakfast establishments, 61
Beverly Hills, 36
   maps, 2, 136
   walking tour, 135–39
Bicycling, 56
Boats. *See* Ship, traveling by
Brea Tar Pits, La, 39
Burke Williams Day Spa & Massage Centre, Santa Monica, 105–6
Bus, traveling by, 12, 44
Business and shopping hours, 22–23

Cabrillo Beach, 108
Capitan Theatre, El, 142
Car, traveling by
   insurance, 13, 16
   maps, 43–44
   renting a car, 13
Cash machines. *See* Automated
   teller machines
Catalina Island, 41
   map, 152
   transportation to and around, 155
   walking tour, 152–55
CBS TV, 100, 131
Cemeteries, 41, 103–5, 145
Central Library, 124
Charter flights, 10
Chinatown, 38, 121–22
Cinco de Mayo (festival), 47
City Hall, 31, 37, 123–24
Climate, 9
Colleges and universities, 49–50, 146–47
Consumer protection, 12
Costa, La, Carlsbad, 106
Credit cards, 22
   telephone calls with, 23–24
Cruises. *See* Ship, traveling by

Disabled travelers, 16–19
   special services, 19
Discounts on scheduled flights, 10–12
Disneyland, 31, 42, 91–92
Donut Hole, 101
Doolittle Theatre, 59
Dorothy Chandler Pavilion, 37–38, 59
Downtown Los Angeles
   maps, 3, 120
   places of special interest, 36–38
   walking tour, 119–25
Driving. *See* Car, traveling by; Tours; *names of individual tours*

El Capitan Theatre, 142
El Pueblo de Los Angeles, 36–37, 113, 119–21
Emergencies
   medical assistance, 24
   telephone number in Los Angeles, 24
Exotic Feline Breeding Compound, 102

Fairfax Avenue
   map, 132
   walking tour, 131–34
Family Feud (participating in), 101
Farmers' Market, 38–39, 92
   map, 132
   walking tour, 131–34
Ferries. *See* Ship, traveling by
Festival of the Arts and Pageant of the Masters, 47
Finley & Gibbons Fashion Flowers, 102
Fishing, 56
Fitness centers, 56–57
Football, 30, 31, 46, 47, 57
Forest Lawn Hollywood Hills, 103
Forest Lawn Memorial Park, 41, 103
FOX TV, 100
Fredericks of Hollywood Lingerie Museum, 142

Game shows (participating in), 101
Gene Autry Western Heritage Museum, 47–48
George C. Page Museum of La Brea Discoveries, 39
Glen Ivy Hot Springs, Corona, 106
Golf, 46, 57, 110
Gower Street, 34

Graumann's Chinese Theatre. *See* Mann's Chinese Theatre
Greek Theatre, 59, 97
Greystone Park, 139
Griffith Park, 40

Handicapped travelers. *See* Disabled travelers
Health care
  emergency number for medical assistance, 24
  hospitals and pharmacies, 24
  insurance, 16
Hermosa Beach, 150–51
Hiking, 94–95
Hillside Memorial Park, 104
Hockey, 57
Holidays. *See* Special events
Hollywood
  maps, 2, 140
  places of special interest, 33–36
  walking tour, 140–43
Hollywood Bowl, 38, 59, 97–98
Hollywood Memorial Park, 104, 128
Hollywood Studio Museum, 33–34
Hollywood Wax Museum, 33
Holy Cross Cemetery, 104
Horse racing, 57
Hospitals. *See* Health care
Hotels, 43, 60–70
  grand hotels and special havens, 61–63, 96

Insurance, 13, 16
International Festival of Masks, 47
International Surf Festival, 47

Japanese American National Museum, 48, 123
Jeopardy (participating in), 101
Jogging, 57–58
J. Paul Getty Museum, 41

Knott's Berry Farm, 31, 42–43

La Brea Tar Pits, 39
La Costa, Carlsbad, 106
Laguna Beach, 108
Legal aid, 25
Leo Carillo State Beach, 108
Little Tokyo, 37, 122–24
Local services, 45–46
Local transportation. *See* Transportation
Long Beach, 108
Los Angeles Bach Festival, 47
Los Angeles Children's Museum, 48, 124
Los Angeles Civic Center and Mall, 37
Los Angeles County Fair, 47
Los Angeles Master Chorale, 38
Los Angeles Museum of Art, 39
Los Angeles Opera Company, 38
Los Angeles Philharmonic, 38, 59
Los Angeles Times Building, 123–24
Los Angeles Zoo, 40
Lotus Festival, 47

Mail, 23
Malibu Beach, 95–96, 108
Malibu Creek State Park, hiking in, 94–95
Malls, 37, 53–54, 92
Manhattan Beach, 149–50
Mann's Chinese Theatre (Graumann's), 31, 33, 142
Maps
  in this guide
    beach towns (Manhattan, Hermosa, and Redondo), 148
    Beverly Hills, 2, 136
    Catalina Island, 152
    downtown Los Angeles, 3, 120

INDEX

Maps (*cont.*)
    Fairfax Avenue/Farmers'
      Market, 132
    Hollywood, 2, 140
    Los Angeles, 2–3
    Melrose Avenue, 126
    Westwood, 144
  sources for, 25, 43–44
Marina del Rey, 109
Marineland, 31
Mark Taper Forum, 37, 58, 99
Max Factor Beauty Museum, 34–35
Medical assistance. *See* Health care
Medieval Times, 42
Melrose Avenue
  map, 126
  shopping, 52–53, 93, 127–30
  walking tour, 126–30
Midtown, places of special interest, 38–39
Monarch Beach, 110
Money
  sending, 22
  See also Automated teller machines; Credit cards; Traveler's checks
Montana Avenue, shopping, 53
Moreno Valley Ranch, 110
Mt. Olympus (in Laurel Canyon), 32
Movieland, 31
Movieland Wax Museum, 42
Mulholland Drive, 32
Museum of Contemporary Art (MOCA), 38, 123
Museum of Flying, 48
Museum of Neon Art, 48
Museum of Science and Industry, 48
Museums, 47–49
  See also specific museums
Music, 59, 97–98
Music Center, 31, 37–38, 58, 59

Natural History Museum, 38

NBC TV, 100
Newport Beach, 109–10
Newspapers, local, 44
Nightclubs and nightlife, 59–60, 98
Nisei Japanese Festival, 47
Nixon. *See* Richard Nixon Library & Birthplace
Norton Simon Museum of Art, 48–49

The Oaks at Ojai, Ojai, 106–7
Odyssey Theatre Ensemble, 59
Ojai Valley Country Club, 110
Older travelers, 20–22
Old Plaza Church, 36, 121
Olvera Street, 37, 119–21
Orange County, places of special interest, 42–43

Pacific Coastal Highway (to Santa Barbara), 43
Package tours, 14–16
  for disabled travelers, 18–19
  for older travelers, 21–22
  for single travelers, 20
  See also Tours
Palace, 59
Palace Court, 59
Palomino Club, 59, 98
Pantages Theatre, 59, 142
Paradise Cove, 108
Paramount Pictures, 34, 128
Pasadena Playhouse, 59, 99
Performing arts, 97–99
Petite Elite Miniature Museum & Gallery, 102
Pharmacies. *See* Health care
Photo Express, 102
Photographing Los Angeles, 110–14
Pierce Brothers Westwood Village Memorial Park, 104–5, 145
Plane, traveling by. *See* Airplane travel

Plaza, the, 36–37, 113, 119–21
Plaza Firehouse, 36, 121
Polo, 58
Ports o' Call Village, 40
Pueblo de Los Angeles, El, 36–37, 113, 119–21

Queen Mary, 41

Radio, 44
Redondo Beach, 40–41, 149, 151
Redondo Beach Marina, 40–41
Renting a car, 13
Restaurants, 70–87, 92–93
   afternoon tea, 86–87
   incredible edibles, 71–73, 96–97
   in Santa Barbara, 43
Richard Nixon Library & Birthplace, 49
Robert H. Meyer Memorial State Beaches, 108
Rodeo Drive
   shopping, 50–52, 137
Rose Bowl, 30, 46, 47, 57
Roxy (night club/music hall), 59, 98
Roy Rogers & Dale Evans Museum, 49

Sailing, 109–10
Santa Barbara, 43
Sending money, 22
Senior citizens. *See* Older travelers
Ship, traveling by
   Catalina Island, 41
   day cruises, 41, 109, 155
   ferry companies, 155
Shopping, 50–56, 102
   discount stores, 54–55
   Farmers' Market, 38–39, 92, 131–34
   malls and shopping centers, 37, 53–54, 92

Melrose Avenue, 52–53, 93, 127–30
Montana Avenue, 53
Rodeo Drive, 50–52, 137
specialty stores, 52–53
Universal CityWalk, 35–36
vintage, 55–56
West Third Street, 53
Shubert Theatre, 59, 99
Silent Movie, 102–3
Simon Wiesenthal Center Beit Hashoah Museum of Tolerance, 49
Single travelers, 19–20
Six Flags Magic Mountain, 40
South Bay beaches
   map, 148
   walking tour, 149–51
Southwest Museum, 49
Spago, dining at, 92–93
Spas, 105–7
Special events, 46–47
Special-interest packages. *See* Package tours
Sports and fitness, 56–58, 107–10
   See also specific sports
Sport Walk of Fame, 102
Strawberry Festival, 47
Subway, 45
Surfing, 58
Swimming, 58

Tax, sales, 44
Taxis, 45
Telephone, 23–24, 44
Television, 44
   participating in shows, 99–101
Temperature. *See* Climate
Temporary Contemporary Art Museum, 38, 123
Tennis, 58
Theaters, 37–38, 58–59, 98–99
   See also specific theaters
Third and Broadway, 37

Time zone, 22
Tourist information, 25, 43–44
Tournament of Roses. *See* Rose Bowl
Tours
  day cruises, 41, 109, 155
  guided, 15–16, 40, 45, 105, 119, 123
  helicopter, 40, 155
  walking and driving, 117–55
    beach towns (Manhattan, Hermosa, Redondo), 149–51
    Beverly Hills, 135–39
    Catalina Island, 152–55
    downtown Los Angeles, 119–25
    Fairfax/Farmers' Market, 131–34
    Hollywood, 140–43
    Melrose Avenue, 126–30
    Westwood, 144–47
  See also Package tours; *names of individual tours*
Train, traveling by, 32, 45
Transportation
  from the airport to the city, 12–13
  getting to and around Catalina, 155
  local, 32, 44–45
  See also Airplane travel; Bus, traveling by; Car, traveling by; Ship, traveling by; Train, traveling by
Traveler's checks, 22

Two Bunch Palms, Desert Hot Springs, 107

Union Station, 121
Universal Amphitheatre, 59, 98
Universal CityWalk, 35–36
Universal Studios Hollywood, 31, 35

Venice Beach, 93–94, 113
Virginia Robinson Gardens, 139
Volleyball, 58

Walking tours. *See* Tours; *names of individual tours*
Walt Disney Concert Hall, 38
Warner Brothers Studios, 34, 35
Weather. *See* Climate
West Third Street, shopping, 53
Westwood
  map, 144
  walking tour, 144–47
Westwood Playhouse, 59, 99
Whales, watching, 94, 114
Wheeler Hot Springs, Ojai, 107
Wheel of Fortune (participating in), 101
Will Rogers Memorial Park, 139
Will Rogers State Beach, 109
Wiltern Theatre, 98

Zoos, 40

Notes

Notes